MANTLE

Books by Tony Castro

Chicano Power:
The Emergence of Mexican America

Mickey Mantle:
America's Prodigal Son

The Prince of South Waco:
American Dreams and Great Expectations

DiMag & Mick:
Sibling Rivals, Yankee Blood Brothers

Looking for Hemingway:
The Lost Generation and A Final Rite of Passage

Gehrig & The Babe:
The Friendship and The Feud

MANTLE

The Best There Ever Was

TONY CASTRO

ROWMAN & LITTLEFIELD
Lanham • Boulder • New York • London

Published by Rowman & Littlefield
An imprint of The Rowman & Littlefield Publishing Group, Inc.
4501 Forbes Boulevard, Suite 200, Lanham, Maryland 20706
www.rowman.com

6 Tinworth Street, London SE11 5AL, United Kingdom

British Library Cataloguing in Publication Information available

Library of Congress Cataloging-in-Publication Data

Name: Castro, Tony, author.
Title: Mantle : the best there ever was / Tony Castro.
Description: Lanham, Maryland : Rowman & Littlefield, [2019] | "Distributed by NATIONAL BOOK NETWORK"—T.p. verso. | Includes bibliographical references and index.
Identifiers: LCCN 2018056819 (print) | LCCN 2018057216 (ebook) | ISBN 9781538122228 (electronic) | ISBN 9781538122211 | ISBN 9781538122211(cloth : alk. paper)
Subjects: LCSH: Mantle, Mickey, 1931–1995. | Baseball players—United States—Biography.
Classification: LCC GV865.M33 (ebook) | LCC GV865.M33 C378 2019 (print) |
DDC 796.357092 [B]—dc23
LC record available at https://lccn.loc.gov/2018056819

Printed in the United States of America

To RENEE
best of wives, best of women, best of friends
and
OLIVER
our first grandchild

"Not everything that can be counted counts, and not everything that counts can be counted."

ALBERT EINSTEIN

Contents

PART ONE

THE BEST THERE WAS

Mickey was the best I ever saw. I never saw Ruth play in person, but I saw all the others: Gehrig, Ted Williams, Willie Mays—and I know how good I was.

And to say there was anyone better in the game, to say there was anyone better than Mantle is what we Italians would call "un sacco di stronzate," a load of crap.

—JOE DIMAGGIO

PROLOGUE

"I've Beaten Gehrig"

THEY SAY THE SOUL OF A NEW YORK CITY SUMMER IS HEDONISTIC IN the most selfless way imaginable. Some make a game of watching how others endure the heat, or wilt in the unrelenting sun. In the dog days of summer in 1961, few people could take their eyes off Roger Maris, Mickey Mantle included. Mickey knelt down in the cathedral that was Yankee Stadium. Of course he did, and he wasn't religious. He just happened to be in the on-deck circle, rubbing the rag of pine tar across the handle of his bat as he watched Roger dig in at home plate. If you happened to be watching the two of them, it was impossible not to see that they were as different as night and day. Maris's muscles seemed to flow; Mantle's bulged. Maris was visibly high strung and intense; Mantle, playfully laid back. Then, Maris swings from his heels. The crack of the bat is deafening.

"This could be '56!" booms the excited voice of Mel Allen, the familiar Yankees radio broadcaster. "She's going . . . going . . . GONE! Maris has hit No. 56 . . . four behind the Babe, and it's only September 9 . . ."

Almost an hour later, a pack of sportswriters surround Maris in the Yankee clubhouse, according to the next day's newspapers.

"Rog, what's it feel like to be this close to Ruth's record?" one writer asks.

"It doesn't feel any different than it did yesterday," says Maris.

Another writer jumps in. "Didya know that with your homer today, you and Mantle have already overtaken Ruth and Gehrig for most home runs by two teammates in a single season?"

"No, I didn't know that," says Maris, who hollers to Mantle. "Did you, Mick?"

Nearby, Mantle looks up. "Nah. How many did Gehrig hit?"

"Forty-seven," the second writer tells Mantle.

"Fuck, forty-seven? I already got fifty-two. I've beaten Gehrig," says Mickey, quickly looking at Maris. "It's up to you to beat Ruth."

There's a roundhouse of laughter as the writers scribble furiously.

Later in the training room, Mickey's immersed in a whirlpool, sipping on a beer. Maris is getting rubbed down on the training table, Yankee clubhouse attendant Pete Sheehy recalled in a 1976 interview with me in which he recounted the scene between Mantle and Maris.

"Mick, I'm losing hair," says Maris. "I'm losing sleep. Something I don't get. How come going for the record doesn't seem to get to you?"

Mickey considers it with a sip of beer.

"It does," Mantle says finally. "It did in '56."

"I read where you had forty-seven going into September?"

"Then I only hit five more the rest of the way," says Mickey.

"What happened?"

"The Babe," says Mantle. "He rose out of his grave and kicked me in the balls."

"What?"

The trainer finishes the rubdown on Maris. He's been listening in.

"Mickey pulled a groin muscle," the trainer tells Roger.

Mantle takes a long swig of his beer. "I was seein' the Babe on the street, in cabs, in bars. Of course, it wasn't, and I mighta been drinkin' too much." Mickey points to the beer Maris has just opened. "Someone else's ghost becomes your monster."

"Tell me 'bout it," says Maris, putting his beer down.

"It's like naming a kid 'junior,'" says Mickey.

"What's wrong with that?"

"Nothing personal," says Mantle. "Well, actually it is." He pauses and remembers something from the past.

"You know, a couple of years ago, Merlyn and the boys were flyin' back to Dallas, and I guess Mickey Jr. was playin' in the aisle. Well, some guy thought he was cute and asked him what his name was. Merlyn says he said, 'Mickey Mantle Jr.' Real proud and all. Well, the guy must've thought here was this little kid who wants to grow up to be Mickey Mantle and made a joke about it. Mickey Jr. started cryin' cause the guy didn't think that was his name. Imagine having to go through life like that."

Mickey is weepy eyed and reflective, as is Maris.

As different as they were, they were bonded that summer, as they would be the rest of their lives, in a pursuit not for fame but for immortality in sports, which are often confused as the same, though they aren't. Mickey would have countless friends and many teammates over his lifetime, but Roger Maris would remain special.

"Roger is the man I wish I could have been," Mantle told me during one of our conversations in the early 1970s. There was no arguing with him. You couldn't tell him that all men are different. They may be equal in the eyes of the law, the founders of America, or perhaps even in some religions. But they are different, and one man's character may be as ill fitting on another as their clothes. As someone to admire, though, you could do a lot worse than Roger Maris. On October 1, 1961, in Yankee Stadium, on the last day of the season, Maris hit his sixty-first home run of the season, breaking the revered, thirty-four-year-old single-season home run record held by Babe Ruth. It was a historic day in sports—and, in many ways, in the social fabric of America. A photograph of Maris in the full extension swing that produced that home run adorned the back of the program handed out to the nine hundred or so as they entered St. Mary's Cathedral in Fargo, North Dakota, on December 19, 1985, for Roger's funeral mass. He was fifty-one years old when he died after a long bout with lymphatic cancer.

Among those braving the snow and a temperature of two degrees above zero to pay their tribute to Maris that day was his former Yankees slugging mate. "Mantle, his blond hair graying," recalled Ira Berkow, the *New York Times* Pulitzer Prize–winning columnist, "held a white handkerchief and wiped his eyes and nose." The handkerchief wasn't for a runny nose from the cold, Mickey later told me when we caught up at a baseball card show in Southern California. "I was bawling, almost like a baby at times," he said. "You know, those dreams I used to tell you about? Now when I have them, Roger's in them, like he was back in the day."

As dreams go, these were doozies, even by Mantle's standards, and he confessed having many, from as early in his childhood.

"I think the only reason you didn't beat me to the record was you didn't really want it . . . or need it."

That was Roger talking to Mickey in one of those dreams. And the circumstances? Well, the company in that dream was incredible. It included Mantle's father Mutt who died in 1952, Roger Maris, Casey Stengel, and Billy Martin. In the dream Mantle recounted in 1970, all except Mutt were still alive—and all were crammed into Mickey's hospital room in 1951 after he had just blown out his knee in the second game of the New York subway World Series against the Giants.

"You were already Mickey Mantle," Maris tells Mickey. "You didn't have to be Ruth or DiMaggio."

"Ah, he coulda been better than both," says Stengel.

"I would've liked to have seen Ruth and the Dago handle night games, the slider and television," says Martin.

"They was different times," says Stengel.

Then Billy gets into Stengel's face in an awkward confrontation.

"But, Case," says Martin, "how could you not put Mick on your all-time all-star team?"

There's an awkward moment. Stengel appears visibly uncomfortable. In 1961, out of baseball for a year, Stengel published his autobiography in which he snubbed Mantle, his pride and joy and the best player on any of his teams. In the book, Casey named two personal all-star teams. One was composed of Yankees he had managed and Mickey was on that list. But the other more meaningful all-star team made up of those he considered the best of his time notably excluded Mantle. Stengel listed six outfielders on his American League team of players from 1912 to 1960, including three center fielders—Ty Cobb, Tris Speaker, and Joe DiMaggio.

"You had DiMaggio, Berra, even Rizzuto on it," says Billy.

"I dunno . . . some writer comes up to you . . . asks names . . ." Stengel offers, lamely.

"Few things have ever hurt like that," Mantle mumbles, breaking into tears. "My own manager."

"I mighta been mad or disappointed with you," says Stengel.

"You tried to treat me like you were my father," says Mantle. He is smoldering. "But you're not. All I wanted you to be was my manager."

Stengel's head hangs down. "You're right. You're right," he says. "You'll have to forgive a man who never had any children."

"There you go again, Case," says Mickey. "Playing head games. You were always the best at that."

Casey's in tears.

"Case," Mickey pleads, "if I weren't the best, then why are they paying the highest price for my autograph?"

1

The Hero's Widow

Merlyn was the perfect woman any man would want to love, marry, have as mother to their kids and grow old with. The problem is I just wasn't the perfect man.

—MICKEY MANTLE

IN LATE SUMMER OF 2009, FEW PEOPLE STROLLING PAST A TREE-shrouded apartment building in Plano, Texas, which strangers often confused with North Dallas, realized that an aging widow spending her last days inside, staring blankly and unable to remember much of her life, had once been the envy of perhaps every woman in America and was held in near Madonna-like status by their husbands. Half a century earlier, perhaps only the beautiful, loving wife of the young Massachusetts senator who would soon be elected president of the United States commanded such high regard. In that decade of American prominence after World War II, in what some likened to a cathedral in the Bronx borough of New York City, she had watched her husband perform spectacular athletic feats that had much of the nation proclaiming him the symbol of his time. He was called "The Last Hero" by many, "America's Prodigal Son" by others, and "The Last Boy" by some. But he was also, as one of his legions of idolizers had put it, a fragile hero to whom we had an emotional attachment so strong and lasting that it defied logic. And yet he was perhaps the most compelling hero of our lifetime. He was also complicated, but as *Sports Illustrated* once said of him, Mickey was proof that "we don't mind our heroes flawed, or even doomed." And as I said about him in *Mickey*

Mantle: America's Prodigal Son, "In America, failure is forgiven of the big swingers, in whom even foolishness is flamboyant, because the world will always belong to those who swing from the heels. He was, then, the hero of America's romance with boldness, its celebration of power, a nation's Arthurian self-confidence in strength during a time when we last thought might did make right."

Merlyn Louise Johnson Mantle—who always looked like a tiny, platinum-blonde high school cheerleader at various stages of life—was a quiet woman who had never yielded to self-pity, though she might have had reason. The wives of American heroes—be they soldiers, astronauts, public servants, or athletes—too often are seen as only extensions of their spouses. Few recognize their sacrifices and that, sadly, they often live with and love a stranger—a husband who not only they don't know but also isn't real. For like most heroes, Mickey Mantle was a construction. If the great switch-hitting home run legend of the New York Yankees had never lived, team broadcaster Mel Allen once said, he would have been invented. Merlyn Mantle, who was married to him for forty-three years, until Mickey's death in 1995, and with whom she had four sons, would have agreed. He was an utter stranger to her much of their lives. So much so that she sometimes joked that she raised five boys, her four sons and her husband. She was married to someone who was part created image and the other part a mystery to himself. What Merlyn may have known best was Mickey's glory, which she had also basked in. And oh, how glorious that ride must have been. In his day—and beyond because his legend only grew long after his retirement in 1968—Mickey Mantle was all that America wanted itself to be, and he was also all that America feared it could never be. In one sense, he truly was Arthurian: he and his country were one, the secret to finding the Holy Grail according to legend.

Postwar America of the mid-twentieth century was like all societies with the need for heroes not because they coincidentally made them up on their own but because heroes like Mantle express a deep psychological aspect of human existence. They can be seen as a metaphor for the human search of self-knowledge. In his time, Mickey Mantle showed us the path to our own consciousness through the power and spectacle of his baseball heroics, particularly his prodigal home runs often backlit by the cathedral solemnity of Yankee Stadium. In the atomic age of the 1950s, the tape-measure blasts in our national pastime took on the form of peacetime symbols of America's newly established military dominance. After all, Hank Greenberg, the first Jewish slugger in the game, said that when he had hit his home runs from the mid-1930s into the 1940s, he was hitting them against Hitler. In the 1950s, Mickey Mantle came to reflect the appearance and values of the dominant society in the world. He was America's golden god of the time, and Merlyn Mantle was right there with him as his goddess.

"I developed an instant crush on Mickey Mantle," she would reminisce in her own memoir, "and by our second or third date, I was in love with him and always would be."

They would have memories, good ones and some pretty awful ones, and she had been surrounded by the great ones throughout her home at the corner of Watson Circle and Jamestown in the Preston Hollow section of North Dallas where they had lived since 1958. Here they also resided with Mickey's trophies and significant memorabilia: his three Most Valuable Player awards, the Silver Bat award he won for his 1956 American League batting title, his 1956 Hickok Belt, his five hundredth home run ball, the tape measure that the Yankees' traveling secretary used to record his 565-foot home run, some World Series home run balls, and seven World Series championship rings. When Mickey died, Merlyn began to store much of the memorabilia, anticipating a move to a fifteenth-floor condominium she could manage more easily. Later, after Mickey Jr. died, she had gone to live in his house in nearby Highland Park where she raised her son's teenage daughter Mallory.

When she still had her own house, visitors who called would discover that the elegant, erect, graying blonde-haired lady was still every bit the performer she had ever been in proudly giving you a guided tour of her house, its decorations, and the mementos that were everywhere, even beyond the fabled den filled with trophies. The Mantle home was a four-bedroom beige house on an acre of emerald green with an inviting swimming pool separating two wings wrapping around it. To a newcomer, the house with its beige-upon-beige decor could redefine Mickey Mantle, for it had a casual elegance about it that looked lived in, especially when the boys were young, but also showed the distinctive touch of someone who loved him and knew that the home had to be as impressive as the American hero who lived there.

"Mick was the star of the family," she loved to tell visitors. "I was just happy keeping my home and my kids and being the wife, and that's what I did."

The trophy room in the back of the house was reminiscent of those you would find in the athletics hall of any major university, filled with glass cases stuffed with shining hardware of all their teams' accomplishments—that is until you realized these trophies weren't of one team but of one athlete. Even in her later years, as Mickey's widow prepared to scale down her lifestyle, these symbols of Mantle's career could be overwhelming and make Merlyn seem like a pack rat. Boxes were opened. Out would come her life with Mickey in photographs, documents, jewelry, and plaques. There was Mantle's collection of balls he hit of special significance: his 512th and 535th home runs and his sixteenth World Series homer that broke Babe Ruth's record. Then there were Mantle's contracts: his first baseball pact, to play for the Independence (Kansas) Yankees for $140 a month, and a $1,150 bonus, in 1949; and each of the eighteen contracts he signed to play in New York, showing his annual salary to have been $100,000 from 1963 to 1968. She was their curator in the years after Mantle's retirement, the keeper of his memory after his death. She had married Mickey Mantle on December 23, 1951, after his rookie season, and she had been faithful. In various rooms of that house, Merlyn had crammed the fading memorabilia of her now distant marriage. However, all those treasures and remembrances were now locked away, somewhere where she could no longer reach them, much less view them. This had been her uppermost fear since Mickey's death when she had waged a legal fight with collectors but none more so than with the woman Mantle left her for and with whom he had spent his last decade. Fate can be cruel, though, and now, alone in her own mind at the hospice facility where she lived her final years, it had played its last deception. Merlyn Mantle could remember little, if any, of Mantle or of her life with him. Merlyn, at age seventy-seven, was suffering from Alzheimer's disease.

However, in those moments of coherence and clarity in her final years, Merlyn seemed almost duty bound to protect and enhance, if possible, Mickey's legacy—not his standing in life and the controversy that surrounded it, the drinking and the womanizing, but how baseball would look at him. In the newspaper accounts she read following Mantle's death, Merlyn wasn't particularly disturbed by the depiction of their troubled marriage as hardly fitting of the fairy-tale story she had once wanted it to be, but she would become furious about comments short-changing the greatness of Mantle's career, those lines often alluding to his Hall of Fame career ending on bad knees and faded dreams. They had still been young when Mickey retired just before the 1969 season. He had just turned thirty-seven the previous October. Mantle had looked better and stronger than half his teammates. The writers, however, made him out to be an old-timer, and that matched no vision that Merlyn could recall from all those Yankees Old-Timers Day games she had witnessed at the stadium. Even before Mickey's death, Merlyn Mantle had committed herself to one holy quest above all others: to rescue her husband's historical reputation from all the innuendo and slanderous attempts to tarnish it. She recognized that Mickey's lifestyle and all the publicity surrounding it had made him easy fodder. She shuddered any time she heard anecdotes like the one in New York that had become a punch line: a drunken Mickey Mantle, having stepped out of a limousine, had tripped and fallen into a gutter outside the St. Moritz Hotel. A friend kneeled down to help, and Mickey looked up with that crooked grin of his and cracked, "A helluva place for America's hero, ain't it?"

Merlyn seethed any time she heard that story. She felt embarrassed for Mickey, who at times admitted that he had regrets about retiring when he did. How did his dream life as the star of the New York Yankee turn into the nightmare from which he had always awakened in a sweat?

I'm in a taxi, trying to get to Yankee Stadium. I'm late and I've got my uniform on. But when I get there the guard won't let me in. He doesn't recognize me. So I find this hole in the fence, and I'm trying to crawl through it, you know? But I can only get my head in. I can see Billy and Whitey and Yogi and Casey. And I can hear the announcer: "Now batting . . . number 7 . . . Mickey Mantle." But I can't get through the hole. That's when I wake up. My palms are all sweaty.

He had been increasingly haunted by the vision of that nightmare, even in the early morning hours of the day in spring training in 1969 when he announced his retirement. He had endured several bad seasons, and he dreaded having another. He had put a good face on his announcement, but he was in horrific pain—and it was from his knees—and that pain would never go away. "The only thing I'd ever known in my life was baseball," he said to me a couple of years after his retirement. "And there I was, barely thirty-six years old—fuck, at thirty-six, Babe Ruth hit 46 home runs, drove in 163 runs and batted .373—but me? I'm finished. I'm a fuckin' has been."

I was amazed Mickey could recite Babe Ruth's statistics by heart, obviously the result of some serious comparison on Mantle's part, and the disappointing realization of just how short he came up in measuring himself against the great Bambino. At age thirty-seven, Ruth had belted forty-one home runs, driven in 137 runs, and batted .341. At thirty-eight, Babe numbers had been more modest: thirty-four homers, 104 RBIs, and a .301 batting average. Babe Ruth hadn't been just a baseball star. He had been a god. Imagine having to be compared to that?

Day after day, year after year, Mantle finally had time to reflect on his career. His mind was on baseball every waking moment. He couldn't believe he didn't finish with a .300 batting average. He wondered what it would have been like if he had played in a different, hitter-friendly ball park. Yankee Stadium in his day was 480 feet to center field, and Mickey was certain that in his career he must have lost at least fifty home runs that had been long outs but would have cleared the fence elsewhere. And of course the legs, especially his right knee that had him in agonizing pain almost every day. Wasn't that the reason so many Mantle fans hated Joe DiMaggio, blaming him for the first and worst of Mickey's injuries that virtually snuffed out his unlimited potential for unquestioned claim as the greatest of all time? Mantle himself would never point a finger at DiMaggio, or say anything negative, carrying responsibility for all that happened to him to his grave. But privately it would gnaw at him. It is no wonder that Mickey would exhaust himself thinking about baseball and his career, what was and what might have been. Mantle wasn't a religious person by nature, but along the way in this retrospective soul searching Mickey reached a freakish epiphany that changed his whole view of his career. He came to a moment of awe and ecstasy. Mickey Mantle, he discovered, had been a rare, extraordinarily great ballplayer—and it was damn time to put aside that act of Oklahoma country boy humility and to start making a case for himself as deserving of a place in any discussion of the greatest players in the game.

"I really do believe I would be way up at the top of everything if I hadn't been injured," Mickey told *Los Angeles Herald Examiner* sportswriter Diane K. Shah in 1980, a dozen years after hanging up his spikes. "When I was healthy, I really believe I was the best of anyone I ever saw play."

Wow! Say that again, Mick.

I was the best of anyone I ever saw play. From the mouth not of The Babe but of The Mick. *I was the best of anyone I ever saw play.* Isn't it ghostly how much that sounds like those lines from *The Natural*, the Bernard Malamud 1952 novel adapted to film in 1984?

"I coulda been better," laments Roy Hobbs, the story's heroic ballplayer who had his athletic promise compromised. "I coulda broke every record in the book."

"And then?" asks his childhood love Iris who has joined him years later.

"And then?" says Roy. "And then when I walked down the street people would've looked, and they would've said there goes Roy Hobbs, the best there ever was in this game."

Is that what The Mick, Merlyn, and certainly his most ardent of fans wanted to hear or would have hoped to hear? People in New York City, Dallas, or anywhere that baseball is played recognizing Mantle as he walked down their street as the one who was the best there is, the best there was, the best there ever will be? Positively, yes! *"There goes Mickey Mantle, the best there ever was in this game."*

That would be the issue argued for years to come. Could that have been Mickey Mantle, with a break or two going his way? Merlyn Mantle, a woman of her time who had loved only one man, would spend the rest of her life devoted to Mickey's memory. I had known Merlyn personally in the early 1970s, meeting her through Mickey with whom I often played golf. She spent an hour on the night I met her, even with Mickey passed out on a couch, giving me a tour of her home and the trophies within.

"Mickey was built up to being the next DiMaggio, another Babe Ruth," she told me in one conversation. "Well he was better than Joe. Look it up. Five hundred and thirty-six home runs, three hundred sixty-one for Joe. Their RBIs and slugging averages almost even. MVPs, even. All-star teams: Mickey eighteen, Joe thirteen. Triple Crowns: Mickey 1956, Joe never."

I was impressed by the litany of statistics she could rattle off from memory, which she might have carried on with had I not insisted to her that she was preaching to the choir. She didn't need to convert me. Mickey, my boyhood hero, I would rank above DiMaggio. But Ruth? She was ready to debate Mickey versus The Babe, too, not so much in statistics, which favor Ruth, but in talking about the eras of which she believed there was no comparison. Babe didn't have to play night games. His era hadn't had the tremendous starting pitching depth and relievers that Mantle faced in the 1950s and 1960s. She made good points. Here, though, Mantle himself had conceded, even as he made a case on his own behalf. "But," he added dolefully in one interview, "you have to go by the records."

After our springs and summers of golf in Dallas in the early 1970s, I saw Mickey again years later at memorabilia shows in California, but I never spoke to Merlyn again even though I tried in the late 1990s. I was working on my Mantle biography, *Mickey Mantle: America's Prodigal Son*, and I had hoped Merlyn would agree to allow me to use her off-the-record comments from our conversations years ago. I sent her several letters with my request, but I never received a response. I was later told by mutual friend Pat Summerall, the former NFL player and television broadcaster, that Merlyn had been miffed that I had already spoken at length with Greer Johnson, the former schoolteacher who had become Mickey's business partner and with whom he lived the last decade of his life. Still, I honored our agreement that I would not quote Merlyn from our conversations of the early 1970s until after her death. Then, several years after the publication of my Mantle biography, I received a message through my agent Mike Hamilburg that Merlyn had called, insisting on talking to me. I presumed she wanted to finally voice her complaints about my book, which had been published in 2002. I delayed returning her call until Mike insisted. I agreed and prepared for Merlyn's fury. I was wrong. When I returned her call, she was as gracious as she had ever been in her home and began talking to me as if we were longtime friends.

Then we talked about my biography of Mickey, and I was pleasantly surprised that she didn't have any complaints about what was in the book. She had complaints about what *wasn't* in it.

"Why didn't you say it," she said, "that Mickey was greater than Joe DiMaggio and that his accomplishments, when you consider different eras and that Mickey played his entire career on only one healthy leg, were right up there with Babe Ruth? All these new ways of looking at statistics in baseball are pointing to that. Look it up. That day is coming."

She was still insistent, still the keeper of Mickey Mantle's legacy. We had a good, lengthy conversation, and I was reminded about her passion about Mick and his place in baseball. She told me she had spoken to other writers who told her about new statistical analyses used in evaluating players. She asked me for a signed copy of my book, and I was happy to send one to her. But I never spoke to her again. On August 10, 2009, Merlyn Mantle died of pneumonia at that hospice where she spent her final days in Plano, Texas. She was entombed next to Mickey and two of their children—Billy Mantle and Mickey Mantle Jr.—at Hillcrest Memorial Park and Mausoleum. She was survived by her two other sons, David Mantle and Danny Mantle and his wife, Kay; and four grandchildren, Mallory, Marilyn, Will, and Chloe Mantle.

Why didn't I say it? It became a mantra I kept hearing from Mantle fans. *Why didn't I say it?* Why didn't I say that Mickey Mantle was the greatest ever? I certainly had believed it when I was young. I had a treasure trove of Mantle memorabilia. Rookie cards, Topps and Bowman. Every Mantle card ever made. Signed baseballs. The huge posters that had hung in my childhood bedroom. More than enough memorabilia to stock a Mantle museum. I'm not certain at what point I determined that it wasn't necessary for me to believe that Mickey was better than Ruth or DiMaggio, or Duke Snider or Willie Mays for that matter. I was reminded about how kids compete, kids in my native Texas, at least: my dad can whup your dad, yes he can. It was all so silly.

Merlyn Mantle had lived long enough to see some of the changes in baseball beyond the designated hitter, the set-up and closer relief pitchers as institutions, and the exaggerated defensive shifts once used only on a few hitters like Ted Williams but that had become commonplace in the game. And yes, all the new statistics that are befuddling traditional fans much as the new math homework confounded parents a generation ago. I don't know how much Merlyn Mantle got into in her exposure to the new numbers that have become part of appreciating the game: the polynomial equations and algorithms of sabermetrics to the ESPN Home Run Tracker that interpolates data from tapes, meteorological conditions, and eyewitnesses and spits out data like what it found on Mickey Mantle's home run off Kansas City Athletics pitcher Bill Fischer on May 22, 1963—the blast that struck the facade atop the right-field upper deck and nearly became the only fair ball ever hit out of the old Yankee Stadium. That home run that left Mickey's bat at an angle of twenty-seven degrees with a velocity of 124 miles an hour was one of the hardest-hit balls in history—and would have traveled 503 feet if it had completed its flight and landed on River Avenue outside the stadium.

Merlyn would have loved anecdotal ammo like that because it could only lead to more. If I could have said anything more to her, it would be to tell her that it's making an even bigger believer, even among members of the choir. I would have also said that I wouldn't be surprised if some time in the future—based on the evolution of analytics in baseball, on his incredible statistics during the golden age of the game, his injuries notwithstanding, and because of his ability to do this as a switch-hit-ter—Mickey Mantle doesn't become widely acclaimed as having fulfilled those great expectations once placed on him: being recognized as the greatest player of all time, greater than Ruth, Gehrig, DiMaggio, and all the rest.

But then she knew. As she said, *that day is coming*.

2

Myths and Curses

I never saw Babe Ruth play. Hell, he mighta been a myth, for all I know. But then who of us is truly real? Fuck, Mickey Mantle may be no more real than Howdy Doody.

—MICKEY MANTLE

MICKEY MANTLE ONCE CORRECTED ME WITHOUT HESITATION WHEN I called 1956, the year he won the Triple Crown and virtually every sports award given out, his "favorite season." It was when he became "Mickey Mantle," a household name in America and the most popular athlete in a culture that worshipped them. It was his best season, he said. His greatest season, without a doubt. He had even put his name on a ghostwritten book about 1956 having been *My Favorite Summer 1956*. But his true favorite season, he insisted, was 1951, his rookie year, despite all the learning bumps and bruises, regardless of the humiliation of having been demoted to the minors in midsummer, and notwithstanding the awful knee injury in the World Series that would affect his abilities for the rest of his career.

"I could be me then," he said about his rookie season. "Nobody really knew me. I was just a wide-eyed kid in the big city. Everything was new. It was fun getting an education to New York, to being a big league ballplayer, to being a Yankee. I had no money to speak of, barely any walking-around money, but I was finding I didn't need any. I was free, but I was also free to succeed and fail, and I guess I did both. But I was playing next to DiMaggio, and day to day I saw how he handled not just being a big leaguer but being Joe DiMaggio. This is important. If I was as good as Case was saying I could be, as good as my daddy always told me I could be, I needed to see and know what that was like. And what better example than Joe. He had come to the Yankees while Lou Gehrig was there and got to see him and learn from him day after day. And I reckon it might have been the same way with Gehrig becoming a Yankee alongside Babe Ruth."

I was surprised that Merlyn Mantle felt the same way. I thought she would have picked any of the years when her boys were born or the years of Mickey's greatest triumphs—the Triple Crown season, the M&M Boys 1961 season chasing Babe Ruth's record with Roger Maris, or Mickey's Hall of Fame induction year in 1974. But then 1951 was the year she married Mickey, the love of her life, she reminded me when I first met her and in our final conversation almost four decades later.

"That was the year that Mickey became a man—the year he had to grow up," she said. "Mickey was on his own in the biggest city in America, and, what is that line Frank Sinatra sang in that song 'New York'? That if you can make it there, you can make it anywhere. That's what Mickey learned in 1951, and that was important for Mickey. That he could make it. I know that when he returned to Commerce after the World Series, Mickey was a different man, a different person than the one who left early that year to go to spring training. He had been through so much. He was a nineteen-year-old young man who had so much pressure put on him by the Yankees, by Casey, by the fans. It would have been one thing if everything had gone his way, and his character hadn't been tested. That didn't happen. Mickey took his lumps, and it would have been so easy for him to give up when he was down. Remember, there was a moment in Kansas City when he was so depressed that I was really afraid he might just quit and come home. But he didn't. That wasn't who Mickey was. I think he looked deep down into his soul and found courage he may not have even thought he had. He stuck it out, proved that he belonged in the major leagues with the Yankees and showed everyone what he was made of and what kind of special character he had."

Indeed, as seemingly ordinary as his rookie season statistics were, Mickey Mantle's 1951 season transcends stat lines in a way that has to be studied beyond its role in baseball. The extraordinary unmatched spring training season, as meaningless as it may have been for career statistics, laid the foundation for the creation of a myth, not unlike Babe Ruth more than a generation earlier.

The unique relationship between America and baseball must be understood to fully appreciate Mickey Mantle's place in the equation. This was the age when baseball players were the princes of American sports, along with heavyweight boxers and Derby horses and the odd galloping ghost of a running back from down South or the occasional lanky basketball player in short shorts. Baseball players were the souls of their cities—Stan the Man in St. Louis; The Kid in Boston; Pee Wee, The Duke, Jackie, and Furillo in Brooklyn; and of course the incomparable Willie Mays for Giants fans. As 1950s historian Jacques Barzun was to aptly observe, "Whoever wants to know the heart and mind of America had better learn baseball."

Long before Mickey Mantle, long before baseball became an industry of multinational owners and millionaire players, Walt Whitman wrote, "Well, it's our game. That's the chief fact in connection with it: America's game. It has the snap, go, fling of the American atmosphere. It belongs as much to our institutions, fits into them as significantly as our Constitution's laws, is just as important in the sum total of our historic life." Baseball is, to be sure, an American cultural declaration of independence. It has come to express the nation's character—perhaps never more so than during the intense, anti-Communist, post–World War II period, when a preoccupation with defining the national conscience might be expected, particularly defining the national self in a tradition that is so culturally middle of the road. As American studies authority Gerald Early told Ken Burns in his 1994 documentary *Baseball*, "I think there are only three things America will be known for 2,000 years from now when they study this civilization—the Constitution, jazz music, and baseball."

By the middle of the twentieth century, baseball as an unquestioned symbol and performance ritual of the best qualities of something called Americanism was an entrenched truism. The fictional literary character Terence Mann perhaps states it more succinctly in the Hollywood film *Field of Dreams* when he says to protagonist Ray Kinsella, "The one constant through all the years, Ray, has been baseball. America has rolled by like an army of steamrollers. It's been erased like a blackboard, rebuilt, and erased again. But baseball has marked the time. This field, this game, is a part of our past, Ray. It reminds us of all that once was good and it could be again."

America in the 1950s was also not so much a stage as a set piece for television, the new national phenomenon. It was a time when how things looked—and how we looked—mattered, a decade of design. From the painting-by-numbers fad to the public fascination with the First Lady's apparel, the television sensation of Elvis Presley, and the sculptural refinement of the automobile, American life in the 1950s had a distinct style in material culture and in art history at eye level.

America in the mid-twentieth century, to be sure, needed a Mickey Mantle to transform from a largely conventional baseball figure into a pop-culture deity of entertainment, which is what the game ultimately became in Mantle's time and thereafter. Mantle would be the cultural equivalent of Elvis, Marilyn, and James Dean. He was young, he was handsome, and he came to be seen on television in millions of homes in ways Ruth, Gehrig, and DiMaggio never were. It should be no surprise that popular biography has reflected this conversion, or that the change parallels the way baseball has come to be viewed in the years since Mantle arrived on the American scene. In a sense the image of all popular figures is a reflection of the public that follows them. But with a dead figure, that reflective process grows exponentially—like the compounding effect of a series of mirrors. As a cultural symbol whose life can now be made into anything with impunity, Mantle has become, in Elvis biographer Greil Marcus's words, "an anarchy of possibilities"—a reflection of the public's mass fears and aspirations and also a constant vehicle for discussing those sentiments. Thus Mantle, Elvis, and Marilyn alike have evolved into a collection of cultural deities—modern-day equivalents of the Greek gods, who were immortal while sharing the characteristics of the human beings who worshipped them.

"We knew there was something poignant about Mickey Mantle before we knew what poignant meant," recalled broadcaster Bob Costas in his eulogy of Mantle. "We didn't just root for him. We felt for him. Long before many of us ever cracked a serious book, we knew something about mythology as we watched Mickey Mantle run out a home run through the lengthening shadows of a late Sunday afternoon at Yankee Stadium."

Perhaps it is all too simple in the modern age of multimillionaire athletes to dismiss the references to sports greats such as Mantle as "heroes" in the context of our common humanity, with rare figures being held in esteem for what the Greeks would call *arete*, or special talent, and less in the religious or spiritual context that hero theorists Joseph Campbell and Carl Jung proposed. On the other hand, as great people pass on, our memories tend to mold them into the collective image of the archetypal hero, interpreting their lives in a more spiritual way as a reflection of society's need for men and women a touch above ordinary, able to live on the plane of existence of basic right and wrong, good and evil, heaven and hell. Sports is an obvious arena from which to draw candidates for this category of immortality, elevating the super athlete's accomplishments on the field to an almost religious pitch and unwittingly interpreting their lives as expressions of unconscious projections of our own dreams.

"The view of Mantle as a Homeric hero is correct, I think," Bryan M. Davis, a specialist on heroes in pop culture, said in an interview discussing Mantle as a heroic figure. "He reminds me much more of Achilles or Hector—heroes we revere for their ability to overcome the shortcomings of simply being human but finally having to succumb to those weaknesses—rather than an archetypal hero such as Moses or King Arthur. But the religion of baseball tends to deify its greats. Perhaps, in a thousand years, another civilization will look back and remember the hero Mantle, who slew the demon baseballs with a mere stick and led the people in ritual song every seventh inning."

Could it have been that, like King Arthur, Mickey Mantle was one with his country, and of course the grail Mickey set off to find—athletic greatness—simply reflected the greatness America believed was its entitlement after World War II. But then baseball was the national pastime. As such, the game has also been a metaphor for American greatness. Not surprisingly, baseball-themed literature and films have often been about what America could and should be: nostalgic for lost idealism; seeking redemption on the baseball field; the game cloaked as religion; and its ballparks as cathedrals. In Mickey Mantle, we also saw baseball as an experience not only about heroes and rebels but also about fathers and sons. Could any other sport be more emblematic of the devoted father reliving his dreams and about the boy in the father made whole. Mantle was the eternal youth forever playing catch with his father.

"I guess you can say I'm what this country's all about—I have to play ball. It's the only thing I know," Mantle once said in a quotation that seemed to sum up his connection with America. Perhaps fittingly, he reportedly made this remark to the Duke of Windsor when the English royal had visited New York in 1953. The former King Edward VIII, who abdicated his throne in 1936 to marry the American divorcée Wallis Simpson, attended his first baseball game when the Yankees hosted the Detroit Tigers on May 19. "Delighted" was his response when he was asked if he enjoyed the game, and he asked "to meet that 'switcher fellow'"—switch-hitter Mickey Mantle. The Duke of Windsor, while wearing a Yankee cap, was then even photographed on the dugout steps with Mantle, Casey Stengel, and Phil Rizzuto.

"I've heard about you," the Duke of Windsor said to Mantle when they were introduced, according to the next day's New York newspapers.

"I've heard about you, too," Mantle replied.

The photograph with the Duke of Windsor became one of Mantle's favorites that Merlyn displayed in their home's den.

"The former king of England wanted to meet Mickey. Can you believe that?" Merlyn said when she showed me the photograph. "Mickey's ancestors came here from England. What are the odds of an American boy of English blood growing up to become an American hero and then meeting the man who was once king of England? A charmed life if ever there was one."

But heroes, even those with the stars in their favor, are nothing without their frailties. And Mickey made no secret about the Achilles' heel that threatened not only his career but also his life. He sometimes talked about a curse on the men in his family as if it were some kind of defensive mechanism denying his own mortality. Of course, no athlete wants to contemplate failure, much less death. Mickey Mantle, though, had come face-to-face with the end of life. When he was thirteen in 1944, he watched helplessly as his grandfather, one of the men who had helped raise him, fell ill and died.

"Grandpa suddenly became old and feeble, almost overnight," Mickey said to me in 1970 while telling the story of his family's tragedy that he had recounted so many times in the past. "My father would help him out of bed and support his wobbly legs that used to stride along South Quincy Street with so much vigor. . . . Dad was worried sick over Grandpa's condition." Mickey's grandfather was suffering from Hodgkin's disease. At the time, Hodgkin's disease was virtually a terminal illness, especially when untreated or diagnosed too late. The disease ravaged Charles Mantle's body quickly.

"I never forgot that moment, standing beside the casket with my little twin brothers, Ray and Roy, the three of us looking down on him, and my father whispering, 'Say goodbye to Grandpa,'" said Mickey. "I was just a kid then. I didn't understand death and sickness very well. Even now I don't remember the order of events from that time in my life. It just seemed that all my relatives were dying around me. First, my Uncle Tunney, the tough one, then my Uncle Emmett. Within a few years—before I was thirteen—they had died of the same disease. I knew Uncle Emmett had it because the doctor had to cut the lymph nodes out of his ravaged body for nearly a year. To no avail . . .

"That [molded] my belief that I would die young. I lost my grandfather, my father and two uncles, all to Hodgkin's disease. None of them lived beyond the age of forty-one. I took it for granted that this would be my fate; it took all the Mantle men."

It came to be known as the "Mantle curse," and it would define the dark side of his nature. "I hope to make it to forty," Mickey first told *New York Daily Mirror* sportswriter Arthur Richman while in his midtwenties in 1956. "Sure, I kid about it, but I think about it, too." Howard Cosell, the legendary sports commentator, even went so far in an ABC profile of Mantle as to call Mickey "the doomed Yankees slugger, playing out his career in the valley of death." Although Mickey tired of talk of the family curse, how could anyone ever completely put something out of his thoughts, or not be reminded of his own immortality when another Mantle man met his premature end?

In 1951, the moment Mantle went down chasing Willie Mays's fly ball in right center field, he knew his first World Series was over. He was disappointed that it had ended so abruptly, but it would be matched by the suddenness of how quickly his personal life would soon take another turn. The next morning, on the steps of Lenox Hill Hospital, as Mantle stepped out of a taxicab, the life he had known since childhood would begin coming to an end.

"[My father] got out of the cab first, outside the hospital, and then I got out," Mantle remembered years later during one of our conversations. "I was on crutches and I couldn't put any weight on the leg that was hurt, so as I got out of the cab I grabbed my father's shoulder to steady myself. He crumpled to the sidewalk. I couldn't understand it. He was a very strong man, and I didn't think anything at all about putting my weight on him that way. He was always so strong."

Both Mantle and his father were rushed into the hospital where Mickey underwent orthopedic tests confirming two torn ligaments in his right knee. At the same time, doctors at the hospital ran a series of tests on Mutt. Their only consolation was that Mutt and his son were put in the same room where they were able to watch the remainder of the World Series on television. Years later, Mickey would say that he had suspected his father had been ill—that he had noticed some weight loss when Mutt had visited him in Kansas City that summer to confront him about "being a man." No one acted on that, though, and Mantle may have even been in denial of anything that threatened the most formidable figure in his life. It may have also been Mickey's own reluctance or inability to assert himself with his father. But now, just three weeks shy of turning twenty, Mantle's world and his relationship with his father were about to change dramatically. "That was the first time," he said in retelling the story in 1970, "that I knew Dad was really sick."

It was the dreaded Mantle curse. Mutt Mantle had Hodgkin's disease, the identical form of cancer that had killed Mickey's Grandpa Charlie and his uncles. Mickey Mantle, the toast of baseball just months earlier and on the cusp of becoming one of the game's immortals, was helpless and could do nothing. The diagnosis offered little of the hope that the suddenly shocked Mantle desperately sought.

"I'm sorry, Mick," the doctor who had examined Mutt told Mantle. Mickey memorized the doctor's words and would repeat them verbatim when recalling his father's diagnosis. "I'm afraid there's not much that can be done. Your father is dying."

With Mantle, however, the course of the self-destruction he would later follow had far less to do with celebrity and fame, and was rooted in his impending sense of doom that would become part of the Mantle legend, even as he attempted to downplay its significance in later years. Mantle became haunted by the fear of an early death. Teammate Hank Bauer told me in a 2001 interview how he once confronted Mickey after seeing him arrive for a game hungover from one of his late-night drinking binges. Mantle, though, wanted no fatherly advice, no matter how well intended. "My father died young," he told Bauer, looking at him through bloodshot eyes. "I'm not going to be cheated."

Mantle would never be convinced that his father hadn't been cheated by his early death—robbed of seeing his boy win baseball's Triple Crown trophy in 1956 and his every accomplishment, robbed of seeing the grandchildren he had asked for, robbed of the chance to grow old and make the peace that is often shared by fathers and sons. While researching *Dynasty*, his history of the 1949–1964 Yankees, author Peter Golenbock heard Mantle reminisce about his father and their relationship—something Mickey often refused to do with Yankee beat writers.

"Do you still miss him?" Golenbock asked. "Do you still think about him?"

Mantle nodded. "Oh, yes," he said. "I dream about him all the time."

Mantle, in a sense, not wanting to get "cheated," was living out not only the dream his father had for him but also the life his father had been denied. A son comes into his own when he surpasses his father, psychiatrists and Shakespeare would attest. Mickey Mantle continued the race with his father the rest of his life, with Mutt remaining a prominent figure in his psyche. Mutt Mantle would forever be present in his son's life, not simply as a memory but also as a patriarchal figure from whom Mickey never severed the ties of a child. The tension between fathers and sons invariably requires some form of break, physical and emotional, but with the Mantles there had been neither. Mickey's nightlife carousing, his sexual infidelity, his showing up hungover for games—it may have been

Mantle not wanting "to be cheated," but it was also the rebellion of a son seeking that break.

Years later, author Robert Creamer, who ghostwrote Mantle's book *The Quality of Courage* in 1964, wrote in a *Sports Illustrated* tribute to Mickey that the only time he ever saw him drunk was in New York in 1963, after the Yankees had been swept in the World Series by the Los Angeles Dodgers. "It was late at night," said Creamer, "and he was standing in the downstairs lobby of a hotel with a drink in his hand, talking with a small group of baseball people. He wasn't loud or belligerent, just a little sodden and a little wistful about the defeat."

Creamer said it was quickly apparent, more than a dozen years after his death, that Mickey's father still remained foremost in his son's consciousness—and that Mantle was still affected by him deeply. "[Mickey] said, 'What about this book?' It was about courage, I said," Creamer recalled, "and Mantle began talking about his father. He described his strength in holding his family together during the Depression and his courage in the last year of his life, when he knew he was dying of Hodgkin's disease but did not tell Mickey, who was in his precarious rookie season with the Yankees. 'My father was the bravest man I ever knew,' he said. I learned that Mantle was more sensitive than I had imagined from the surly image he had been projecting, and I found he had a subtle sense of humor. After our book was published, I took a copy to Yankee Stadium and asked him to autograph it for my children. When he handed it back, he had a little grin. In his strong, clear hand he had written, 'To Jim, Tom, John, Ellen and Bobby, my best wishes—from the man who taught your father a few lessons in journalism—Your friend, Mickey Mantle.' That was a nice little zinger, and I got a kick out of it."

3

Of Fathers and Sons

Mantle, Elvis, and Marilyn alike have evolved into a collection of cultural deities—modern-day equivalents of the Greek gods, who were immortal while sharing the characteristics of the human beings who worshipped them.

—*Mickey Mantle: America's Prodigal Son*

MICKEY RARELY SLEPT WELL AND ALMOST NEVER THROUGH THE NIGHT. He first experienced this as a youth, and the condition followed him when he left Commerce to play professional baseball. In New York, especially in late spring and summer when he would sleep with the windows open, he would stay awake listening to the cacophony of crowd noises, the neighbors' radios, and the sounds of the city that would build slowly in the background. Sometimes he would fall asleep, and the sounds and noises would transport him to a dream scene that was always the same. Reddish clay filled the image; then the top of a player's left baseball shoe would dig once, twice, three times. Then he would see the top of the right shoe digging in at the same time that he would catch, from the top, two muscular thighs as they swiveled just slightly. And then the view began to broaden, revealing first home plate, then the grassy edge of a baseball infield, and finally, a slowly unfurling magnificent panorama.

It was Yankee Stadium in the afternoon in all its storied glory, the legendary House That Ruth Built was abuzz and dressed in majestic red, white, and blue bunting. The Washington Senators, dressed in the visitors' traditional gray uniforms, were on the field. It is Memorial Day, 1956. A crescendo of cheers and boos builds in the crowd, and we hear the voice of announcer Bob Sheppard echoing over the public address system. His words are clipped but distinct: "Batting. Number seven. Centerfielder. Mick-ey Man-tle." The deafening cheers and boos loom hauntingly in the cavernous stadium, as at last we see at home plate the ballplayer who is the target of all the passion and pathos: Mickey Mantle. Blue-eyed, blonde hair, and surprisingly boyish looking for his age, which is twenty-four. His Yankee pinstripes make him look much taller than he is, and he poses an incredible physical presence: forearms rippling and the shoulders of a Greek hero. He appears oblivious to the crowd, which is on its feet, both those cheering and those booing. Mantle's eyes momentarily catch a glimpse of a father and his young son in the box seats in his sight line. They are seated in front of two nuns whose white habits resemble spinnakers. Then Mantle turns to the pitcher as we hear the loquacious, almost syrupy voice of radio announcer Mel Allen. "Mickey stands in against Ramos," Allen tells his audience. "Runners on first and second." From a stretch, the pitcher sweeps into his motion and delivers a ball. "Mickey takes the first pitch," says Allen. "Ball, low and away. Pedro Ramos works carefully. He knows Mickey's had a great month of May. Thirteen round-trippers. And he's looking for fireworks to celebrate this Memorial Day doubleheader."

Mantle steps out of the batter's box and checks for a sign from third base coach Frank Crosetti. He remains oblivious to the fans' screams: "Mantle, yo're a bum!" "You lazy draft dodger!" "Bury one, Mick!" "Hit it to Washington, Mickey!" Unfazed, Mantle is about ready to step back into the batter's box when he sets his gaze in the direction of the father and son he saw moments earlier. But instead of this father and son, Mantle sees another father and son sitting in the exact same seats—set apart from other fans by sepia tones, like an old, faded photograph. We are drawn to a sudden silence. Then a gust of wind swirls and whistles mysteriously in the hollow of the stadium. Mantle is momentarily flushed but composed. He stares hard. This second father and son are Mickey's father, Mutt Mantle, and Mickey as a young boy. Mantle told me in 1970 that he had "felt my father being with me at the stadium" even after he was dead. There were times, he said, when he had looked into the stands and there, then, for just a fleeting moment, he would catch a glimpse of Mutt sitting with him when he was a young boy. One of those times had been the day that the Senators' Pedro Ramos tried to throw his fastball past Mantle only to see Mickey slug the ball against the facade of the upper deck in Yankee Stadium. That was this day. In the stands, the young Mickey reaches over for his father and tugs at his coat sleeve. "Dad," says young Mickey. But he's unable to get his father's attention. "Dad," he says again. Mutt still doesn't hear him. "Dad?" Young Mick is more insistent. Our attention turns to the adult Mickey, about to take his at-bat but grim with determination, as if this game is more than it is. Then we hear this Mickey mutter under his breath, "Dad."

Mantle resets himself in the batter's box, preparing to hit. Right-hander Pedro Ramos goes into his windup and throws, as Mickey swings from his soul. His bat arced upward, its tan, grainy wood bearing the familiar black legend—*Louisville Slugger*. The ball and bat explode on impact. Mickey, following through gracefully, watches the ball lift skyward, as we hear Mel Allen's voice through a radio: "Mantle swings. There goes a long drive going to deep right field!"

The ball rockets toward the outfield so fast that the Yankee players sitting on the bench along first base almost get whiplash jerking their heads to look. The soaring baseball appears to be at a point higher than the Yankee Stadium roof, 120 feet from the ground, and it strikes the upper deck's filigreed facade only eighteen inches from the top of the roof. "It's soaring up high!" says an excited Allen. "It's going. It's going. It is gone! A home run for Mickey Mantle! It's almost gone out of the ball park! Mickey Mantle has come within a foot of becoming the first man to ever hit a ball out of Yankee Stadium!"

The ball strikes the facade so hard that it rebounds back through the sky. We can see the sharp image of a baseball, very close and in super slo-mo as it appears, its white cusp and red silk seams breaking into our vision like the sun at the dawn. The ball floats upward, gyrating like a planet, extending on into the sky. In lazy revolutions we can make out the bleached white horse hide bearing the blue legend—*Rawlings . . . American League*. The ball hovers, then falls, and when we focus on it again we see that it is now an old tennis ball that lands with a loud metal thud on the dented roof of an old tin shed, rattles around, and then rolls down into the dirt backyard of the Mutt Mantle home in Commerce, Oklahoma.

Stories of the young Mickey Mantle learning to switch-hit and being pitched to for hours on end every afternoon by his father and grandfather became as much a part of the Mantle lore as the young Arthur pulling out Excalibur from the stone is central to the legend of Camelot. In 1934, when Mickey was three years old, Mutt took a job as a shoveler at the Eagle-Picher Zinc and Lead Co. and moved his family from Spavinaw to Commerce, near the Interstate 44, which connects Tulsa and Joplin, Missouri. Commerce was a small town of fewer than 3,000 people, where the main street was only seven blocks long. This was a town so small it was once called simply North Miami because it was only four miles north of Miami, Oklahoma, in Ottawa County. But in 1914, lead and zinc mines were booming, so business people thought Commerce would be a better fit. The same year the Mantles moved to Commerce, on April 6, 1934, the notorious outlaws Bonnie and Clyde got stuck in the mud on the road between Commerce and Miami. At gunpoint, they forced a trucker to pull them out. A passing motorist happened to notice a bullet hole in Bonnie and Clyde's car's windshield and called the police. In the ensuing shootout, the Commerce police chief was taken hostage and the constable was killed.

Life was a lot calmer at 319 South Quincy Street, a four-room clapboard house that became home to the Mantles for the next ten years. Mutt, by this time, had become a ground boss in the Eagle-Picher lead and zinc mines, earning $75 a week, extremely good pay in the 1940s in Oklahoma or anywhere else in the country. Mutt, however, was supporting not only his growing five children and a wife but his father Charlie as well. The house on Quincy Street would become the one that Mickey would most associate with his youth. It was situated some hundred yards off the highway on a gravel road leading down to the house from the family mailbox. Often Mickey would wait at the mailbox for his father to come home from the mines, and they would walk together down the road to their house talking about baseball. From the time Mickey had been in his crib, Mutt had made sure his son had a baseball cap nearby. Lovell Mantle had used material from some of her husband's old baseball pants and shirts to fashion miniature uniforms for her son. Here, on Quincy

Street on the edge of town, sometimes in uniform and sometimes without, young Mickey began honing his swing with a tin shed for a backstop.

———

Now the year is 1937. The home is a weather-beaten wood frame house, which acts as a backstop to a little backyard baseball field, with the tin shed situated where center field should be. Mutt Mantle, standing on a makeshift pitching mound, shows a proud, elated smile as he looks at his six-year-old son, Mickey, standing at the plate, obviously having just hit a long home run off his father.

Mutt Mantle is in his midtwenties. He is slender with well-muscled arms and a darkened hue to everything about him. He is a miner, and coal soot clings to him and his clothes. A spry, middle-aged man retrieves the old tennis ball and throws it back to Mutt. He is Charlie Mantle, Mickey's grandfather. Both men have a grace in their movements that shows they have played the game seriously in their time. Mutt, who throws left-handed, approaches his son.

"Now, Mickey, there's one other thing I want to tell you," he says. "When I throw the ball, you go ahead and swing the way you're doin' it now. But when Grandpa Charlie throws the ball, I want you to turn around and swing left-handed. Understand?"

Mickey nods several times. Then he shakes his head.

"Grandpa Charlie's right-handed," his father tells him. "So you hit left-handed when he pitches. I'm a left-hander, so you want to bat right-handed against southpaws."

"But, Dad," pleads Mickey. "I can't hit the other way. I can't hit left-handed."

Mutt stops him with a look. "Mickey," he tells his son. "Some day all the great big-leaguers will be switch-hittin'. Battin' righty against southpaws. Battin' lefty against righties. Come on, let's try it."

Then he looks to Grandpa Charlie: "Pa, come pitch to Mickey."

Mickey sets up awkwardly to bat left-handed. Grandpa Charlie winds up and soft-tosses the tennis ball to his grandson. Whiff. Mickey misses. He misses a second time, a third, and a fourth. When he misses a fifth time, Mickey's young face begins showing an anxious look that is almost fear. When he misses again, tears begin running down his little cheeks.

"Dad, I can't do it. I can't." His pleading is accented with sobs he tries to hold back.

Mutt bites his lip but can't hide his obvious disappointment. "Yes, you can, Mickey," he insists. "I don't want to hear you say you can't. Understand?"

Mickey nods and takes his stance again. Uncle Charlie winds up and throws another soft strike. Mickey swings, harder than ever, and misses once again—his face a mixture of pain and panic as he turns, looking for his father. Mutt is shaking his head, visibly disappointed.

Mutt's wife and Mickey's mother, Lovell, has been watching from the kitchen through the tattered screen and calls out, "Mutt, Mickey, Grandpa Charlie. Y'all gotta stop. Supper's ready."

Inside, as the family settles down for dinner, the Mantle house is typical of those in the mining community, small but tidy. Photographs of Mutt in a baseball uniform and with a team adorn a wall. Baseball trophies read "Mayes County, Oklahoma Champions." Stacks of schoolbooks lay scattered on the floor. Around the dinner table are Mutt, Grandpa Charlie, Lovell, Mickey, and four younger siblings, including twin boys, a little girl, and a baby. As she eats, Lovell reads from several handwritten sheets of paper, as Mickey recalled that she often did at dinner. "Oh, Mutt, I can't read my own writing," she announces. "One day you're goin' to get me one of those fancy scorekeeping books, if you expect me to listen to the game on the radio and tell you what happened."

"You're doin' fine," he assures her.

"Oh, okay. Here's what happened." The entire table seems to hang on Lovell's words. "So, in the bottom of the ninth inning, Johnny Mize pops up to short for the first out, Pepper Martin singles, Joe Medwick walks."

Excited at what he's hearing, Mickey blurts out, "They had the tying run on base?"

Mutt delights at young Mickey's interest and observation.

"But then the Cubs' pitcher makes a wild pitch," says Lovell.

"Oh, no!" moans Mutt.

"What's wrong with that, Dad?" Mickey asks. "It's a wild pitch. The runners move up."

"Mickey Owen's up," says Mutt. "Takes the bat out of his hands."

"How?" Mickey doesn't understand.

"The Cubs walked Mickey Owen intentionally," says Lovell.

"Loads the bases," says Mutt. "Sets up a force at any base. Maybe even a double play."

Lovell eyes her husband with a smile. "The next batter, Enos Slaughter, grounds into a double play."

Mickey and the twins groan in disappointment.

"A lot more baseball to be played," said Mutt. He had a way of saying things that let everyone else know that that part of the conversation was up. "My dad indulged idle conversation about as much as he did fools," Mickey later recalled. "You knew when it was time to shut up or move to something else."

"I can't wait for school to be over," Mickey told the dinner table, "so I can listen to the games with Mom."

Lovell, though, moved on from baseball talk for the day. She looked directly at her husband: "Well, you know who didn't wait for school to end? The Ramseys. They lit out for California today. Packed up and left. Just like that. Can you imagine?"

"Things are bad in the country, Lovell," Mutt said. "Someone at the mines said they read in the paper that they call Oklahoma the Dust Bowl."

"It's that darn Roosevelt," said Grandpa Charlie. "He ain't done nothin' for the workin' man like he promised to do."

"It's the Depression, Pa," said Mutt.

"Oughta go to war, I say," his father shot back. "That'd get people workin'."

"Charlie! I dare say!" said Lovell. "We have food on the table. Mutt's workin' steady at the mines. We have lots to be thankful for."

"Then why don't we ever say grace?" asked Mickey. "And why don't we go to church? Everyone else goes to church."

There is an awkward pause as everyone continues eating. Lovell looks at Mutt, her eyes suggesting that he should give Mickey an answer.

"Well, Mickey," said Mutt, "religion doesn't necessarily make you good."

"Amen," Grandpa Charlie chimed in.

"As long as your heart is in the right place and you don't hurt anyone," said Mutt, "I think you'll go to heaven—if there is one."

The front door opens, and a teenage girl enters the house: Anna Bea Mantle, Lovell's daughter by a previous marriage. The first thing she does is walk over to the radio and turn it on. A staticky Glenn Miller tune comes on, and Anna Bea sways to the music.

"Anna Bea," her mother asks. "Where have you been? You're late for supper again."

The twins jump up out of their chairs and start poking fun at their half sister: "Anna Bea's late! Anna Bea's late! Anna Bea's late!" She ignores her mother, sticks her tongue out at the twins—who squeal and laugh—and walks over to the table, where she picks at Mickey's plate.

"Your momma's talkin' to you," Mutt tells his stepdaughter.

"I'm late. I'm sorry," she says in an empty apology.

From his seat, Mickey eyes Anna Bea with distrust. There is an obvious uneasiness in his reaction.

"So where have you been all afternoon and evening?" her mom asks.

"Studyin'."

Mickey smirks. Anna Bea tries to kick him, but his reaction is too quick. He smirks again.

"At least my bed's dry," she says loudly as she walks away.

Mickey is so angry that he shoots daggers at her as she leaves the room.

Half an hour later, the music is still playing as Mutt and Lovell sit in the living room listening to the radio. Lovell stitches a homemade baseball uniform by hand. Mutt pensively draws on a Lucky Strike. The windows are wide open, and now they seem enchanted by the night sky filled with fireflies and the sound of crickets.

"You know, Mutt. Mickey really does love the game," Lovell says this matter-of-factly, almost as if she's got something else on her mind.

"I know," he says.

"But, you know, Mutt, he hates it that he has to learn to bat left-handed."

"I know that too," says Mutt. "But it's for his own good. Once he starts seeing some right-hander's curve ball, he'll understand too. If he's battin' right-handed, that curve's gonna run away from him faster than a greased pig at the fair. No, Lovell, Mickey's gonna be a switch-hitter."

4

The Boy Who Would Be Best

Mick was from Oklahoma. That's a hard part of the country to be from. It's a testament to Mick—and to his character.
—JOE DIMAGGIO

THE MINING TOWN OF COMMERCE, OKLAHOMA, LIES AN ENTIRE OCEAN and half a country away from Brierley Hill in Shropshire, England, a distance of 4,347 miles to be exact. In the Victorian Age of the nineteenth century, Brierley Hill was notoriously famous for its hellish appearance in the choking environment of England's Black Country. It was said that Queen Victoria once visited the area and had been so startled from the overwhelmingly unpleasant sight that she asked for the blinds of her railway carriage to be drawn to hide the view of the hideous industrial landscape, this dreadful Black Country her couriers had brought her to. The Black Country had been christened with that ignominious name because of the dark clouds produced by thousands of ironworking foundries and forges that Charles Dickens said made it a "cheerless region" in which "tall chimneys, crowding on each other and presenting that endless repetition of the same, dull, ugly form poured out their plague of smoke, obscured the light, and made foul the melancholy air." So abominable were living conditions that residents at that time composed a rhyme comparing Brierley Hill to hell:

> When Satan stood on Brierley Hill
> And far around it gazed
> He said, "I never more shall feel
> At Hell's fierce flames amazed."

Almost a century later, in Commerce, Oklahoma, the environmental conditions in the Depression era of the 1930s were almost identical to those of Brierley Hill in the Victorian Age. The thriving mining industry there disposed of its mine waste, known as "chat," in huge mounds right on the ground, creating huge artificial hills across the community landscape. The chat was toxic, and the fine grains from the chat piles created dark, threatening clouds that the wind blew all over town, settling on everything, all while residents young and old inhaled the smoke.

The George Mantle family detested the living conditions in their English hometown. Seeking a better life, they immigrated to America to escape the conditions of Brierley Hill, leaving much of their extended family and their homeland. Back in the old country, the Mantles had been part of the environmental debacle, as well as longtime residents. It is believed within the Mantle family, which has kept a meticulously recorded history, that Mickey's great-great-great-great grandparents were George Mantle and Ann Jordin who married on August 20, 1765, in Cleobury Mortimer, Shropshire. Their son Thomas was born in June 1776, a month before the signing of the American Declaration of Independence, there in Hopton Wafers, Shropshire. Thomas Mantle married Mary Gittins and named their first son after Thomas's father, George. He was born in Shropshire on January 22, 1805, and his wife Maria Scriven was born in Staffordshire on April 20, 1808. They were married at Tipton Parish Church on June 16, 1828. Their children grew up in Brierley Hill, among whose foundries by this time were the Mantle Family and Old Level Ironworks that George would eventually pass on to his son Harry George as George Mantle and Co. George and Maria's eldest son, James David Mantle, was born in Brierley Hill on May 10, 1841. Seven years later, on August 23, 1948, George Mantle and his young family sailed from Liverpool on the *Sailer Prince*, landing in New Orleans on November 20. The family ferried up the Mississippi to St. Louis where they lived for a short while before settling in Osage near Linn, Missouri. There the only work George could find was as depressing as what he had left behind in England. He worked the mines, and it appeared the Mantles would see its next generation growing up as if it had never left England's Black Country. After George's death in Linn in 1879, James moved on to

Missouri and Illinois. He had already married Eliza C. Moore in 1863, and they had three sons: Robert, Richard, and Charles Edwin. It was Charles Edwin Mantle who later married Mae Clark and came to be known as "Grandpa Charlie" by his oldest grandson whom he would help teach to switch-hit.

Had he been born in the family's homeland, Mickey Mantle might have grown up to be the greatest cricketer in England's history, the Ian Botham of his time. Who hasn't wondered who they might have been had they been born two or three generations earlier in their family, and in the country from which they immigrated to America? For Mickey Mantle, he didn't even have to go that far back. There was a good chance Mantle could have been born his aunt's son. That was certainly who Elven Clark Mantle had his eye on. By then Charles Edwin Mantle had relocated to the mining town of Spavinaw in Mayes County, Oklahoma, where his wife Mae died of pneumonia a month after giving birth to her fifth child. Charles was left a widower with five children; Elven, who was eight years old, was the oldest. Relatives raised the baby, while the single father struggled until the two boys were in their teens and could join him working in the mines.

In 1929, Elven "Mutt" Mantle happened to meet Lorene Richardson, who was also from Spavinaw, and set about courting her. Elven, who had been born March 16, 1912, was seventeen years old. Lorene was five years older, but Mutt didn't seem to mind and asked her out. Not much is known about Lorene's family dynamics that brought about what happened when Mutt called on her at the Richardson home on South Choctaw Avenue in Spavinaw. He was met at the door by Lorene's older sister Lovell Thelma Richardson Davis, a divorcée with two kids from her marriage. At the age of seventeen, Lovell had run off with William Theodore Davis, a farm boy from nearby Craig County. She had two children with Davis, Theodore and Anna Bea, before divorcing. She would one day explain her marital breakup to Mickey by telling him, "We had a bad misunderstanding." To say that Lovell was desperately looking for a husband to get her out of her father's house yet a second time is an understatement. But Lovell's looks were still easy on the eyes. She was a tall, slender woman with gray eyes and reddish-blond hair. A few months after they met, on December

29, 1929, Mutt and Lovell were married. Lovell was eight years and one month older than her teenage groom, causing some relatives to cruelly joke that "Mutt married himself a mother."

Lovell, though, made life bearable in Spavinaw for a young man taking on the serious responsibility of a young family. They shared a common background of coming from a long line of Oklahoma people, five generations of Americans with family bloodlines of English, Dutch, and German stock. At one point, there was unfounded speculation, in part spurred by Mickey's pride in the American Indian heritage of his beloved Oklahoma, that his mother was part Native American. Spavinaw had been the heart of Cherokee Indian country, and during this time in the Depression it was in the midst of the legendary Dust Bowl, the plains in Oklahoma where red dirt blanketed everything when the wind blew. It was here that Mickey Mantle was born October 20, 1931, in an unpainted two-room house on a dirt road. It was a time of America's worst economic depression. Anyone who has looked at black-and-white photographs in James Agee and Walker Evans's *Let Us Now Praise Famous Men* couldn't help but be moved by the stolid and stunned faces of tenant farmers immortalized in the book and in literature like John Steinbeck's *Grapes of Wrath*. In Spavinaw, the Mantles saw many neighbors give up trying to make a living and move to California, like the mythical clan of Dust Bowl farmers in *The Grapes of Wrath* who migrate to California after they lose their Oklahoma farm.

For people like the Mantles, though, there was hope and there was baseball. For Mutt Mantle, the 1931 season during which he and Lovell were expecting their first baby just happened to be a fortuitous one. Mutt's favorite ballplayer was Mickey Cochrane, a catcher and sparkplug of the Philadelphia Athletics' championship teams of 1929/1930/1931. "If my child is a boy," Mutt told his friends, according to Dick Schaap's 1961 biography, *Mickey Mantle: The Indispensable Yankee*, "he's going to be a baseball player. I'm naming him Mickey—after Mickey Cochrane."

True to his word, Mutt named his son Mickey, giving him the middle name Charles after his own father. Mutt apparently was unaware that Cochrane's name at birth had been Gordon Stanley and that he took on "Mickey" as an informal name derived from the nickname "Black

Mike" that Cochrane had been given at Boston University for his competitiveness on the football team. But then Mutt had never been one concerned about the exactness of names. Mutt's given name of "Elven" became "Elvan" on his Oklahoma driver's license and ended up back as "Elven" on his headstone at the Grand Army of the Republic Cemetery between Miami and Commerce, where he was buried after his death in 1952. Mutt's name was also spelled "Elven" on the birth certificate of Mickey's youngest brother, Larry. Meanwhile, Mickey always spelled his father's name "Elvin." Yet, still, the federal government recorded Mutt as "E. C. Mantle," in the 1940 U.S. Census.

By 1940, Mutt Mantle had weathered the bad times of the Depression and survived. Not long after marrying Lovell and Mickey being born, Mutt lost his job grading county roads and thought long and hard about moving his young family to California, as many others from Oklahoma had done. Instead he became a tenant farmer and worked eighty acres of land that finally led him to relocate in Commerce. He returned to the underground life of mining, which Mickey would lament his entire life.

"I always wished my dad could be somebody other than a miner," a regretful Mickey would reminisce in one of our conversations in the early 1970s. "I knew it was killing him. He was underground eight hours a day. Every time he took a breath, the dust and dampness went into his lungs. Coughed up gobs of phlegm and never saw a doctor. What for? He'd only be told it was 'miner's disease.' He realized that if he didn't get cancer, he'd die of tuberculosis. Many did before the age of forty. 'So what the hell? Live while you can,' he'd say and light another cigarette. [My dad was] a confirmed chain-smoker, I hardly remember him without one stuck in the corner of his mouth."

A man that tough, a father that tough, be he "Elven or "Elvin," the nickname Mutt was perhaps more fitting. It is also safe to say that with Mickey's eventual fame, Elven or Elvin Mantle would be known simply as Mutt in New York Yankee lore. As such, he would come to epitomize the American image of the doting father on a gifted son. Some, like Merlyn Mantle, would even come to view Mutt's dreams for Mickey as bordering on the obsessive. "The feeling between Mutt Mantle and his son," Merlyn Mantle wrote in her 1996 memoir *A Hero All His Life*, "was more than love. Mick was his work of art, just as much as if his father had created him out of clay. He spent every minute he could with him, coaching, teaching, shaping him, and pointing him toward the destiny he knew was out there. Baseball consumed Mickey. He talked, when he talked, of little else. It was the number one priority in his life and, in a way, always would be."

"Mama says dad showed me a baseball before I was twelve hours old and it almost broke his heart when I paid more attention to the bottle," Mantle wrote in his own 1985 autobiography *The Mick*. "Baseball, that's all he lived for. He used to say that it seemed to him like he just died in the winter, until the time when baseball came around again. Dad insisted on my being taught the positions on the baseball field before the ABCs. He was that crazy about baseball.... I was probably the only baby in history whose first lullaby was the radio broadcast of a ball game. One night, mama says, I woke up during the seventh-inning stretch. She pleaded with dad to please cut off that contraption and let me sleep. 'You got Mickey wrong, hon,' dad said. 'I don't blame him for screaming. He knew the situation called for a bunt instead of hitting away.'"

For his part, Mickey looked upon his father as a near saint.

"No boy, I think, ever loved his father more than I did," Mantle told author Mickey Herskowitz in *Mickey Mantle: An Appreciation*. "I would do nearly anything to keep my father happy.... He never had to raise his hand to me to make me obey, for I needed only a sharp look and a word from him and the knowledge that I had displeased him to make me go and do better.... I knew from the time I was small that every small victory I won, and every solid hit I made or prize I was awarded, brought real joy to my father's heart."

How many fathers haven't had a similar dream as Mutt had for his son? Thousands, even millions, no doubt. What made his special? Or was it just fate and good fortune? There was no annunciation, no angel from the baseball gods. Mutt Mantle was a simple lead and zinc miner who had played semiprofessional baseball. His father Charles Mantle had played baseball on another mining company team. They had little to pass on to Mickey beyond their work ethic and perhaps something in their genes that ultimately produced an incredible, almost mythic physical strength that one day would produce his prodigious home run power.

"My father was a quiet man, but he could freeze you with a look," Mickey said in a 1970 conversation. "He never told me he loved me. But he showed that he did by all the hours he spent with me, all the hopes he invested in me. He saw his role as pushing me, always keeping my mind on getting better. I worked hard at doing that because I wanted to please him. He would drape an arm around me and give me a hug. . . . I adored my dad and was just like him in many ways—I was shy and found it hard to show my emotions. I couldn't open up to people, and they mistook my shyness for rudeness."

Sadly, the way he was molded by two unemotional parents would influence the way Mickey himself would model his relationships with his own sons. "He had been brought up a certain way," son Mickey Jr. said of his father in a family memoir, "and if he couldn't deal with his feelings, he buried them. He paid a high cost for packing away the affection that was so close to his surface. For most of our lives, when we greeted each other after a separation of weeks or months, we would shake hands. It wasn't just him. Everybody in his family, my uncles, his cousins, kept the same distance."

Mickey had a different, more distant relationship with his mother. Lovell Mantle, the daughter of a carpenter, had difficulty showing her feelings with her loved ones. Mickey would later say in *The Mick* that his mother "didn't lavish affection on us either . . . when mom wanted to show her love, she fixed a big meal."

In her memoir, Merlyn Mantle's recollection of her mother-in-law seemed to capture the essence of Mickey's mom best: "Lovell was not a warm or openly affectionate woman, but she was a tireless and protective mother. She had seven children, two by a first marriage, and I never saw anyone do as much laundry. She did it by hand, on a washboard in the backyard, and hung it on row after row of clotheslines to dry. They lived in the country and didn't yet have electricity."

Lovell Mantle, though, had a dark side to her, which Mickey acknowledged in a 1976 interview with *Dallas Times Herald* columnist Blackie Sherrod. Mickey reluctantly talked about whippings he had been given by his mother. He would also see some of his mother's dark side in her treatment of little David Mantle, who would describe his grandmother as "always mean to me."

"She used to chase me around and hit me with a broomstick," David remembered with sadness in a family memoir. "Maybe it was because I was so hyper. One day I was sitting on a stool in her kitchen, and I did something a kid would do. Dad told me she just backhanded me and knocked me off the stool. After that, he never let her watch me any more because it really hurt him that she would give me that kind of swat. He said she used to whip him, too, something he didn't like to admit. She was still dad's mother, and I respected her, but I didn't have the love for her that I did for mom's folks."

Perhaps most surprising about the Mantles as Mickey was growing up in Oklahoma was that they did not have much of a traditional spiritual life, especially considering that they lived in a community of God-fearing neighbors in the heart of the Bible Belt. "Nobody in my family took religion seriously," Mantle told Sherrod in 1976. "I suppose it was my dad's influence. He used to say, 'Religion doesn't necessarily make you good. As long as your heart is in the right place and you don't hurt anyone, I think you'll go to heaven— if there is one.' Mom felt the same way. She backed him no matter what he believed."

Merlyn Mantle would go to her grave convinced that Mutt's overbearing fathering unchecked by Lovell's own detached manner left Mickey emotionally and psychologically traumatized, and unable to turn even to his loved ones for help.

"The early pressure on Mickey to play ball and his self-imposed drive to play it better than anyone, caused real emotional problems for him," she wrote in her memoir. "A lot of the conflicts in him later had their roots in those years. Mick wet his bed until he was sixteen years old. I would hope that this would not be taken as demeaning him. But it is important, I think, in understanding what he went through, and how much he wanted to please his dad. This is what the pressure of wanting that approval did to him. He told me that he knew from the time he was five years old that he wanted to be a ballplayer, and how he could never face his father if he didn't make it to the major leagues. Interestingly, the bed-wetting stopped when the Yankees sent him to Independence, Kansas, for his first season in Class D. He had to solve the problems before any of his teammates found out. He could not abide anyone making fun of him. He stopped by asserting his own pure willpower, because the pressure didn't end then, or with the Yankees. It never ended. I know exactly how much he ached for his dad's approval. . . . His father had this wonderful but obsessive dream for Mickey, and only for Mickey. He was anointed from the cradle. When his dad would pitch to him for hours, out of a hundred pitches, Mick would be in terror of missing one and looking bad, and having his father frown or criticize."

Mantle talked about the bed-wetting on a 1970 *Dick Cavett Show* on which songwriter Paul Simon was also a guest. In that talk show, Simon was dumbstruck by the revelation of another of his heroes and expressed the shock of millions: "Mickey Mantle wet his bed?!"

But there was one childhood trauma that Mickey never spoke about publicly. When he was four or five years old, his half sister Anna Bea and some of her teenage friends sexually molested him. He admitted this to wife Merlyn later in their lives. Earlier, though, he had shared this secret with Holly Brooke, his New York girlfriend in his 1951 rookie season.

"It had devastated him, as you can imagine it would," Holly told me in a 2009 interview. "He was humiliated."

According to accounts from Holly as well as Merlyn in her memoir, Anna Bea on several occasions had molested him by pulling down his pants and fondling his penis, often as her girlfriends watched and giggled, howling their laughter and derision at the times when he would get a tiny erection. The molestation and the teasing continued for several years until Anna Bea moved out of the house, but the traumatic scarring lasted a lifetime. Merlyn said she suspected that the molestation was the source of what she considered Mickey's womanizing—that it was a reason he never respected women, his affairs, his one-night stands, and the crude and vulgar language he used around women when he drank.

Mutt apparently never knew of Mickey's molestation.

"It was tragic, and it's probably best Mickey's father never knew of it," Holly Brooke said in a 2015 interview. "Heaven help anyone who would have harmed Mutt's son. I can't imagine any father loving a son more than the way Mutt loved Mickey."

5

Eyeing The Babe

With his combination of speed and power, Mickey Mantle should win the triple batting crown every year.

—Casey Stengel

Was Mickey Mantle ready to play big league baseball at the age of nineteen in 1951, or was he rushed in a move that would likely determine his future? Is greatness seen in just a few powerful swings and home runs in spring training, when statistics can be so incredibly impressive but yet disappear from the records because they don't really count? This will long be debated. Should Mantle, who had been in lowly Class C baseball only months earlier, have been groomed slower, perhaps in Double-A ball, with a jump to Triple-A at midseason and then a call up to the Yankees in September? In 1950, Mickey had been promoted to the Yankees for the final two weeks of the season, his reward for his sensational season on the Class C Joplin team. Mickey led the Western Association in four offensive categories, winning the league batting title with a .383 average and also leading the league with 199 hits, 141 runs, and 326 total bases. As soon as the season ended, the Yankees called Mickey up to join the major league team for a series against the Browns in St. Louis, and to travel with them as a nonroster player on their final two-week road trip.

Mantle arrived in Sportsman's Park in St. Louis carrying a straw suitcase with only two pairs of pants, on a Sunday, September 17, 1950. A month shy of being nineteen, he was terrified at just the thought that he was stepping into the dugout with his childhood hero Joe DiMaggio and the defending World Champion Yankees. He was so scared that he stayed in the Yankee clubhouse, unable to join the rest of the team. It was not until two of the players, Jerry Coleman and Bobby Brown, urged him to go on the field that he joined his teammates. But then, after the workout, Mickey hesitated about returning to the carpeted clubhouse while wearing his spikes until he noticed that all his teammates didn't think twice about it.

"I was that fish out of water you're always hearing about," he told me in 1970. "I couldn't believe I was there. I had dreamed of being a Yankee growing up, hearing about Ruth, Gehrig, and DiMaggio, and now here I was. I didn't know how to act or what to say."

Yankee pitcher Whitey Ford, who would become one of Mickey's closest friends in the future, had been brought up from the minors to the Yankees in the second half of that season and recalled, "I remember Mantle joining us in St. Louis, and that was the first time I ever saw him. I didn't meet him. He was so shy, he didn't talk to anybody but [lefty rookie pitcher Bob] Wiesler for the two weeks he was with us. But I remember him and Moose [Skowron, another September call-up] taking batting practice with us before the games, and they put on a great show of power hitting."

The Yankees went on to win the 1950 World Series, sweeping the Philadelphia Phillies for the second of their record five straight titles. Mantle left New York inspired and couldn't wait for spring training at the Yankees' traditional camp in St. Petersburg, Florida. St. Petersburg was where the Yankees had trained for the upcoming baseball season since the days of Babe Ruth except for three years during World War II. But in 1951 the Yankees switched their spring training camp to Phoenix, Arizona. Yankee co-owner Del Webb, a resident of Phoenix, arranged to showcase his world championship team to his influential friends on the West Coast by swapping spring training sites with New York Giants owner Horace Stoneham. Casey Stengel, in his third year as manager of the team, had also persuaded Webb to establish a special three-week instructional camp preceding spring training for rookies, bonus players, and promising minor leaguers. In 1950, the Yankee farm teams had produced sixty all-star minor leaguers, including Mantle. Of these, forty were invited to the 1951 instructional camp. Yankee general manager George Weiss feared that rushing a young prospect like Mickey could harm his development and didn't want Mantle at the camp. Stengel didn't agree with the decision and began a campaign to change Weiss's mind. Casey was joined by Tom Greenwade, the Yankee scout who had signed Mantle and now lobbied Yankee minor league director Lee MacPhail, insisting that Mickey be invited to the camp. They convinced the Yankee executives to include Mantle, but Mickey was noticeably absent when the instructional camp opened. Stengel was understandably irate.

Mickey was still back in Commerce. After receiving a letter from the team shortly after New Year's Day, instructing him to report to the instructional camp, he had waited for additional instructions and a plane or bus ticket but heard nothing more. In Phoenix, Stengel kept pressing the Yankee brass about his young phenom who still had not shown up even as the camp got underway. From Phoenix, the Yankees tried contacting Mickey but couldn't reach him because the Mantles did not have a telephone in their home. Finally, a reporter and photographer with the *Miami (Oklahoma) Daily News Record* showed up at the Mantle home in Commerce to find out why Mickey wasn't in camp.

"They didn't send no ticket or nothing," Mickey told them, according to the Miami newspaper.

"Yeah? Well, we got a call from Lee MacPhail, saying to get hold of you because he doesn't have your home telephone number or any idea in the world where you work."

Mantle headed straight for the Blue Goose Number One mine, where Mutt worked, to call MacPhail. "Where are you?" Mickey recalled MacPhail demanding to know. "Why aren't you here in Phoenix?"

"I'm broke," Mickey told him. "I don't have any money for transportation."

Meanwhile, a story was going out nationwide on the Associated Press wire service that began, "Mickey Mantle, heading for Yankee stardom, has not yet reported to the team's spring training camp because 'I haven't gotten my ticket yet.'"

The next day, Tom Greenwade arrived in Commerce to personally deliver a ticket and expense money to the rookie he had signed. Mickey was quickly on his way to join the Yankees. In Phoenix, Weiss explained to Stengel and other Yankee management brass that he had forgotten to send Mantle the expense money. Stengel and others didn't buy the story.

Weiss was an extremely meticulous man; Stengel suspected that he had never intended to send Mickey his transportation money.

Mantle arrived in Phoenix stressed, anxious, and needing a good night's sleep. He still had trouble sleeping in camp. When he did fall asleep, Mickey would drift back in dreams to the place most familiar to him: Commerce, Oklahoma. Looking almost bleak and mournful, the place where he had grown up now appeared to him with a flat, paved highway road in rural Oklahoma lined by telephone poles leading into a tiny, seemingly deserted, desolate, windblown, dust-bowl town. There, in his backyard, he saw images of his childhood practicing his switch-hitting, batting successfully right-handed against Mutt, struggling left-handed against Grandpa Charlie. . . . Then on the driveway, with baseball glove in hand, Mickey saw himself greeting his father, a smile relieving his weariness from a long day working at the coal mines. Mickey opens Mutt's lunchbox to find a chocolate cupcake he's saved for his son. . . . Another day pint-sized Mickey plays catcher in equipment that dwarfs him, but he acquits himself well behind the plate, comes up to bat and smashes a double. . . . A couple of years older, Mickey batting right-handed slugs homer after homer off the tin shed's roof. Then, batting left-handed, Mickey again struggles and shows his frustration.

These memories swept in and out of his dreams in no particular order. It was a jumble of stream of consciousness: Outside the Mantle house, Mickey, Mutt, and Grandpa Charlie creep outside and into an old LaSalle. Then they are on a highway. In the back seat of the LaSalle, Mickey watches the Kansas countryside as they pass signs of cities ahead, including one that reads, "St. Louis 41 Miles." . . . Inside Sportsman's Park in St. Louis, in total awe, Mickey watches a major league baseball game with his father and grandfather. . . . The next moment, at a rickety Oklahoma ballpark, Mickey is sitting in the dugout with his Douthat travel club teammates watching the opposing team's pitcher—a right-hander—who is bringing serious heat and mowing down batter after batter. A teammate, Mickey's neighbor Leroy Bennett, has just struck out and returns to the dugout. Mickey has a bat in his hands and is sitting next to another good friend, Nick Ferguson. Mantle later recalled the incident from memory.

"What'd he get you with, LeRoy?" Nick asks.

"Dunno," says Leroy. "Can't hit what I can't see."

As Mickey gets up off the bench and heads to the on-deck circle, Nick catches his attention. "Man, Mickey," says Nick, "we gotta break up this no-hitter."

"Yeah, Mickey," says Leroy, "it's gonna be up to you."

From the on-deck circle, Mickey surveys the bleachers. He sees his mother, but there's no trace of Mutt. He walks back toward the dugout's edge and calls Nick and Leroy, who huddle close to Mickey.

"Dad was working a double shift today and said he didn't think he'd make it to the game," Mickey tells his teammates. "You don't see him anywhere, do ya?"

Nick and Leroy scan the crowd.

"He's not here, Mickey?" says Nick. "Why?"

"Are you going to switch, Mickey?" Leroy asks.

Mickey nods. "I've struck out batting left-handed three times," he says, "but I know I can hit this pitcher if I bat right-handed."

Just then, the batter strikes out. Mickey's up. He walks purposefully to the plate, takes a couple of practice swings right-handed, checks the third base coach, then steps into the right-handed batter's box where he starts to dig in.

Suddenly, a booming, frightening voice reverberates over the field, stopping play.

"Go on home!"

Mickey and everyone else turn to see Mutt, who has shown up behind the backstop.

"Go on home!" Mutt yells angrily. "And don't you ever put on that baseball uniform until you switch-hit like I taught you."

Devastated, Mickey breaks into tears as he runs off the field. That night, still upset and distraught, Mickey seeks his mother's consolation. Lovell is ironing a large stack of clothes. There are sounds of the other Mantle kids playing in the living room.

"I just can't be what Dad wants," Mickey, near tears, tells his mother.

"Mickey, your daddy just wants you to be the best ballplayer you can be," his mom tells him.

Now crying, Mickey shakes his head. "He wants more. He wants me to be the best ballplayer ever. That's impossible."

"Mickey, if your daddy has dreams for you, it might be because he didn't have a chance to live out his." His mother says this in a matter-of-fact tone, without any sense of sympathy for her child. "Your daddy has spent his life in those mines, it seems, and it's been for us. You know, your daddy was only seventeen when we got married, and he took on a family. I already had Anna Bea and Theo. I'm ten years older than your daddy, did you know that?"

Mickey shakes his head. He is enchanted by the story of his father and mother.

"He was the handsomest thing I ever saw," Mickey's mother tells him. "I couldn't wait to have his children. That's why you're so special. To me, as well as to him."

The front door opens. It is Mutt. Mickey's eyes light up, and he looks at his father with renewed admiration.

"Dad, I'm sorry," he says, bursting into tears. "I won't ever do that again. I promise."

Mutt nods and rubs Mickey's head. But Mutt's face is wrought with emotion over something weightier than baseball.

"Where's Grandpa Charlie?" Lovell asks him. "Wasn't he with you?"

Mutt nods again. "Pa's sick." His announcement is met with stunned silence from Lovell and Mickey. "He collapsed," says Mutt. "We took him to the hospital. They're gonna keep him for a few days."

Mickey starts crying again. "I hate hospitals," he says.

Suddenly, a distant siren begins to wail, becoming increasingly louder and foreboding. Mickey rushes to the window, followed by the kids from the other rooms.

"Oh, heaven," says Lovell, recognizing the siren and what it means. "There's been an accident."

"I've gotta be there," says Mutt wearily.

The stream-of-consciousness daydream ends. Mantle later remembered that it was dusk outside the Blue Goose Mine, and there is an urgent, chaotic scene. Soot-covered miners slowly filter out of the mine so dirty and filthy that you almost can't tell them apart. Makeshift lights have gone up. Everything looks damp and dark.

Lovell and Mickey join other families that wait for word outside the mine. Lovell recognizes one of the men leaving. He is Eugene Mantle, Mutt's brother who was known as Tunney.

The family calls out to him, and Tunney sees them and rushes toward them. The conversations stuck in Mickey's steel-trap memory.

"I saw Mutt down there," he says. "He's fine."

"What happened, Uncle Tunney?" asks Mickey.

"A cave-in in one of the tunnels," he says.

"How bad?" Lovell asks him.

"We got some men trapped down there," says Tunney. "It was a bad one. Mutt told me about pa. I'm headin' to the hospital."

The faint sound of a bell tolls, then tolls again clearer and increasingly louder, just as it begins raining.

It is still pouring at a cemetery as a steady rain blankets the graveyard. Umbrellas offer cover to the mourners. The Mantle family sadly watches a wooden casket being lowered into a grave.

Mutt Mantle, an arm loosely around Mickey's shoulders, walks slowly with his oldest son past the grave behind other mourners who sprinkle dirt onto the casket as they pay their last respects. Lovell, the twins, and her other children are right behind. Then it is Mutt and Mickey's turn.

Almost expressionless, Mutt sprinkles dust and starts to say something—but doesn't or can't. He is a man who has a difficult time showing his emotions, even now. It leaves Mickey uncertain as to what to do.

"Say good-bye to Grandpa," he tells his oldest son.

"Good-bye, Grandpa Charlie," Mickey recalled saying. "I'll miss you. Dad'll miss you."

Tears well in Mutt's eyes, but he quickly restrains himself. Then, leaving Mickey with his mother and siblings, Mutt continues walking alone out of the cemetery through the rain. Mickey is torn between following after his father and allowing him to mourn alone. You sense that he wants to join his father. But he is unable to act on his feelings and does nothing.

Just then the alarm clock rings. Mickey breathes hard as he tries waking up in the spring training dorm where his roommates race to get dressed.

6

The Child of Stengel and Destiny

When I first came to Yankee Stadium I used to feel like the ghosts of Babe Ruth and Lou Gehrig were walking around in there.
—MICKEY MANTLE

WHEN MICKEY ARRIVED IN THE YANKEE SPRING TRAINING CAMP IN 1951, an uncanny sense of destiny and history was already at work. The man with the acumen to pick up what was happening was not the manager, Casey Stengel, nor anyone else in the Yankee's upper echelons. Rather it was a man who for more than half a century worked in virtual anonymity with the Yankees, obscure except among the Yankee players and the Yankee family. He was Pete Sheehy, the clubhouse attendant, a short, wispy man who was later memorialized when the home locker room at Yankee Stadium was named the "Pete Sheehy Clubhouse."

Sheehy obviously recognized that there was a historic symmetry to the Yankees' line of succession: Lou Gehrig had assumed the superstar role after Babe Ruth; Joe DiMaggio's debut had come toward the end of Gehrig's career; and now Mantle appeared headed to join the Yankees in DiMaggio's last season. Sheehy was known as one of the few people who could joke around with the somber, stoic DiMaggio, who was like an ice god emotionally. Sheehy loved to tell the story of the time DiMaggio asked him to check out a red mark on his backside.

"Hey, Pete, take a look at this," Joe said. "Is there a bruise there?"

"Sure, there is, Joe," Sheehy replied in a matter-of-fact tone. "It's from all those people kissing your ass."

Sheehy's duties included assigning new players uniforms and, in particular, keeping track of uniform numbers that were not already worn by a player or retired to honor Yankee legends like Ruth and Gehrig. One of the great though not well known stories of the Yankee clubhouse was that Sheehy had originally issued the young Joe DiMaggio the number 18 when he joined the team in 1936. It was a number that had previously been worn by a tempestuous pitcher named Johnny Allen who was traded to the Cleveland Indians. As he got to know DiMaggio and sensed that he would be the historical successor to the legacies of Ruth and Gehrig, Sheehy decided Joe should wear number 5. When numbers were first put on uniforms, most of them had been issued by the player's place in the batting lineup. So Ruth, as the third batter in the Yankee lineup, was given number 3, and Gehrig, who followed Babe in the batting order, was issued number 4. When Mantle arrived at the Yankee instructional camp amid much anticipation in 1951, Sheehy didn't hesitate in issuing him the only number that made historical sense—number 6. "Around this club," Sheehy told Dick Schaap, "you always had the feeling that great things would happen. It started with Ruth and kept going on."

"When I came up, Casey told the writers that I was going to be the next Babe Ruth, Lou Gehrig, and Joe DiMaggio all rolled up in one," Mantle recalled in one of our conversations years later. "Casey kept bragging on me and the newspapers kept writing it, and of course I wasn't what Casey said I was. I don't mind admitting that there was incredible pressure on me because of what Casey was saying, and the fans were expecting so much, which I wasn't able to deliver."

The memory of that pressure in his rookie year was always troubling to Mickey. Equally upsetting, he said, was how casually Stengel would talk about it, even in his presence. Or perhaps his manager wanted Mantle to hear him say those things. He recalled one time in particular that spring training when he was standing clearly within earshot of Casey as he talked to reporters about the team and Mickey.

"Well, the Dago, he ain't what he used to be," Stengel told that day's collection of writers gathered around the Yankee manager in the late morning Arizona sun. "And Tommy Henrich, remember, is now saying he's three years older than anyone thought, and that makes me feel older just thinkin' about it."

"How's Tommy comin' as a coach?" one of the writers asked.

"Well, he's got his hands full tryin' to teach Mantles how to play the outfield," said Stengel. "But iffen Henrich can't get him ready to replace the Dago, who can?"

"You're grooming Mantle to succeed Joe?" asked another writer, almost not believing what he's just heard.

"Well, iffen we're grooming him to succeed anyone," Casey said. "I'm sure not groomin' him to succeed me, now would we?"

The writers shared a good laugh, and Stengel continued: "Well, as far as his hitting, he's a big-league outfielder right now. He can run the bases and his speed kinda keeps you on edge. His speed is so big that maybe he can use it in the outfield. And his arm is so strong that he won't have to think out there. All he'll have to do is throw the ball in. He made a lot of errors, I understand, at shortstop, and it might take him a couple of years to make it there. He'd have too many things to learn and if he wasn't playing, I couldn't keep him up there, but would have to send him down to the minors."

The writers scribbled furiously into their notebooks.

"All I know is that he has me terribly confused," said Casey, "and he's getting me more so every day. I know he's not a big league outfielder yet. He should have more minor league ball under his belt. That's the only logical thing. But this kid isn't logical. He's a big league hitter now."

If Casey Stengel sounded more like a carnival barker than a major league manager, the confusion was understandable. In his early days in baseball his clownishness had included entertaining the fans with stunts. Once he had hidden a sparrow under his cap, which had flown out when he tipped it to the crowd, delighting the fans. Now he was using Mickey Mantle, an unsophisticated nineteen-year-old straight out of Class C baseball, as his sparrow. Another manager might have known better than to have placed outlandish expectations on such a young ballplayer, no matter his potential. But then Stengel had his own personal agenda. He was trying to leave his own legacy in a game for which he had had only a fraction of Mantle's talent. Baseball was all Stengel had left in his life. He was already sixty-two and childless. He had been a journeyman in the game, kicking around with the Giants, the Dodgers, the Pirates, the Phillies, and the Braves. If Casey had a reputation, it was for being a clown, both as a player and as a coach. No one took him seriously while managing with Brooklyn and Boston, and then he had won baseball's lottery when he was hired to manage the Yankees in 1949, a team with the most popular player in the game, Joe DiMaggio. Was it any wonder that the Yankees won back-to-back World Series championships in 1949 and 1950?

In 1951, Stengel faced the challenge of proving he could win with teams he had developed and not just with the talent he had inherited. He also faced the challenge of winning with an aging team. None of Stengel's starting pitchers—Vic Raschi, Eddie Lopat, Allie Reynolds, and Tommy Byrne—was younger than thirty-one. His top reliever, Joe Page, broke down in training camp and never pitched for the Yankees again. Henrich, the Yankees' "Old Reliable," had called it quits before the season. DiMaggio had been plagued with injuries, and the 1951 season would be his last. The Yankees of the prized Joe McCarthy managing era would soon be history. In their place would be a team built around Mantle, Yogi Berra, Whitey Ford, and others who would come to represent the new Stengel era. Once during that spring training, Stengel had looked around at all his promising young players and, with mixed feelings, complained, "I wish I didn't have so many green peas, but I can't win with my old men. We have to rebuild."

And rebuild Stengel did, much to everyone's surprise. In doing so, whether he rushed Mantle into the majors is debatable. Who is to say whether Mickey might have lingered another season or two, squandering the time moving through the minors, had Stengel not pushed him? What was most impressive about the kid was his ability to hit—and hit with incredible power—from both sides of the plate. No one except Mutt Mantle could take credit for developing the slugger who would become baseball's greatest switch-hitter. Stengel recognized this and even joked that perhaps he should add Mickey's father to the Yankee coaching staff as its hitting coach. But Mantle was still a project defensively. No one knew that better than Casey, who was hoping he and his coaches could develop him if not into a major league infielder then into an outfielder.

Did Casey Stengel, though, see greatness in Mantle? How many scouts, coaches, and managers had seen hints of incredible talent in a young player only to be disappointed after a month or two of testing in the major leagues? The history of the game is littered with the tales of unfulfilled potential. The same was true with managers, and Stengel knew all too well the difficulty of any championship team staying on top. He longed to etch his name into a special place in baseball history and to prove himself. Casey knew that there were still doubters in New York and throughout baseball who wondered what kind of magic he had used to win those back-to-back pennants and world championships. It was the source of his ongoing conflicts with DiMaggio, who was still a great talent, to make some question what Stengel would do without him. The Yankees also still had the heart of an outstanding pitching rotation anchored by Allie Reynolds and Vic Raschi. So the pieces were there for another title run by the Yankees, even as DiMaggio announced that 1951 would be his final season. Stengel felt he just needed a couple of the younger players along with Mantle to develop enough to make the Yankees competitive.

At the same time, Stengel looked for inspiration from his own role model, the great Giants manager John McGraw, for whom he had once played. Stengel also had to manage under the shadow of the Yankees' own legendary manager Joe McCarthy. He had managed the great Yankee teams of the 1930s, earning the admiration and love of his players. When McCarthy resigned in 1946, DiMaggio had been among those lamenting their manager's departure, telling the *New York Times* that "he was like a father to most of us." What made those managers so beloved was that McGraw had won four straight pennants, and McCarthy not only did the same but also topped it by winning four straight World Series. Stengel loved to say that when he had played with the Giants, he was in awe of John McGraw and would boast, "I learned more from McGraw than anybody."

Stengel especially admired McGraw's knack for molding and developing young talent. He had seen McGraw take special pride in developing Mel Ott from a sixteen-year-old into a Hall of Famer. McGraw was so protective of young Ott that he had refused to send him to the minor leagues for development, fearing that some manager or coach would alter or ruin his unorthodox swing. Ott's distinctive batting style, which would become his trademark, involved an exaggerated stride produced by lifting his front foot high off the ground, something no batting coach would ever teach. So Ott spent his first two seasons sitting close to McGraw on the bench where he was nurtured and taught the intricacies of the game. Ott would go on to become the National League's home run king of his day.

Cleveland Indians manager Al Lopez was one who would come to admire Stengel and compared him to John McGraw when he did an interview with *Sport* magazine: "He took chances with kids, and he won with them. McGraw was that way. He'd stick with a young guy and nurse him along. McGraw and Stengel were both very good with young kids. Casey would sit and talk to them by the hour. He never had any children of his own, so he had a lot to give them. Come to think of it, McGraw had no children of his own either. Just thirty years' worth of baseball teams."

Could Mickey Mantle be Casey Stengel's own Mel Ott? It must have been a tempting question to ask oneself for someone who was such a student of baseball in the first half of the twentieth century, especially someone like Stengel who had modeled himself after John McGraw. Did Stengel now have on his team the next great ballplayer, maybe even the greatest who would ever play the game? The best there ever was possibly, and he would be taught by Stengel! "Can you imagine," Casey once asked Pete Sheehy, "what McGraw would say if he saw this kid?"

Stengel's fascination with Mantle had its beginning in 1950 when Mickey had given the Yankees a sneak preview of what to expect. That spring training, Mickey had spent most of the time with other minor leaguers away from the attention of Casey Stengel. Without the benefit of the pre–spring training instructional camp for rookies that would begin the following year, Stengel could mostly only hear of the promising youngster from other coaches. Mantle was as fast as the wind, certainly recording the fastest wind sprint times in the entire camp. But it was Mantle's hitting that caused jaws to drop. And this freckle-faced kid who was a virtual unknown could do it from either side of the plate. Mantle slugged sound-breaking shots from both sides of the plate— unusual majestic home runs rarely seen in spring training. Infielder Gil

McDougald vividly remembered Stengel showing up to see the rookies in camp and being awed at the sight of one of Mantle's blasts. The sixty-year-old manager ran out on the field, waving a fungo bat and chasing after Mickey as he circled first base, demanding of his coaches, "What'sis name? Mantle?"

By the next spring training, other veteran baseball men were equally unable to contain themselves. "This is the kind of kid a scout dreams of," Bill Essick, the Yankee scout who signed DiMaggio, said to reporters at spring camp. "You come up with one like this in your lifetime, you're lucky. I had that moment when I got DiMaggio."

Stengel began calling Mickey "Mantles." No one is sure why. Some, such as Pete Sheehy, have suggested that it was simply "Stengelese," the special use and misuse of the language that Stengel came to be known for as much as for his championship Yankee teams. Others thought the origin may have been in Stengel believing he had two Mantles because of his switch-hitting talent, which by itself was a rarity. At the time of Mantle's arrival, the American League featured just one regular switch-hitter, Dave Philley of the Athletics. Moreover, switch-hitting was seen as a device employed by hitters who were lacking other weapons. Of the switch-hitters that had preceded Mantle—among them Frankie Frisch, Red Schoendeinst, and Max Carey were the best—nearly all were disdainful of the long ball. In 1951, the career leader in home runs by a switch-hitter was Rip Collins with 135. The idea of tape-measure power from both sides of the plate was enough to get anyone's attention. As a switch-hitter, slugging home runs from both sides of the plate, Mantle quickly began to impress the other Yankees as well. Beyond running faster than any player Stengel had ever seen, his hitting talent and potential were prodigious. Only his defensive skills underwhelmed. Mickey had a tremendous arm, but he was no major league shortstop. The Yankees had left him at the position he had played in high school, but at Joplin in his first full minor league season, he had committed fifty-five errors, unusually high for a shortstop. Nevertheless, Stengel had plans for Mickey. The thinking among the front office brass and others had been that Mantle might ultimately be converted into an outfielder. Once an outfielder himself, Stengel also wanted to shift Mantle. Within days of Mickey's arrival at the instructional camp, Stengel made him his own project, personally trying to teach him the new position and then retaining the newly retired Tommy Henrich to coach his young protégé. Stengel could barely contain himself and, in a burst of enthusiasm, invited the sportswriters at the camp to come watch.

"Mantles," Stengel told the writers in one of his meetings with them that spring, "is a shortstop and he ain't much of a shortstop, either. But he sure can switch-hit hard, and run as fast as anybody I ever saw. I've seen some pretty good runners and ol' Case was a pretty fair runner himself. You fellers be out here tomorrow and you might see this Mantle at a place that could surprise you."

Although they dismissed Stengel's comments as more Stengelese, the sportswriters who came by early the next morning caught Mantle taking outfield practice under Henrich's tutelage. The Yankees were determined to turn Mickey into a major leaguer, and Mickey was soon to learn that there was little room for sentiment. Yankee coach Frank Crosetti worked with all the infielders, and the first thing he noticed about Mickey was his glove.

"Where'd ya get this piece of crap?" the former Yankee great recalled asking Mantle.

Mickey didn't hear exactly what Crosetti said about the glove and perhaps didn't want to hear it. Neither could Mantle bring himself to tell him just how special the glove was. It was a Marty Marion autograph model, designed for infielders and endorsed by the shortstop on the great St. Louis Cardinals teams Mantle and his father had rooted for. The glove had been a Christmas present from his father when he was sixteen and that Mickey had used throughout high school and his two seasons in the minors. "I knew exactly what it cost, for I had yearned after it for a long time," Mickey would recall to Dick Schaap of that special Christmas gift. "It was $22, about one-third of my father's weekly salary. And I knew, as all poor boys do, exactly what that amount of money meant in a family like ours. Of course, I doted on the glove with an unholy passion, loving even the smell of it, and I caressed and cared for it through the winter as if it had been a holy relic. But most of all, my heart was bursting with the realization of what a sacrifice like this said about my father's love for me and about his pride in my ability."

Crosetti didn't care about the glove's sentimental history. The next day he replaced it with an expensive, professional-model glove that Mickey had little choice but to break in and use. The new glove was slightly bigger than the one Mickey retired, but for a reason. It was an outfielder's glove, the first step in converting Mantle into a defensive player who could help the Yankees. Mickey Mantle was never going to be a major league short-stop, no matter how many ground balls his father had hit to him back in Oklahoma. Mantle began working with Tommy Henrich in learning how to play the outfield, which he did in that day's intra-squad game. Mickey played center field where he made one putout and didn't make any mistakes. Then, at the plate, he tripled in his first at-bat and followed that with a home run over the right field fence.

Mickey Mantle's 1951 spring training was one out of fairy tale books, and it appeared that the torch of Yankee greatness was being passed to him. If he was bothered by anything, it was not Stengel's expectations, nor the spotlight of the news media, but instead the crowds that came to the Yankee spring training games. The butterflies almost forced Mantle out of the Yankees 1951 exhibition opener against the Cleveland Indians in Tucson. Mickey was so nervous and frightened that he could barely raise his arms high enough to catch a ball. But he had to play center field that day because DiMaggio was aching from his chronic heel spur problem. Replacing Joe in center field, Mantle singled twice and added a double off veteran right-hander Early Wynn. Mantle quickly got over his nervousness, becoming the Yankees' most consistent hitter from both sides of the plate, no matter whether pitchers threw curves, sliders, fastballs, or changeups. The ease with which he was hitting reminded Mickey of those days when he was taking batting practice off Mutt and Grandpa Charlie on South Quincy Street. His teammates were as impressed as the writers and the fans. "I've always had to be sold on these rookies," veteran first baseman Johnny Hopp told the *New York Mirror*, "and at first I thought Mickey was just ahead of the rest in the intra-squad games. But he's still going. He doesn't look like an accident any more."

In baseball Mantle became the most exciting young player since Jackie Robinson, the Brooklyn Dodgers star who four years earlier had broken baseball's color barrier. That spring, among the people who saw Mantle play was Branch Rickey, the Dodgers general manager who had signed Robinson. Now the general manager of the Pittsburgh Pirates, Rickey watched Mantle hit home runs from each side of the plate against his team. He was sitting next to Yankee co-owner Dan Topping and could barely restrain himself after seeing Mantle homer. Rickey, who was known as unusually tightfisted, then did something that was extremely uncharacteristic of him. He tore a blank check from his checkbook, signed his name, and gave it to Topping. "Fill in the figures you want for that boy," Topping recalled Rickey saying to him, "and it's a deal." Topping smiled politely but left the check untouched. Mickey Mantle was his and only his.

"Mantle was so incredibly good on the field that even the men who praised him wondered, at times, whether they were maintaining their sanity," author-journalist Dick Schaap recalled in his book about Mickey.

Among those writers who didn't know what to make of the new Yankees phenom was Jack Orr, who was then covering the team for the *New York Compass*. "Some of us were kicking it around in a compartment on the Yankee train speeding through Texas," he wrote in one column. "We worked over a couple of subjects, but, as always, we got back to the same old one. It was bed time when somebody said: 'Cripes, we've been going for three hours and we've talked about nothing but Mickey Mantle.'"

In another column, Orr quoted Yankee pitching coach Jim Turner who said he had never seen anybody who could excite other ballplayers the way Mickey was doing that spring. "When he gets up to hit," he told Orr, "the guys get off the bench and elbow each other out of the way to get a better look. And take a look at the other bench sometimes. I saw [Pittsburgh Pirates slugger] Ralph Kiner's eyes pop when he first got a look at the kid. [Cleveland Indian] Luke Easter was studying him the other day, and so was [fellow Indian player] Larry Doby. . . . Here's one sure tip-off on how great he is. Watch DiMag when Mantle's hitting. He never takes his eyes off the kid."

What impressed the aging DiMaggio most about Mantle wasn't his hitting alone but his unbelievable foot speed, which reminded Joe of how quick he had also been in his early years with the Yankees. Speed has always been an intangible quality in sports. Even in the sports where speed is not usually considered the most important of attributes, raw, natural swiftness afoot can be impressive. At a pre–spring training instructional camp, Stengel and his coaches as well had been immediately awestruck by Mantle's speed. In the footraces, Mickey outran other players by such margins that Stengel at first thought he was cheating with head starts. Stengel and the coaches had Mantle running sprints against everyone at the camp, including some of the roster players who were there under the guise of being "instructors" to avoid violating the restriction against major leaguers coming to camp before March 1. Mantle outran everyone. He was clocked running from home plate to first base, and his times were 3.1 seconds from the right-handed hitter's side of the plate and 3.0 seconds from the left-hander's side. No one in the major leagues was that fast.

Watching Mantle, DiMaggio made all the politically correct comments about the rookie who was being groomed to replace him. "He's a big-league hitter right now," he told the *New York Post*. "Who does he remind me of? Well, there just haven't been many kids like him. Maybe he has something to learn about catching a fly ball, but that's all. He can do everything else." In San Francisco, Joe's hometown where the Yankees played an exhibition that spring, DiMaggio was asked if he resented Mantle moving in on his center field position. "Hell, no," said DiMaggio. "Why should I resent him? If he's good enough to take my job in center, I can always move over to right or left. I haven't helped him much—Henrich takes take of that—but if there is anything I can do to help him, I'm only too willing. Remember what I said back in Phoenix about those Yankee kids and how great they were? Well, the more I see of the ones we have now, the more convinced I am the Yankees won't even miss me."

"Mickey," said fellow rookie Gil McDougald, "had a spring training like a god."

Veteran first baseman Johnny Hopp, who had the locker next to Mickey that spring, was among Mantle's early fans on the team and would later be one of Mickey's roommates in New York. Soon he also began calling him "The Champ" because of his phenomenal power hitting.

"You're going to make a million dollars out of this game, the Lord behold," Hopp told me he recalled telling Mickey after one spring game.

Mantle let out his country boy laugh. He didn't think he was doing anything special.

But some longtime baseball writers remained unconvinced about the prize rookie and all the media hoopla. Among them was Stan Isaacs, Orr's fellow staff writer on the *New York Compass*, who wrote, "Since the start of spring training, the typewriter keys out of the training camps have been pounding out one name to the people back home. No matter what paper you read, or what day, you'll get Mickey Mantle, more Mickey Mantle and still more Mickey Mantle. Never in the history of baseball has the game known the wonder to equal this Yankee rookie. Every day there's some other glorious phrase as the baseball writers outdo themselves in attempts to describe the antics of this wonder: 'He's faster than Cobb . . . he hits with power from both sides of the plate the way Frankie Frisch used to . . . he takes all the publicity in stride, an unspoiled kid . . . sure to go down as one of the real greats of baseball . . . another Mel Ott.'"

Behind the scenes, the Yankees were surprised by how quickly Mantle's defensive work in the outfield had improved under Tommy Henrich's coaching. Of course, there were still occasional glitches, such as the embarrassing moment when Mickey failed to flip down his flip-down sunglasses and lost sight of a fly ball, which hit him squarely between the eyes. Only Mantle's pride was hurt. All the while, Stengel was having to defend moving Mantle to a completely new position.

By the end of spring training, Mickey was surprising even his critics with his improved outfield play. One game in particular dramatized his new defensive skills. After making a spectacular running catch off of a low line drive, Mantle made a perfect throw to home plate that froze the runner at third base and kept him from scoring.

"How do you like that?" an admiring Stengel bragged in the dugout. "He caught it and threw it the right way, and he's only been taught that play for a week and a half. He's going to be tremendous."

Stengel was now campaigning hard to have Mantle stay with the Yankees, even though the team's front office was usually hesitant about promoting minor leaguers, especially youngsters from the low minors. But Casey wanted Mickey with him, sitting next to him on the bench, if necessary, the way Mel Ott had learned from John McGraw. "This kid ain't logical," Stengel kept telling his coaches. "He's too good. It's very confusing."

"The kid's got to play in New York this year. He'll help me."

7

DiMaggio and Mantle

You guys got to see this kid we have in camp. Out of class C ball, hits
'em both ways—five-hundred feet both ways! You've got to see him.
                                                              —BILL DICKEY

NO MATTER THAT HE HAD BEEN TO GRAND CENTRAL TERMINAL BEFORE,
Mickey Mantle still marveled like a newcomer to New York at the sight
outside where hundreds of red-capped porters scurried about helping
passengers with their luggage. Many of the passengers, especially those
dressed stylishly, which to Mickey seemed like almost everyone in New
York, looked like movie stars and celebrities. But then, he was a raw
rookie in more ways than on the baseball field, and almost every aspect
of the city was a new experience to a nineteen-year-old from Oklahoma. When he hopped into the Checker cab with two fellow rookies in front of the Concourse Hotel in the Bronx where the team had
housed them, Mickey had announced to the cabbie, "Grand Central
Station, 15 Vanderbilt Avenue." The cabbie eyed him and gave him a
piece of smart advice.

"Son," he said, "there *are* places in New York where the name alone
is enough."

Inside Grand Central, Mickey struck the pose of a newly arrived
sightseer: awestruck by the extravagant interior with its marble floors,
Corinthian-style columns, stained-glass windows, a marble fireplace,
and a restaurant. Once inside the concourse, he stopped for a moment
to stare at the 125-foot ceiling vault painted with constellations. Mickey
had described it to his mother as looking like an Italian cathedral, to

which his mother had teasingly remarked, "Mickey, how would you know what an Italian cathedral looks like?" In fact, the concourse, which, when it opened, was hailed as the finest example of beaux arts architecture in America, looked as though it could have been transported from 1870s France. Atop the symmetrical main facade was a large clock and sculptures of an American eagle and Roman deities.

It was what passed through the concourse every day, however, that gave Grand Central its buzz and always brought Mickey down to earth of where he was: "It's a place everyday New Yorkers pass through, whether they are taking a train or not," John Belle, the architect in charge of a lavish restoration in the late 1900s, later told *Architectural Digest*. "Grand Central is our town square." Each day drew upward of a million people, some by subway, some on suburban commuter trains, and others simply walking through the building to get somewhere else, but most at that time arriving or leaving on the railroads that in 1951 were still the heart of long-distance transportation in the country. In the 1940s and the 1950s, a popular NBC radio show closed each program with the line "Grand Central Station—crossroads of a million private lives, a gigantic stage on which are played a thousand dramas daily."

Among those dramas unfolding from the spring through fall of each year was the New York Yankees baseball team, which would depart Grand Central, or Penn Station, for some of its out-of-town trips, to Boston to play the Red Sox, to Chicago for a series with the White Sox, to Detroit for the Tigers, to Cleveland to face the Indians, to Philadelphia to take on the Athletics, to St. Louis for the lowly Browns, and to Washington, D.C., as they were this afternoon for their presidential Opening Day of the season the next day against the Senators, where President Harry S. Truman would throw out the first pitch.

It was the morning of April 16, 1951, and Joe DiMaggio and Mickey Mantle were with their New York Yankees teammates about to board a train to Washington. They were being detained for a few minutes for recorded interviews for CBS Radio's famous news program *Hear It Now* when a remote microphone picked up DiMaggio and Mantle's unrehearsed conversation, a conversation that unfortunately would be soon forgotten and overlooked.

"Well, Mickey, this is another season for me," Joe DiMaggio said to the Yankees' celebrated rookie, who wasn't even sure if he was starting his first season in the major leagues or back in the minors. "Of course, this is the first season for you here in the major leagues. How do you feel about this first trip for the first game you're going to play?"

"Well, Joe, I'm pretty nervous about it all," said a shy and, yes, nervous Mickey Mantle. "It's all really new to me."

"Well, I'll tell you, Mickey, I felt pretty nervous the first game I played," said DiMaggio, obviously trying to make Mantle feel at ease. "As a matter of fact, I can recall I missed seventeen games at the opening of the season and finally I got back in there. When I did play my first game, I swung at the first pitch and was very fortunate to get a base hit and that took all the tension out. Now are you going to do the same thing for us?"

There was a moment of nervous laughs the two shared.

"Well, I don't know," said Mickey. "I'll probably swing at the first pitch no matter what, but I don't know if I'll get a hit."

"Well, I hope it's a hit, Mickey," said DiMaggio, offering encouragement, "because from there on in, you'll go from there."

The veteran DiMaggio appeared enthusiastic and supportive, engaging Mantle in a genuine manner that was both refreshing and surprising. All spring training much of what the press had been reporting was young Mantle's superman-like heroics at the plate, especially since the Yankees appeared to be grooming him as DiMaggio's replacement.

DiMaggio's surprisingly gracious remarks to Mantle were all the more unselfishly magnanimous because in the following years much of what was written about the relationship between the two men would suggest just the opposite. They were, after all, the legends of the greatest team in the greatest era of the game at the greatest time in America— Joe DiMaggio and Mickey Mantle—and seemingly forever they have been depicted as bitter enemies who could make each other physically ill over just which of them could be, or was, the greatest New York Yankee. DiMaggio almost always had been cast as an aloof, bitter aging star who resented the presence of any heir apparent but especially someone as different from him as Mantle appeared to be.

Unfortunately, deeply held notions can be long lasting, especially if they have been repeated without question and then reinforced by reports and books based on little more than misperceptions, no matter how mistaken. There were also the misguided recollections of teammates who might have been put off by DiMaggio's aloofness and his unwillingness to party and carouse with them, while they may have been more receptive and sympathetic to Mantle, who quickly in his career became a party animal and a favorite among his fellow players.

If you believe the stories that have been retold many times in the biographies of both players, DiMaggio never said anything to Mickey all season long in 1951, not until the second game of that year's World Series. That was when Mantle tore up a knee when he caught his cleat in an outfield drain while avoiding DiMaggio as they both chased Willie Mays's fly ball. After making the catch, DiMaggio ran over to check on Mantle, offering reassurance and trying to allay his immediate fears. "Mantle said it was their first conversation of the year," *The Last Boy: Mickey Mantle and the End of America's Childhood* maintained. However, that was far from the truth, as the April 16 recorded conversation shows. It is also at the heart of an overwhelming amount of material documenting that the true relationship of DiMaggio and Mantle, much to the contrary of the long-held myth as unfriendly antagonists, was actually that of symbiotic teammates and heroes cast into the national spotlight in 1951—DiMaggio's final season and Mantle's rookie year—and lasting until Mantle's death in 1995.

It was a changing of the guard for the Yankees, and of stars in the Golden Age, as America had come to call that period not only of the national pastime but of the country as well. DiMaggio had come to symbolize the greatness of America and its conquest of Adolf Hitler and the Nazi threat to freedom. Americans sang songs about Joltin' Joe, as he was known, and his nickname The Yankee Clipper conjured up the image of elegant New England schooners developed in the Chesapeake Bay before the American Revolution. And in 1951, America seemed united in sad regret that the great DiMaggio, after many glorious years in baseball, was about to hang up his spikes and that his pending retirement threatened to extinguish the glitter that his heroics had bestowed on the nation.

Of course, it may not have been coincidental that DiMaggio was leaving the baseball stage, making a farewell tour, though it never was that, in the same year that Mickey Mantle was making his debut. It was in essence a changing of the guard not unlike the significant changes that were underway in the world. President Harry S. Truman was nearing the end of his tenure in the White House as the country had used his caretaker years to acclimate to life without Franklin D. Roosevelt. In a sense, then, America was looking for new heroes to lead the nation into the second half of the century and to cheer on in its national sports obsession.

For America, just six years removed from World War II, was already involved in another foreign conflict, the Korean War, and a new conflict at home, the war against Communism and the "Red Menace." In 1951 Ethel and Julius Rosenberg were sentenced to death, eventually becoming the only two American civilians to be executed during the Cold War for espionage-related activity. The United States had opened the Nevada atomic test site and tested its first hydrogen bomb in May. It was a new age, even in sports, which witnessed the first coast-to-coast telecast of a live sporting event and two landmark shows, *I Love Lucy* and *Dragnet*.

It was the age of America, television, and Mickey Mantle.

Indeed, and it officially began that day when the Yankees boarded that morning after DiMaggio and Mantle's radio conversation. This was the way major league teams had been traveling to their out-of-town games since early in the century. The trains were part of the national pastime lore that kept fans close to the players they read about in the newspapers and whose exploits they cheered on the radio, if they were not fortunate enough to live in a big-league city. For players, the trains were extensions of the clubhouse, filled with card games and baseball chatter. For Mickey, these team train rides began with spring training to the West Coast for exhibitions and then back east through Texas. He loved eating in the main diner with its art deco lights and etched glass dividers. But he was still unaccustomed to walking through a speeding train. This is what he found himself doing on the ride to the nation's capital, following Casey Stengel from car to car toward the bullet-shaped smoking lounge.

"Casey, can you tell me something?" he asked Stengel, according to Mickey's account in *The Mick*. "Am I going to play at [minor league] Beaumont this year?"

Mantle saw Stengel wink at him. "I think you'll stay with us," he said. "When we get back there, just be quiet, and I'll do the talking."

Mantle then stood quietly in the smoking lounge as he heard Stengel tell general manager George Weiss that Mickey should open the season with the Yankees. Weiss didn't agree. Mickey was too young, he said.

"I don't care if he's in diapers," Stengel shot back. "If he's good enough to play for us on a regular basis, I want to keep him."

Stengel had the support of Yankee co-owners Del Webb and Dan Topping.

"George," said Webb, "they've been writing so much stuff about Mickey, I feel we have to keep him."

"The thing is, George," added Topping, "we're not opening in New York. We're opening in Washington. After two or three games under his belt, I think he'll be all right."

Mickey was both surprised and excited. He couldn't believe that he was going to start the season as a New York Yankee. It was true. They were discussing his salary, with Casey negotiating on Mickey's behalf with Weiss. It was a deal structured to the Yankee's best interests, but Mantle could have cared less at this point. Mickey would earn $7,500 for the season, $2,500 above the minimum. But he had to continue playing in the majors because if he slumped and was sent to the minors, his salary would be reduced to the minimum.

Mickey couldn't wait to get to Washington to call home and tell his father that he had just signed his first big league contract. This had been his father's dream, and now it had come true. He was happy and also stunned. He had not expected to make the Yankees major league team this season. It was a long-shot dream that he would make the majors before the age of twenty. But he had. From his seat, he stared at the passing countryside, even as raindrops began covering the train's windows. Mickey had never been this happy in his young life.

When the opening series against the Senators was rained out, the Yankees returned to New York, where the opener would also be Mantle's major league debut. After Mickey's sensational spring, Stengel was indeed beginning to look like another John McGraw. The Opening Day lineup Casey posted in the dugout had Mantle playing right field and batting third behind left fielder Jackie Jensen and shortstop Phil Rizzuto and ahead of DiMaggio who was batting in the cleanup slot. Catcher Yogi Berra was batting fifth, first baseman Johnny Mize sixth, followed by third baseman Billy Johnson, second baseman Jerry Coleman, and starting pitcher Vic Raschi.

And then there was Mickey Mantle, a nineteen-year-old who was as surprised to be a major leaguer as the Yankees were with his presence. He looked like a kid serving shakes at a malt shop or a teenage heartthrob in a Hollywood movie. He was perfect for the age of innocence that baseball represented. Mantle laughed at dugout jokes like a kid. He eyed baseball stadiums where he played with the delirium of a kid. He played and ran with the enthusiasm of a kid. It made some people uncomfortable to see a kid having this much fun on a public stage when many kids his age were being drafted as fodder for the army in the war in Korea. So Mantle was called in for his draft physical once, twice, three times, which he kept failing because of osteomyelitis in one of his legs. Angry, threatening letters would soon start pouring in. Mickey was oblivious to the politics and concerns swirling around him. All he knew, all he would ever know, was baseball. So he pulled down his Yankee cap and kept playing. Other country boys had played major league baseball, of course. But Mickey Mantle had come along at a unique time when America was bulging with its postwar muscle in full view of a national transformation of how the country saw itself and its culture. Television was in its infancy, inheriting its first poster boy hero as if Mickey were the Gerber baby ready to play ball.

"My childhood was part of what made me popular with the fans in New York and elsewhere," Mantle himself said. "I was a classic country bumpkin, who came to the big city carrying a cardboard suitcase and with a wardrobe of two pairs of slacks and a pastel-colored sports coat."

"I remember my impression of him the first time I met him," said Yankee pitcher Whitey Ford. "I thought, 'What a hayseed.'"

Yogi Berra had a similar recollection: "I remember he was a big, scared kid who we already knew could hit the ball out of sight. You know something else I remember? Even when he was a kid, we already knew he was a helluva guy."

On Opening Day at Yankee Stadium, Mickey was flabbergasted at the sight of the towering triple-deck stands already filling up. He had already been to Yankee Stadium, when he joined the team for the final two weeks of the previous season. Mickey was ineligible for the World Series roster. However, at general manager George Weiss's invitation, he had attended the two home games of the Yankees' 1950 World Series sweep of the Philadelphia Phillies. Mantle had been joined in New York for those games by his mother and father, his twin brothers Roy and Ray, and his girlfriend Merlyn Johnson in what she would remember as "a visit to paradise." But now, on Opening Day of the 1951 season, Mickey was about to make his major league debut, and at Yankee Stadium. In the moments before the Opening Day ceremonies, he stared around the stadium for the first time from the playing field. As he studied the famous Yankee Stadium facade above the upper deck, Yogi Berra came up behind him. "Hey, what kind of an opening day crowd is this? There's no people here!" Mickey had quickly come to realize that the Yankee catcher didn't say things so much as growl them out. He stared at Yogi, then understood he was joking. Jim Turner, one of the coaches, then came up to them.

"How many people watched you play at Joplin last year?" he asked Mickey.

"I'd say about 55,000 all season," he answered.

"Well, take a good look," said Turner. "We got about 45,000 here today for one game—almost as many people as saw you in Joplin all year."

Mantle gulped. "No!" he muttered.

"Yes," said Turner, trying to put Mickey at ease. "And most of them came to see what you look like."

An hour and a half before the game, sportswriter Red Smith recalled watching Mantle looking nervously into the stands from the top step of the Yankees' dugout. From the bench, Stengel could only see Mickey from the chest down, but he noticed that the sole of one of his baseball cleats had torn loose. The Yankee skipper got up to talk to Mickey and then returned shaking his head. "He don't care much about the big leagues, does he?" Stengel said. "He's gonna play in them shoes."

"Who is he?" asked a visitor in the dugout who hadn't seen Mantle that spring.

"Why, he's that kid of mine," said Stengel.

"That's Mantle?"

"Yeah. I asked him didn't he have any better shoes, and he said he had a new pair but they're a little too big."

The visitor chuckled along with Stengel. "He's waiting for an important occasion to wear the new ones."

Stengel was also trying not to show his apprehension, not about how Mantle would do but about this team he was patching up with Band-Aids, mirrors, and smoke. Pitcher Whitey Ford and infielder Billy Martin had been drafted and were lost to the team for this season at least. DiMaggio was ailing, and aging as well. All of the team's starting pitchers—Allie Reynolds, Vic Raschi, Eddie Lopat, and Tommy Byrne—were in their thirties. If this Yankees team were to compete for the pennant again, Stengel knew it would have to be with the help of at least two or three prized rookies. Gil McDougald looked ready to take over one spot in the infield. Mantle appeared set to play in the outfield. Then there was another highly touted youngster, Jackie Jensen, to whom the Yankees had given a $40,000 signing bonus. A year earlier Jensen, who had starred in the 1949 Rose Bowl for the University of California, had been the spring training golden boy thought to be DiMaggio's successor. However, Jensen had trouble hitting major league pitching. During 1951 spring training, Stengel tried to convert Jensen into a pitcher. That experiment failed, and now his hopes were that Jensen might hit just well enough to stay with the Yankees.

On the day when Mantle finally played his first game in the majors, the Yankees hosted the Boston Red Sox. Since their season-opening series against the Senators in Washington had been rained out, this was the Yankees' season unveiling as well. So Mickey had the distinction of sharing the Yankee Stadium surroundings of his career debut with his own two personal baseball heroes, teammate Joe DiMaggio and Ted Williams of the Red Sox. They would go down in baseball history for one of the greatest seasons in the game. In 1941 they established records that would stand the test of time, possibly never to be broken. DiMaggio hit safely in fifty-six consecutive games, while Williams's .406 batting average would make him the last player to hit over .400 in a season. Although DiMaggio was given the league's Most Valuable Player award, it is Williams's 1941 season that is often considered the best offensive year of all time.

"If I had known hitting .400 was going to be such a big deal," Williams said on the fiftieth anniversary of that season in 1991, "I would have done it again."

Williams won Triple Crowns in 1942 and 1947, and would go on to hit 521 home runs and finish with a .344 average for his career, of which he lost almost three seasons because of military service as a pilot in World War II and the Korean War. But in 1951, Ted was coming back from a broken arm suffered in the 1950 All-Star Game that cost him the second half of that season. At age thirty-two, Williams was already known as baseball's consummate hitter, which undoubtedly pleased him. As a rookie in 1939, Williams had even been so bold as to tell reporters what he wanted his epitaph to be. "All I want out of life," he said, "is that when I walk down the street folks will say, 'There goes the greatest hitter who ever lived.'" Novelist Bernard Malamud later appropriated this line and changed it ever so slightly—"Sometimes when I walk down the street I bet people will say there goes Roy Hobbs, the best there ever was in the game."—for his mythical slugger in *The Natural*, which would be published in 1952.

Mantle had actually already seen Williams play in person in September 1950, when he was brought up for two weeks after the end of his season at Joplin. "I saw Ted hit two home runs off Vic Raschi," Mickey said, "and I became convinced he was the greatest hitter I'd ever seen."

The 1951 season was to be DiMaggio's final one, but Williams was in the prime of his great career. He and Mantle would match up again for much of the 1950s. But there, that afternoon, they would meet for the first time when Williams walked over to the Yankee dugout to greet DiMaggio. Mickey was standing next to Joe, awed and nervous.

"You must be Mick," Williams said to Mickey. Mantle later told me he was so surprised that Williams spoke to him that he almost swallowed the wad of bubble gum he was chewing.

A few moments later, photographers crowded around them and snapped pictures of DiMaggio, Williams, and Mantle that would become collectors' items in future years.

Nearby Bill Dickey, the former Yankee catcher and manager who was now one of Stengel's coaches, was answering questions from a couple of other sportswriters, with the talk quickly shifting to the rookie sensation. "Gosh, I envy him," said one of the writers, according to Dick Schaap's biography of Mantle. "Nineteen years old and starting out as a Yankee!"

"He's green," said Dickey, "but he's got to be great. All that power, a switch hitter, and he runs like a striped ape. If he drags a bunt past the pitcher, he's on base. I think he's the fastest man I ever saw with the Yankees. But he's green in the outfield. He was at shortstop last year."

"Gosh, Bill," said the writer, "do you realize you were in the big leagues before he was born?"

"He was born in 1932," said Dickey, misstating Mickey's birth year by a year, "and that was the year I played my first World Series."

Half an hour later, New York and Yankee officials delivered the traditional Opening Day speeches at home plate, and then a soldier walked to the mound. It was Whitey Ford wearing his army uniform, and the Yankee southpaw threw out the first pitch of the season.

Mickey Mantle's big league debut began with him fielding a leadoff single to right field hit by DiMaggio's brother Dom. Mantle fielded the ball cleanly and threw to second base. In his first at-bat, Mick swung at the first major league pitch he saw, broke his bat, and almost beat out the infield grounder. In his second at-bat, he popped up harmlessly. Mantle came to bat again in the sixth inning with the Yankees leading, 2–0, with nobody out and runners at first and third. DiMaggio was on deck behind Mickey and called him aside. He said something to Mantle who nodded, then stepped to the plate and, batting right-handed, smashed a fastball off left-hander Bill Wright past the outstretched glove of shortstop Johnny Pesky into left field, driving in the runner from third base.

It was Mickey's first big league hit.

Mantle made a wide turn around first base. As he hurried back to first base, Mickey glanced toward DiMaggio watching his heir apparent from the on-deck circle. A small smile formed on DiMaggio's face as he nodded in the rookie's direction.

"I would have given anything for his approval," said Mantle. "And I'd gotten it."

8

Scouts, Taxmen, and Swindlers

I wish I'd been a baseball bonus baby. My folks could have used the money, that's for sure. And I don't think they could have sent me down [to the minors] if I'd had that bonus baby tag. But it was what it was. Let's face it: Beyond signing me, Tom Greenwade didn't do us any favors.

—MICKEY MANTLE

IF HE HAD BEEN BORN IN NEW YORK, MICKEY MANTLE WOULD HAVE been most likely another of those stickballers he saw playing every morning on 162nd and Sheridan Avenue just outside the Concourse Plaza in the Bronx where he was staying his rookie season. It wasn't baseball, but it was close enough for a nineteen-year-old kid who knew baseball and not much else about life. Stickball was also a poor kid's game, something Mickey could relate to. Stickball bats began life as brooms or mop sticks, possibly borrowed from your mother. You played with wonderful pink rubber balls that came to be called "spaldeens," even if they weren't made by Spalding. In parts of the city, like the Bronx around the Concourse, the game ran a block long and was the center of neighborhood life.

"The Concourse Plaza was *the* hotel in the Bronx during the '40s and '50s," one of those stickball players, Stephen Swid, recalled years later. "Visiting teams and Yankee ball players who weren't married would stay at the hotel. Every once in a while, one of the players would come down and join in one of our games. Now back then, you'd measure a guy by how many sewers he could hit the ball. Each sewer [manhole cover] was ninety feet apart. I was a two and a half sewer guy, not bad at all. A really big hitter would be a three-sewer guy. One day Mickey Mantle came down. We gave him a bat and pitched in. He swung and missed, swung, and missed again. A few more swings, a few more misses. Finally he connected. Boom. It was the deepest shot any of us ever saw, more than four sewers. That was it—the news spread all over the neighborhood and then throughout the Bronx: Mickey Mantle was a four sewer man!"

That Mickey could become so enthralled with stickball and the kids playing it showed just how difficult his transition to New York was in those early days. Mickey was overwhelmed by the city, especially living alone as he did those first few weeks at the Concourse, just a few blocks from Yankee Stadium. Mantle spent most of the nights reading the sports pages from the various New York newspapers and staring at the walls thinking about the next day's game. Sometimes he would walk down to a diner where, unrecognized by anyone, he would sip on a cup of coffee or eat a hamburger while listening to die-hard Yankee fans talk about their team.

Mickey had no real friends. Worse for a young guy in New York, he had little money. He had been in this position since turning pro, and he had occasionally angrily mired himself with self-retributions and pity. He was not the first professional ballplayer who bitterly resented having naively signed a contract that paid him far less than he was worth, and he would not be the last. The Yankee scout who signed him, Tom Greenwade, became a family friend, but he had also taken on the role of family scourge among the Mantles. Now, Mickey had too much time to wallow in thinking, reflecting, and dreaming on how he had gotten here.

At those times Mickey recalled games like one at a ball field in Baxter Springs, Kansas. It was 1947. The area around the field is a vista of shorn wheat where tall, ripe yellow shoots stretch endlessly to the horizon. The baseball field, the wheat fields, and even a river beyond center field are tinted in gold and gray by the setting sun. This is the home of the Whiz Kids, a high-powered Baxter Springs team. Among its players is young Mickey, only fifteen but looking older and already muscular. As Mickey comes to bat, we see Mutt sitting with other parents in the stands.

"Mick, gotta be your pitch," yells his father.

Almost as if on cue, Mantle slugs the first pitch an incredible distance. There's no fence, and the ball rolls maybe four hundred feet to the riverbed. The crowd goes wild.

Moments later, as Mickey steps into the batter's box as a left-handed hitter, Mutt's distinctive voice can be heard again: "Bases loaded, can't pitch around ya, Mick."

Again, Mickey crushes a pitch to holy hell.

Still, moments later.

As Mickey comes to bat against a new pitcher, a lefty, and stands in the righty batter's box, Mutt's voice rings out again: "Comin' with heat, Mick."

And one more time, Mickey connects on a prodigious drive that sends the team and crowd into a frenzy.

In the excitement after the game, Mickey is mobbed by friends and well-wishers. The team's coach, Barney Bennett, comes up to Mutt with three baseballs—Mickey's home run balls.

"Mutt, here's three more for your collection," says Bennett.

"Thanks, Barney." Mutt beams from ear to ear. "He sure buried 'em, didn't he?"

"Just incredible, 'specially when you consider he almost lost that leg just a few months ago," says Bennett.

Mutt winces at the memory of it. "Don't remind me."

"I won't, but there's people who may." Bennett shoots a glance at a middle-aged lanky man nearby. He's Tom Greenwade, a scout for the New York Yankees. He talks with a flat, ridge-runner accent. "Come over here a minute, Mutt."

Bennett leads Mutt toward Greenwade. "Tom, this is Mickey's father," says Bennett. "Tom Greenwade, Mutt Mantle. Mutt, Tom here's a scout for the Yankees."

Mutt raises an eyebrow and nods, appropriately impressed.

"Scout's just a fancy name for bird-doggin' every sandlot I can feast my eyes on," says Greenwade. "I was just askin' Barney here about Mickey's leg. Heard he'd banged it up pretty bad."

"Ain't nuthin', just a football injury." Mutt tries to assure him. "He's fine."

"Someone said it was a bone disease," says Greenwade. "Osteomyelitis?"

"I think so, but they gave him this new drug, penicillin," Mutt tells him. "Good as new."

Bennett tries to help. "Heck, Tom, you saw 'im out there," he says. "Can outrun a jackrabbit."

Greenwade nods in agreement. "Yep. Guess you don't havta really worry about the runnin' if you hit the ball like he does."

"Mutt, you gotta watch out for this one!" Bennett's cautionary joke comes off friendly. "Tom used to be a tax collector. He'll short-change ya!"

They all have a laugh.

"Just that there's slim picks, lemme tell you," says Greenwade. "But I like your son, Mutt. How old is he?"

"Fifteen," says Mutt, "but he hits like a man."

"I'll say," says Greenwade. "Don't often spot a natural. Take care of 'im."

Mantle's dream bank clicks on another ball game in 1948.

Watching Mickey's team play, Mutt makes eye contact with Tom Greenwade. They nod to each other.

Looking stronger than ever, Mickey blasts another mighty home run. Pandemonium breaks out among the players and fans as the Whiz Kids win the game.

Mutt shoots a glance at Greenwade, who is madly scribbling some notes. He looks up and makes eye contact with Mutt. They nod to each other again.

Then came the crisp spring day in 1949 when Tom Greenwade drove up to Commerce High School in his 1948 Oldsmobile. He walks with purpose into the school and to the office of Principal Bentley Baker, a friendly fatherly type who obviously enjoys Greenwade's company as he later walks him back to his car. There, Greenwade pulls a thick envelop from his car's glove compartment and hands it to Baker, who quickly pockets it and shakes Greenwade's hand—all in a manner suggesting that some kind of deal has been struck.

A few weeks later, there is a similarly disturbing scene. Another heavily sunbaked man drives up to the front of Commerce High School. Inside the high school, minutes later, Principal Baker follows a secretary out of his office. He greets the man cordially but with a subtle nervousness.

"Hello, I'm Bentley Baker, the principal," he tells the visitor as they shake hands.

"Principal Baker, I'm Hugh Alexander," says the man, handing the principal his business card.

The principal studies the card. "Yes, a scout for the Cleveland Indians, I see. What can we do for you?"

"I was here to check out one of your baseball players," says the scout. "Mickey Mantle."

"Oh, of course, Mickey," says Baker. "That's interesting."

"He's still in school here, isn't he?"

The principal is slow to answer. "Of course, it's just . . . well, let's go outside and talk."

A few minutes later, outside the front of the high school, Hugh Alexander's body language shows disappointment—like he's heard his hunting dog's just been shot.

"Oh, it was one of the worst football injuries I've ever seen," the principal tells the scout. "He must've been in the hospital for weeks. I heard they wanted to amputate and might've except that Mickey's momma said, 'Not my Mickey!' and they took him outa the hospital here and drove him all the way to Oklahoma City. That youngster's got one messed up leg, and I think arthritis set in too. I don't see him playing much baseball. Besides, here at Commerce High School, we haven't had a baseball team in a couple of years. Oklahoma's football country."

"I've heard," says Alexander. "Well, too bad about Mickey. It's hard enough to make the majors if you're healthy. Sorry to inconvenience you."

"No inconvenience," says the principal.

When Alexander gets back into his car, he sees a piece of paper on the passenger's seat. It's got Mickey's name jotted down along with his high school and address. As Alexander drives off, he throws the paper away—and in the rearview mirror sees it blowing across the parking lot.

Mickey remembers his high school graduation a few weeks later. A sign on the schools' front lawn announces that graduation commencement exercises are taking place that night. Inside the school, Mutt, Mickey, and Tom Greenwade are meeting with Principal Bentley Baker, and the Yankee scout is interceding on the Mantles' behalf.

"I think what Mutt's trying to say, Baker," Greenwade says, "is that he and his family wouldn't be askin' this favor if it weren't for somethin' special."

"Well, anyone else in my place probably would say no," says Baker. "Mickey can't miss graduation to play a baseball game. But if there's a chance that it could lead to Mickey one day playing for the New York Yankees, well, I think then those are the times when exceptions need to be made."

Elated, Mickey jumps up and shakes the principal's hand. "Gee, Principal Baker, thank you so much!"

"Hit a couple for me, Mickey," the principal tells him.

"We're certainly grateful, Mr. Baker," adds Mutt.

That night an electrical storm threatens on the horizon. The thunder and rhythmic flashes of lightning are mesmerizing. Each recurring flash of light draws our attention to the sky. Mickey comes to the plate, looking more confident than ever, despite a clap of thunder that shudders across the darkening field. The scoreboard shows that the score is tied, and it is the bottom of the seventh inning.

Mickey wipes his palms on his pants and twitches his cap. The pitcher, chewing bubble gum vigorously, springs into his windup, kicks and throws . . .

Mickey swings, and a heavy explosion of thunder fills the sky. The ball skyrockets off Mickey's bat, soaring far past the lights in right center field. The outfielders remain frozen and watch the ball's flight. Rounding first base, Mickey breaks into a home run trot as the skies release a thunderstorm. The Whiz Kids jump up and down in the dugout, the home run winning the game.

At Tom Greenwade's Oldsmobile a few minutes later, soaking wet, Mickey and Mutt and the Yankee scout all jump into the car almost at the same time. The mood is one of elation and celebration.

"Whada game, Mickey!" yells a rain-drenched Greenwade. "Whada game!"

"I reckon that's what you came here to see," says Mutt. "I told Mickey you and the Yankees were the ones we needed to wait for. We haven't so much as said hello to anyone else."

Mutt winks at Mickey.

"Have we, son?"

"Nah, I wanna be a Yankee," says Mickey, looking at Greenwade, "if you'll have me."

"Well, I'll tell ya," begins Greenwade, "bein' real honest with ya both, there are some concerns."

Mickey and Mutt eye each other apprehensively.

"There's Mickey's defense," continues Greenwade. "He makes a whole lot of errors as a shortstop. Then some people think he might not be big enough. And of course there's the Yankees. Contrary to what you may have heard, they're a tightfisted bunch. But we might just be able to come up with somethin' if we can make the numbers right. Mutt, what would you want for Mickey to sign? Be reasonable now."

Mutt gathers himself to make his best pitch for his son's future: "Well, you'll have to give him as much as he'd make around here all summer, working in the mine and playin' ball on Sunday. Mickey's pay in the mine is eighty-seven and a half cents an hour, and he can get fifteen dollars on a Sunday playing semi-pro ball."

Greenwade jots down some numbers on the back of an envelope.

"Okay, I hear ya," says Greenwade, writing down more numbers. "I hear ya. And I think I can come up with something that you might like. Mutt, I figure that if Mickey went to play in Joplin, we could pay him a monthly salary of one hundred forty dollars for almost three months for the rest of that summer. Now that's about four hundred dollars. Now suppose we spice that up with another eleven hundred dollars bonus. All total, we're talkin' fifteen hundred dollars. I think I could get that for Mickey. Would that work for ya'll?"

Mutt and Mickey can barely contain their excitement.

"Tom, just tell 'im where to sign," says Mutt.

At the Mantle home a few days later, an old sedan pulls up. A middle-aged man carries a bundle of newspapers to the front door of the house. He is Joe Payton, a linotype operator for the local newspaper.

Mutt meets him at the door. "Joe, what brings you out . . . ? It's in the paper?"

"Yep. I thought you might want some extras."

Payton hands a copy of the *Miami (Oklahoma) Daily News Record* to Mutt and points to the front-page article on Mickey's signing with a photograph.

"Mickey! Lovell! Come quick!" Mutt's pride and excitement fill the house.

Payton hands a copy of the paper to Mickey and his mother and delights in seeing them read the news.

"Oh, wow," says Mickey, "this is like signing all over again!"

"You must be so proud of Mickey," Payton tells Lovell.

"Of course," says Mickey's mother. "Of course, we are."

"It says here there's another story on the sports page," Mickey tells his parents, as he tears through the paper to get to the sports pages.

"Yep, actually, that's a story about a youngster from Broken Bow, on the other side of the state," says Payton. "He signed with the Chicago White Sox."

As Mickey pours through that story, his elation subsides noticeably, and then he calls out to his father.

"Dad, it says here that this other shortstop signed for fifty thousand dollars," Mickey says, so startled that he can't believe what he's reading.

Mutt is visibly flushed, and the house goes silent.

"What's his name?" Mutt finally asks.

"Jim Baumer," says Mickey.

"Never heard of 'im." Mutt appears too flabbergasted to read the story himself.

Mickey continues reading: "It says here 'New York Yankees scout Tom Greenwade camped outside the Baumer home for several days and said the Yankees offered Jim Baumer twenty-five thousand dollars, but they were outbid by the White Sox.'"

Lovell walks over to read the newspaper story herself.

"Mutt, did Tom Greenwade tell you any of this?" she asks her husband.

Speechless, Mutt starts to walks out to the front porch but then stops and sits down, pausing as if to allow this surprising news to sink in.

"Yeah," says Mickey, "and here in the story about me, Tom Greenwade predicts that I'll probably set records with the Yankees that equal Babe Ruth's and Joe DiMaggio's."

Mutt eyes Mickey, then Lovell, and finally stands up, tosses the newspaper aside, and starts to walks outside.

"Well," he says, "I reckon that old tax collector just outslicked us."

———

Mickey would forever be tormented by how he and his father were duped by Tom Greenwade, and the memory of it would resurrect itself any time the mention of "bonus babies" came up. In 1970, he told me how he had used the slight and the presence of a "bonus baby" to motivate him to overachieve. At spring training in 1951, Mickey met the first of these prized young prospects, Jackie Jensen. Just a year earlier, many thought that it would be Jensen who would eventually become Joe DiMaggio's successor in center field. Jensen, an all-American in two sports at the University of California, was a college golden boy with a national reputation. He had pitched and hit his Golden Bears team to the 1947 College World Series championship. Then he had led his football team to a perfect 10–0 season in 1948, finishing fourth in the Heisman Trophy balloting. He had given up his senior year to sign a $40,000 contract that made him a baseball bonus baby. As such, under baseball rules, Jensen had to be kept on the major league roster, though he had proven to be a disappointment in 1950.

In 1951, the presence of Jackie Jensen and Mickey Mantle together would make many wonder, especially those who knew how the Yankees had gotten Mickey for a fraction of the money paid out to Jensen. If Jackie Jensen, who looked like he would be a bust, at least for the Yankees, could command forty grand, the thinking was, what kind of bonus did the ball club have to put out to sign a phenom like Mickey Mantle? When other ballplayers and others learned that Mantle had been signed for a mere $1,500 bonus, most thought they had misheard. For Mickey Mantle, the kid Casey Stengel and others were already raving about? For the next Ruth and DiMaggio? Fifteen hundred dollars? Not fifteen thousand? Joe DiMaggio, for one, found it hard to believe.

"I thought they were joking, to be honest," DiMaggio said. "I couldn't believe it. I figure he either was a rich kid who didn't need the money or some kid off the farm who had no idea of what he was worth. Oh, my, what he had to learn. And can you imagine, if I'd had another few years, what kind of bargaining unit we could have been? We would have owned [part] of the Yankees."

Tom Greenwade would later say that signing Mantle had been the crown jewel of his scouting career. Signing Mickey Mantle, in fact, had been a well-designed plan that had been in the works for the better part of two years back in the day—a plan on which he misled and lied to Mantle at every turn. Greenwade had first laid eyes on Mantle in 1948 when he went to scout a teammate of Mickey's on the Whiz Kids team on which he was playing while still in high school. Of course, a baseball scout needs to be a consummate poker player, rarely letting on his true feelings about a prospect. It was to Greenwade's advantage to downplay Mickey's potential as a future professional player when he spoke to Mutt Mantle, who used this as motivational fodder for his son. Mickey, consequently, came to believe what Greenwade had said to his father—that he had not been overly impressed in his first view of what would ultimately become his prize signing. That wasn't just downplaying his hand; it was a flat-out lie.

"When I first saw him," Greenwade eventually admitted, "I knew he was going to be one of the all-time greats." Still, on another occasion Greenwade would say, "The first time I saw Mantle I knew how [Yankee scout] Paul Krichell felt when he first saw Lou Gehrig. He knew that as a scout he'd never have another moment like it."

Tom Greenwade, of course, shared that feeling. When he first saw Mantle with that great power and foot speed, he mistook him for being a year or two older. Later he even admitted having been so impressed when he first saw Mickey that he wanted to sign him on the spot. He had no idea the kid was only a fifteen-year-old high school student. For Greenwade's part, he was also fortunate that Mickey's father, while so knowledgeable about the game of baseball, was so naive about its business side and didn't know that big signing bonuses were becoming part of the sport.

In contrast, the $50,000 Chicago White Sox bonus baby from Broken Bow, Oklahoma—Jim Baumer, who was half a year older than

Mickey—would go directly to the majors and then become a journeyman minor leaguer for the entire 1950s before playing briefly with the Cincinnati Reds in 1960. Eventually Baumer made it big himself—as a scout whose signings included Hall of Famer Robin Yount. In an interview, Baumer later boasted of how on his high school graduation night his parents' living room had been filled with scouts, including Tom Greenwade—who seemed confident he had Mickey Mantle safely in his pocket.

"That amount *is* a pittance even by the standards of that day," said Kevin Kerrane, author of the classic *Dollar Sign on the Muscle: The World of Baseball Scouting*, of the Mantle signing for $1,500. "It's amazing when you think that he was signed for so little."

The signing of Mickey Mantle was actually far more complex and involved that even Mantle fully realized, although over time he came to understand that all had not been as the Yankees and Greenwade made it out to be. Signing Mickey, in fact, would be a steal, not only in the incredibly unfair deal the Yankees made with the Mantles but also in that the Yankees appear to have violated baseball's rules against dealing with youngsters still in high school. The Mantles, however, apparently didn't fully understand that major league teams were prohibited from even making *contact* with Mickey until he had graduated, much less making a signing offer.

Cleveland Indians scout Hugh Alexander, who was interested in Mantle, would later suggest, and the facts certainly would support, that the Yankees effectively monopolized what should have been a healthy competitive bidding for Mickey, with the help of his high school principal who, for reasons he took to his grave, was scaring off Greenwade's scouting competitors. The shrewd and resourceful Greenwade, a former Internal Revenue Service tax collector, had obviously ingratiated himself with Mickey's principal as much as he had with his father.

Mutt Mantle can perhaps be forgiven for his impatience about getting his son signed to a professional contract. He knew only about the hard life in the mines, made even tougher during the Great Depression. Although he was filled with optimism about Mickey's potential, a cold wind sometimes blew through the back of his mind—the knowledge that the world could collapse. Even as Mutt managed to overcome obstacles, the 1930s of his young adulthood whistled thinly through his memory. Those bleak years gave him an ambience of expectation about life and its pitfalls. Not too surprisingly, the Mantles used almost all of Mickey's signing bonus to pay off the mortgage on the family home. It is understandable how Mutt may have been extremely anxious to get Mickey playing professional baseball as soon as possible that summer; nevertheless, Mutt's decision to have Mickey sign so soon after becoming eligible to even talk to the pros appears to have been ill advised at best. At the time, Mickey was one of the area's most talented amateur athletes, and legendary coach Bud Wilkinson even tried to recruit him for his football program at the University of Oklahoma.

Undoubtedly, Mutt could have used the college football offers as negotiating leverage with the Yankees. As Al Campanis, the late Dodger baseball executive and himself a former scout, would later say in reflecting on Mantle's signing, "[Baseball's] rule against signing someone before he graduates from high school doesn't mean that on the day you graduate you have to sign a contract. That just marks the start of the race. Mantle was just coming into his own then. The only reasons I can see for him signing so quick would be if there'd been a big bonus—and there wasn't. Or if there'd been a contract that put him on the major league team roster—and there wasn't that either. Mantle could've played [amateur] ball that summer and built up his value the more he was seen and scouted. There's no telling what he could've signed for."

In fact, the Yankees had authorized Greenwade to pay up to $25,000, if he needed to. Yankee general manager George Weiss later told friends that he had told Greenwade to offer that much—the same bonus Bill Skowron would receive—to sign Mantle and the Baumer youngster in nearby Broken Bow. Once Baumer signed with the White Sox, Greenwade had even more money to use on Mantle. Weiss, a brilliant businessman who had been with the Yankees since 1932, had been the architect of the organization's farm system, which he had shrewdly built by signing a lot of Depression-era players cheaply and often making incredible profits when he sold some of them to other teams. After one of those deals, then Yankee general manager Ed Barrow asked Weiss, "George, doesn't your conscience bother you?"

Ultimately, the signing of Mickey Mantle would become part of Americana and heroic fable, befitting a *Saturday Evening Post* cover by Norman Rockwell. As author David Halberstam would later put it, "The myth of Tom Greenwade, the greatest scout of his age, blended with Mantle's myth to create a classic illustration of the American Dream: For every American of talent, no matter how poor or simple his or her background, there is always a Tom Greenwade out there searching to discover that person and help him or her find a rightful place among the stars."

Mantle's signing would also forever cement Greenwade's place with the Yankees and in baseball. Greenwade would remain with the organization for forty years, retiring in 1985, a year before his death. Throughout his life, Greenwade would deny violating the high school tampering rule. Although he admitted to being worried of other scouts moving in on Mickey, he claimed to have waited patiently until the Sunday after Mickey's graduation before offering him a contract that was ironed out in fifteen minutes of negotiations between himself and Mutt. Mickey signing for a total of $1,500 was a tenth of the money Elston Howard received from the Yankees a year later.

"It was not until the signing was announced in the paper and I read Tom Greenwade's prediction that I would probably set records with the Yankees, equaling Ruth's and DiMaggio's, that I began to wonder if my father and I had been outslicked," Mickey said years later.

"Greenwade, by *his* account, had just been going through Oklahoma on his way to look over a *real* prospect, when he stopped to talk to us. I never did find out who that *real* prospect was."

9

Life in the Big Apple

The only thing I knew about New York before I played there was that it was the home of the Yankees, as well as a whole lot of people.
—MICKEY MANTLE

IF SOMEONE HAD OFFERED TO SELL THE YOUNG MICKEY MANTLE THE Brooklyn Bridge, there's a chance the Yankee rookie would have been interested. He might have even fallen sucker for buying Grant's Tomb, though his onetime girlfriend Holly Brooke told me she felt fairly certain "Mickey wouldn't be foolish enough to think he could buy the Statue of Liberty or part of Central Park." Holly, though, wouldn't put money on it. She got to know Mickey too well in 1951. And anyone who knew him then will tell you that it was fortunate that Mickey Mantle was a gullible but not yet well-heeled rube at the time. He was an Oklahoma boy too trusting of strangers in the big city. In those early days, he was easy prey for con men and scam artists there on the streets of New York. He didn't have much money, so he believed the hustlers hawking cheap sweaters claiming to be worth hundreds. But then perhaps this was in the Mantle DNA. His father, after all, sold Mickey to the Yankees for $1,500 when the scout who made the deal paid $50,000 for an Oklahoma prospect and was even authorized to pay $25,000 for Mantle. Truly, the apple didn't fall far from the tree.

But Mickey might never have met the great love of his life, Holly, had he not been such a sucker. Holly Brooke was Mantle's consolation prize in the crazy scam with a Broadway opportunist named Alan Savitt. He convinced Mickey that as his agent, he could guarantee him $50,000 a year in endorsements and personal appearances, all for a fifty-fifty split. Mantle was ready to make the deal, never even bothering to ask the advice of teammates who had taken an interest in his safety and well-being. It wasn't as if most Yankee players, other than DiMaggio, were swarmed with moneymaking endorsement deals. But when those opportunities did come up, Frank Scott, who had been the team's traveling secretary through the late 1940s, represented several other players. He was an honest guy always looking out for the players.

One of those players was Hank Bauer, who had already taken Mickey shopping and bought him two suits with his own money. Bauer soon learned about Mickey's deal and enlisted both Scott and the Yankees' help in trying to extricate Mickey. Bauer and Scott even developed a clever plan for Scott to seek out Mickey as a client. For a country rookie, however, Mickey could be unusually stubborn.

"I've got bad news for you," Mantle told Scott when he approached Mickey about representing him. "This fellow wants to be my agent, and he's giving me a contract that guarantees me $50,000 a year."

Although skeptical, Scott said he couldn't offer any guarantees but would only take 10 percent, which was a more typical agent's fee. Scott also advised Mickey to have the Yankees' lawyers read over the contract. Mickey, however, was naive enough to believe he had somehow latched onto a better deal than anyone else. When Scott again ran into Mantle a few days later, Mickey informed him he had signed the contract.

"Did you take it to the Yankee lawyers?" Scott asked.

"Nope," said Mickey, confidently. "I didn't have to. This fellow had a lawyer for me."

Indeed, as Whitey Ford used to often say about this friend, Mickey Mantle was a hayseed.

Alan Savitt himself didn't have any money, so to pay Mantle the advance he promised him, he tried selling shares in the deal. But he was a con man. He had no legitimate investors, nor access to any. So he tried hustling shares to struggling actors and Broadway show people and anyone else he could find in midtown Manhattan.

"There was an ice cream parlor and drug store in the fifties—it was the most inexpensive place around, and Alan Savitt came in and asked if anyone knew Mickey Mantle," Holly told me in our interviews more than half a century later. "The fellas in the crowd did. I didn't. He asked if we'd invest $1,500. No one had $1,500. I asked my brothers and father. They knew of [Mantle], and they got the money together for me. Alan Savitt asked me if I wanted to meet him. I said, 'Yes, if I'm investing money, I want to meet him.' I was staying at a hotel for women. Danny's Hideaway was across the street from me. So I said that's the best place to go because the models and actresses would go in there and eat lunch because Danny's would always give us everything at half price and then sometimes we'd get things free. So we'd all go in there to eat. So I asked him if we could come in there. Mickey and I and Savitt, and he asked, 'Do you mind if we take pictures?' and I said, 'I don't mind. Ask him.' He didn't mind. So he took photographs of Mickey and me, that's the one you have in [*Mickey Mantle: America's Prodigal Son*]. And Mickey and I, I don't know. For some reason we clicked. I don't know what it was. And he asked if he could see me again, and I said yes. And then I saw him after that every single day that he was in town. . . . He was incredibly handsome and muscular, and he was very young. I told Savitt I was in and I thought, 'Okay, Holly, I've just bought a quarter interest in a ballplayer.' I started to leave, and that's when Mickey asked if he could see me again."

It didn't matter to Mickey that he was engaged to his high school sweetheart, Merlyn, who was still in Oklahoma. Holly Brooke was stunning, as beautiful as any of the starry-eyed young actresses who hung around the Stage Deli or Danny's Hideaway in those days. "I thought she looked a little like Rita Hayworth," Mickey said years later. "I had never seen anyone that beautiful in the movies. You know how people wondered later why Joe [DiMaggio] fell so hard for Marilyn Monroe? Well, when you've grown up the way Joe did in San Francisco and I did in Oklahoma, poor and the smell of fish and coal in your nostrils so you want to choke, and then someone like that—someone you would only see in your dreams or on the movie screen—taking any kind of interest in you, well, there's no goddamn way you're going to walk away from that."

Mickey began seeing Holly every day that the Yankees were in New York. Holly, who was seven years older than Mickey, showed him the New York nightlife that he wouldn't see with any of his Yankee teammates that year. "I guess I developed my first taste for the high life then," Mantle later said, "meeting Holly's friends, getting stuck with the check at too many fancy restaurants, discovering scotch at too many dull cocktail parties."

However, that wasn't exactly true. Mickey didn't get stuck with many checks. That's something that he quickly learned from Holly—that his celebrity and fame opened doors and were a commodity that he could trade. The Stage Deli in particular was often Mickey's security retreat from the intimidation of the big city. Max and Hymie Asnas, who owned the delicatessen, befriended Mickey and often made him special meals that were not on their menu. "Like all shy people," said Mantle, "I had a hard time going into new restaurants, not knowing whether to grab a table or wait to be shown, afraid to order something different for fear of making a jerk of myself, unable sometimes to tell the waiter from the busboy. But in the Stage Delicatessen I might have been in my home town." Much the same was true at Danny's Hideaway and many of the places where he went, where there was always someone picking up the tab. If someone wasn't paying for Mickey and whomever he was with, the places he went to were always too happy to comp him his meals and his drinks. It was a big deal to have a New York Yankee who was a regular hanging out in your place, and early in the season Mickey was the toast of the town.

"Mickey was the prince of the city," Holly said. "And he was having the time of his life. He loved every minute of it."

It didn't even seem to matter to Mantle that Savitt had failed to deliver on the $50,000 guarantee he had promised him to sign a contract for representation. Soon the Yankees got involved, as general manager George Weiss called on Arthur Friedlund, Yankee owner Dan Topping's personal lawyer, to finally extricate Mickey from the contract with Savitt.

No one, though, was going to separate Holly Brooke from him.

In Mantle's own words, Holly Brooke—a young divorced mother from New Jersey—would become "the love of my life" who would hold on to his affection for years. The New Yorkers who knew her, or more accurately, knew of Holly, dismissed her as the Broadway showgirl who in the spring of 1951 had been involved in some reportedly sketchy scam to take advantage of the dazzling Yankee rookie. But she and Mantle would carry on a love affair even after Mickey's marriage later that year and through much of his Yankee career. It ended only after she married a Broadway producer in the late 1960s who left her well taken care of.

"I became the showgirl who tried to scam Mickey Mantle," Holly reminisced half a century later. "Oh, if they had only known. I loved Mickey. Mickey loved me. Mickey had great years in his career. I was with him in New York those years, too. Many of his fans would tell you that 1956, when he won the Triple Crown, was his favorite year. And it was his best season. But if you had asked him, he would have said that 1951 was his favorite year. It was his favorite year because it was our year."

So who was this Holly Brooke who captured the heart of Mickey Mantle as no girl or woman ever had?

Holly Brooke had been born Marie Huylebroeck in Bayonne, Hudson County, New Jersey, a girl so striking and lovely that in 1948 she won the Miss New Jersey Pageant, qualifying to compete for Miss America. There was only one problem. She was a divorcée, a violation of the pageant rules. She was also a twenty-three-year-old single mother with a young child. Any scandal was quickly avoided when Huylebroeck agreed to quietly relinquish her newly won crown. A cover story was quickly produced, and a new Miss New Jersey took her place.

"I knew I was beautiful and had talent and I guess I just wanted to see how I kind of stacked up against other beautiful, talented women," she told me in explaining why she had even entered the pageant, knowing she was in violation of its rules. "And if anyone in the pageant had said to me, 'Young lady, you're going to win,' I would have dropped out or not even entered. I wouldn't have wanted to put myself in that kind of predicament. Who would?"

The experience, though, was a validation for a Jersey girl with grand dreams and great expectations but an unusual name of Belgian and French origin. The Americanized pronunciation of Huylebroeck was Holly Brook, and as a teen that was the artistic name she chose, spelling it Holly Brooke. She later moved to Manhattan where she appeared in several small parts in off-Broadway productions and bit roles in films.

By early summer 1951, she was effectively living with Mickey Mantle and spending every off-the-field moment with him when the Yankees were home. His Yankees teammates, those who knew of the relationship, feared she was a femme fatale who would ruin Mickey. Mantle would call her his first and great love. All was well as long as Mantle played well and continued to hit the way he had in the early weeks of the season. Mickey, however, had begun drinking heavily and had no control, especially since he could always find someone to pay for his drinks or buy the booze he would take home.

"He moved from the Concourse Hotel to 53rd near the Stage Delicatessen—I think they were on the fourth floor—and he wanted me there all the time," Holly told me in one of a series of interviews, "and I couldn't because I had to work as an actress and model. I would come there after my work, and sometimes I'd work on a movie until ten or eleven at night. One night I came home late, and he had started drinking and was so sick that I had to stay there with him all night, rubbing his back and helping him to the bathroom because he was so sick he kept throwing up. I felt bad that I hadn't been home earlier, and I kept telling him, 'Mick, you can't keep doing this. This isn't good for you.'"

Was Mickey Mantle a nineteen-year-old kid unable to hold his liquor, or was he already hooked, already an alcoholic, something he would finally admit to years later but that in his rookie season was quickly becoming a problem?

"I remember the first weekend the Yankees were home and me telling him I had to go home for the weekend, and Mickey begged me not to go," Holly recalled. "And I said, 'Mick, I've got to. I see my son on weekends.' I had already told him I was a working mom, and that my family kept my son during the week, and I'd go home on the weekends. He said, 'Well, okay, Holly, bring him up here, and we'll spend the weekend together.' I couldn't believe he'd said that, but I thought, 'Well, let's see.' And I brought my son Harlan up, and I swear Mickey took to him like he was his own."

Those early weeks of Mickey's 1951 rookie season were significant for Mantle because they put in place a relationship and friendship with Joe DiMaggio that would become misunderstood, misrepresented, and flatout lied about in the coming years. The two men were seventeen years apart in age, and that only began to hint at how different they were. DiMaggio was the veteran legend about to retire, but no one on the team could truly say they knew him, certainly not away from the ballpark. Everyone in the clubhouse from Pete Sheehy, the attendant, to the lowliest player had their own imitation of DiMaggio, Mickey told me, and they would often do these impersonations while Joe was sitting in front of his locker, his back to his teammates, seemingly self-absorbed in his brooding.

"Joe was just too easy to make fun of, and I guess I saw all the other players do it that it seemed easier to be that way than to be as serious as Joe always was," said Mickey. "He wasn't much for having friends on the team, and I think it was that way his entire career."

What Mantle saw in those first weeks of his rookie season was watching how an old pro like DiMaggio handled playing day after day when his body was telling him to quit. "I know that by '51, which was the only year I played with Joe, he was someone you just left alone," Mickey said of that time. "If he wanted to say something to you, he would. He did offer advice, I'll say that for him, and I think he might have wanted to be a good teammate—and don't get me wrong, on the field, in a game, there was no better teammate, and he was hurtin' that last year. Later in my career, when I practically needed a wheelchair almost at times just to make it on to the field, I thought of Joe in '51, and it occurred to me that that son-of-a-bitch was hurtin' just like that. And to be honest, it became a kinda backhanded inspiration because I figured if old man Joe DiMaggio could suck it up and go out that last year the way he felt, well, goddamn if I wasn't gonna try to do the same."

One of the first times Mickey recalled DiMaggio coming over and saying something to him was shortly after Mantle hit his first home run, off of right-hander Randy Gumpert on May 1 in Chicago, a 450-foot drive into the White Sox bullpen beyond right field.

"Joe came over to me on the dugout bench and said, 'Mickey, Gumpert oughta thank you. You just put him in the history books,'" Mantle said. "I wasn't sure what the hell he meant until later. He meant people would remember he was the first pitcher I homered against. So I guess Joe knew I was going to amount to something."

Meanwhile, Mantle's strong start to his rookie season had stolen much of the thunder from DiMaggio's struggles. Mickey's father had already seen some of his games, but it was not until the Yankees traveled to St. Louis to play the Browns that his mother was able to attend a game. At Sportsman's Park that day were Mickey's mother, his girlfriend Merlyn, and her mother. A reporter even approached Merlyn after the game and asked her what she thought of Mickey having hit a home run. "I expected it," she said. "He promised me he'd do it."

The Mickey Mantle of 1951 was an unusual sight to behold, not as a slugger—that was still a year or so ahead—but as a ballplayer. It mostly had to do with his daring speed, chasing down fly balls in right center field or down the right field line and on the base paths. There was a game against Detroit in which Mickey was bunted over from first base to second. Mantle, though, never slowed up and rounded the base knowing full well there was a routine throw being made for the putout of the bunter at first base. That is the normal play, with the first baseman then checking to make sure the runner at second base hasn't been careless. But in this game, the first baseman was startled to see that Mantle was streaking to third base and slid in safely ahead of the late throw.

Casey Stengel immediately jumped up from the bench in the dugout, yelling, "He went from first to third on a bunt!"

Mantle did something similar in a game against Cleveland when he lined a hit that Indians center fielder Larry Doby quickly cut off and, intending to hold Mickey to a single, prepared for a routine throw to second base. Mantle, though, had rounded first base at full speed without breaking stride and slid into second with a double well ahead of Doby's throw.

"You ain't seen nothing yet," Stengel bragged to the writers traveling with the team. "The kid doesn't run—he flies. He's positively the fastest man on the bases I've ever seen."

It was Mantle's speed in the outfield, though, that endeared him to the Yankee pitchers as Mickey quickly showed signs of becoming an outfielder possibly capable of taking over for DiMaggio in center field. No outfield in the American League was as cavernous as Yankee Stadium, especially in the gaps. Inexperienced outfielders had been known to get lost in that outfield, or at least embarrassed. But Mantle was so fast that his speed could help him overcome getting a late jump on a fly ball. DiMaggio had noticeably lost a step or two in playing the gaps to his right and left, so Stengel had already quietly urged Mickey to hustle harder for any balls in the gap between him and the aging Yankee Clipper. "You can run faster than any other outfielder in the business," Stengel told Mantle, "but one never would know that from watching you out there. Put on a show. Run hard for the ball. Haul off. Throw a foot high into the air when you heave the ball. Don't be afraid to throw."

Stengel, of course, took great pride in the quantum leap of Mickey's defensive play, but Mantle's real tutor was Tommy Henrich. The Yankee outfielder-turned-outfield coach had spent long hours teaching Mantle the intricacies of playing the outfield in the big leagues. Mantle responded well to Henrich because nothing he was teaching him conflicted with anything he learned from his father. Mickey reacted differently when anyone, especially Stengel, tried to change anything having to do with his hitting and what Mutt had taught and drilled into him.

Just how well Henrich had taught Mickey became most evident in a game early that 1951 season when Mantle caught what looked like a routine sacrifice fly in right field. Jim Busby of the Chicago White Sox had tagged up at third base and broke for home the moment the ball hit Mickey's glove. But then in almost the same motion, Mantle planted his right foot the way Henrich had taught him and gunned a strike to catcher Yogi Berra at the plate so fast that Busby had to stop halfway home and retreat to third. Henrich was among the first to jump to his feet in the Yankee dugout.

"That's the best throw I've ever seen anyone make," Henrich proudly told Stengel nearby. "I don't think I have anything else to teach him. He's got it down pretty good."

10

The Fateful Day

I know that some people say, "Mick blamed Joe [DiMaggio] for ruin-ing his career"—that the injury in '51 was Joe's fault. Well, that's a lot of crap. I never said that. I never thought that. Jesus Christ, Joe wasn't my boogyman. He was my teammate.

—MICKEY MANTLE

MICKEY MANTLE'S FIRST WORLD SERIES, PLAYING IN YANKEE STADIUM next to childhood hero Joe DiMaggio with his father watching from the stands, was like something out of a boy's fairy tale. The Yankees' oppo-nent was baseball's Cinderella team, the New York Giants who had just made a miraculous National League pennant run after trailing the Brooklyn Dodgers by thirteen and a half games in the middle of August. The Giants won thirty-seven of their last forty-four games, finishing in a tie with the Dodgers and then capturing a three-game playoff in an implausible comeback on Bobby Thomson's famous ninth-inning home run—what became known in baseball lore as the "shot heard 'round the world." The Giants' magic carried over to winning the series opener, but the late-afternoon sun the next day seemed to cast a foreboding shadow over Yankee Stadium in the second game.

Before the World Series began, Casey Stengel had taken Mantle aside and instructed him to be especially aggressive from his right field posi-tion. "Take everything you can get over in center," Stengel told Mickey. "The Dago's heel is hurting pretty bad." It wasn't an intended slight of DiMaggio but just the reality of Joe now being only a shadow of his for-mer self in center field. With his knees, back, and shoulder often hurting,

Joe had become a defensive liability. All season long, shortstop Phil Riz-zuto and second baseman Jerry Coleman had been going unusually deep into left and right center fields to take cutoff throws from the increasingly weak-armed Yankee legend. Joe had also misjudged more fly balls than ever before in his career. So Mickey was prepared to cover for DiMaggio.

Still, this was DiMaggio. There had once been a time when a fly ball like this one would have been routine for DiMaggio, who was notori-ous for selfishly guarding his territory in center. One time in 1949, then rookie Hank Bauer had eased over into right center to take a fly ball, much as Mickey had now been instructed to do. DiMaggio had stared at the young outfielder between innings in the Yankee dugout until Bauer asked him if he had done anything wrong. "No, you didn't do anything wrong," replied DiMaggio, "but you're the first son-of-a-bitch who ever invaded my territory."

On deck when Thomson hit his home run had been Willie Mays. Like Mantle, he was playing in his first World Series, and this would be the last of DiMaggio's ten fall classics. It would be the only time the career paths of all three New York future Hall of Fame center fielders converged, but none of them had much to do with the outcome of the 1951 World Series, which the Yankees won in six games. When Mays led off the top of the sixth, the Yankees were ahead, 2–0, having scored single runs in the first and second innings. Mantle in right field shaded over a couple of steps toward center field. Looking over at DiMaggio, it was still hard for Mantle to imagine the great Joltin' Joe even a step slower than in his prime. He still moved so gracefully under fly balls and made every catch appear easy and effortless.

The Yankee's coy, junk-ball left-hander Eddie Lopat fooled Mays, as he had most right-handed batters, with a screwball that faded away. Mays managed to slap a fly ball into short right center that looked as if it might drop in, with Mel Allen telling his radio audience that "Mantle gives chase." Mickey was hollering "I got it! I got it!" when suddenly, at the last second, DiMaggio surprised him, calling for the ball. Mantle immediately pulled up to avoid crashing into DiMaggio, but the spikes on his right shoe caught on the rubber cover of a drain hole in the outfield. Mantle's right knee twisted and collapsed, as he let out a blood-curdling cry, falling to the ground as if he'd been shot. He was sprawled on the grass with one leg down and the other scissor-kicked up in the air as DiMaggio made the catch, and then rushed over to Mickey's side to check on him. For a split second, DiMaggio thought that Mickey might have been shot.

"I was afraid he was dead," DiMaggio later recalled. "I shouted, 'Mick! Mick!' And he never moved a muscle or batted an eye. Then I waved to our bench to send out a stretcher."

"Fans, Mantle appears seriously hurt," Allen told his broadcast audience. "DiMaggio is calling for help, and Yankee teammates have surrounded Mickey."

From behind the Yankee dugout, Mutt Mantle jumped up, his face drained of any color and with a look of concern. Joe Payton was in the seat next to him.

"Mutt, that ain't Mickey's bad leg, is it?" Payton asked Mutt.

"No . . . it's his good leg," said Mutt. "Dammit to Betsy, it was his good leg."

With DiMaggio kneeling next to him, Mickey regained consciousness and began moaning and writhing.

"Don't move, Mick," said DiMaggio. "They're bringing a stretcher."

Two teammates from the bullpen were the first to reach Mantle, joined soon by Casey Stengel and two clubhouse men with a stretcher. After a moment, as fans stood in hushed concern, the trainers lifted Mickey onto the stretcher. Several players came over to Mantle and tapped him on the shoulders. Then the trainers carried Mickey on the stretcher through the infield dirt on the right side of the diamond toward the Yankee dugout along the first base line as the stadium erupted into a tremendous ovation.

By the time the trainers arrived at the Yankee dugout, Mutt had already made his way down there. The moment was an emotional one for father and son. Mickey, already in visible pain, broke down in tears.

Stengel had been next to Mantle as he was carried off the field. "Hang on, Mickey, we're gonna take care of ya," he said to his young star as he turned to Mutt. "Mr. Mantle, go on with Mickey."

The calamitous result of Willie Mays's short fly ball that day would be repeatedly relived and debated in the coming years by fans, commentators, and Mantle himself. Mickey had suffered the injury on a play that no right fielder would have been required to make unless he was cover-ing for a washed-up center fielder who had become a defensive liability. So who was to blame? Or was it just a case of bad luck? "I knew there was no way DiMaggio could get to it," Mantle would recall, "so I hauled ass. Just as I arrived, I heard Joe say, 'I got it.' I looked over, and he was camped under the ball." Mickey would later say that as he saw DiMag-gio, he thought, "Oh, shit! I'm gonna hit DiMaggio. I'll put him in the hospital. They'll never let me play again! That's when I slammed on the brakes. My spikes caught on the rubber cover of a drain hole buried in the outfield grass. Pop. There was a sound like a tire blowing out, and my right knee collapsed. I fell to the ground and stayed there, motionless. A bone was sticking out the side of my leg, [and] the pain squeezed like a vice around my right knee." Mickey was convinced from the cracking sound he had heard that he had broken his leg and feared that his career was suddenly over.

In the trainer's room after the game, Yankee trainer Gus Mauch put splints on the sides of the leg and wrapped it up to protect the knee. That night the knee swelled to almost twice its size, and Mickey had barely slept when he and Mutt took a taxi the next morning for an appointment at Lenox Hill Hospital.

"D'ya think about just takin' the ball yerself?" Mutt finally asked his son the question that had been on his mind since the nightmare of seeing him so badly injured that he had to wonder if Mickey would ever play baseball again.

"I guess I was afraid of runnin' into him and hurtin' him," said Mickey.

Mutt bit his lip as he measured his next words.

"Someone in the clubhouse was sayin' he wouldn't call that ball until he was damn sure he could make it look easy," he said.

Mantle considered that for a moment, then became silent as the taxi pulled up at the hospital entrance.

"[My father] got out of the cab first, outside the hospital, and then I got out," Mantle remembered years later. "I was on crutches and I couldn't put any weight on the leg that was hurt, so as I got out of the cab I grabbed my father's shoulder to steady myself. He crumpled to the side-walk. I couldn't understand it. He was a very strong man, and I didn't think anything at all about putting my weight on him that way. He was always so strong."

In the commotion Mutt collapsed under Mickey's weight.

"Dad, what's wrong?" asked a visibly startled Mantle.

Mickey caught his father, who came to rest leaning on his son. Mutt's head rolled aimlessly with a forced smile on his face as he stared at Mickey's frightened gaze. As Mutt tried to speak, Mickey lowered his head to hear his father's whisper.

The noisy street drowned out their voices, but you could hear a wail in the October morning wind.

Two hospital attendants who had just come out of the entrance rushed to their aid. One of them supported Mickey while the other one helped Mutt get to his feet. The look on Mickey's face was one of utter disbelief.

Both Mickey and Mutt were rushed into the hospital and into separate examination rooms. In the Yankees clubhouse the previous afternoon, team physician Sidney Gaynor originally diagnosed Mickey's injury as a torn muscle on the inside of his right knee. Now at the hospital, he revised the diagnosis to a torn knee ligament. The leg remained badly swollen. Two weeks later, Mantle was sent to Johns Hopkins Hospital in Baltimore where specialists concluded surgery wouldn't be necessary but that Mickey would have to undergo extensive physical therapy during the off-season. He would likely be ready for spring training for the 1952 season.

The diagnosis for Mutt Mantle was another matter. Doctors concluded he was suffering from Hodgkin's disease, which had been what had killed Grandpa Charlie, Uncle Tunney, and several other Mantle men.

"But you can do something, can't you?" Mickey pleaded to the doctor who informed him of his father's fate.

"I'm sorry, Mickey," Mantle later recalled the doctor's words, which had been embedded in his memory. "I'm afraid there's not much that can be done. Your father is dying."

Your father is dying. The words kept repeating in his head, he remembered, as he fell back on the pillow onto his hospital bed, stunned, resigned, and watching the ceiling fan blades spin slower and slower until there came an almost blinding flash of hard white light and we are into a dream sequence going through Mickey's mind:

Mickey undergoing grueling physical rehabilitation work on his knee at Lenox Hill Hospital and then using crutches to leave. Mantle limping with a cane in Central Park, arm in arm with girlfriend Holly Brooke, during an early New York winter. Then a storm of hard white-light flashbulbs of photographs being taken of Mickey at his wedding in December 1951—to hometown fiancée Merlyn Johnson—in her Oklahoma family home decorated for Christmas. Photos include the newlyweds taking their vows with Mutt's pal Turk Miller, the best man, the bride and groom with their families, and the young couple separately with Mutt, looking very gaunt. Sad recollections of the funeral and burial of Mutt in the spring of 1952 and Mantle throwing a violent temper tantrum in the Yankee clubhouse when he hears the news. Then Mickey ecstatic over the birth of Mickey Jr. in 1953, and the 1952 and 1953 World Series championships. He remembers yet another hospitalization after another injury, undergoing several army pre-induction physicals in which his records are marked "4F" every time. There is carousing—a lot of it—with Billy Martin and Whitey Ford, meeting President Eisenhower before a World Series game, and Mickey frustrated after making an out pinch-hitting, losing the 1955 World Series to the Brooklyn Dodgers.

We get a sense of Mickey changing and maturing as the memories dissolve to a blue sky and in the foreground the sharp image of a baseball, very close and moving in super slo-mo with its white cusp and red silk seams breaking our vision from right to left, like a sunset. The ball floats downward, gyrating like a globe, coming down from the sky in lazy revolutions, its bleached-white horse hide bearing the blue legend: *Rawlings . . . American League.* There is a moment's pause before we see Yankee Stadium, Memorial Day 1956, from the earlier scene, with the baseball floating back from striking the right field facade and ricocheting halfway between the fence and the infield grass. As the ball hits the grass, there is an explosion of wild cheering and celebration in the stands.

On the bases, we see Mickey running head down, his customary home run trot to avoid embarrassing the pitcher, circling the bases, getting a handshake from third base coach Frank Crosetti, and crossing home plate . . .

"How about that?" an excited Mel Allen yells into his broadcast microphone. "Mickey Mantle came within inches of puttin' one out of the House That Ruth Built, something no one's ever done—not even the Babe."

As he gets a congratulatory handshake from Yogi Berra, the next batter waiting near home plate, Mickey turns to look back at the box seats where he had seen his father and himself when he was a child. But the father and son he sees now are the father and son he saw originally.

Mantle is slightly red-eyed, tiny tears mixed with sweat rolling down his cheeks.

An hour later, in the postgame jubilation, Yankee teammates and reporters surround Mickey's locker. His friends tousle his hair, hug him, and congratulate him on his dinger, as Mickey visibly enjoys the fuss. He sits on a stool, a can of beer in one hand, taking it all in. His uniform is off, and he is wearing only a baseball undershirt and his sliding shorts. But what grabs our attention is his legs—or, to be more accurate, the thick layers of white Ace bandages that encase both legs, from his thighs down to his ankles. He resembles someone with a mummified lower body. Mickey starts unwrapping the bandages as he answers reporters' questions.

"Mickey, is that the hardest ball you've ever hit?" asks one reporter.

"Nah, I hit one in my rookie year . . ." Mantle says. "Spring training . . . an exhibition in L.A."

"But in a game that counted," says a second reporter, "that's the hardest ball you've hit, isn't it?"

Mantle easily becomes impatient. "Fuck, how am I supposed to know?" he says. "I just hit 'em."

"Mick, you've taken Ramos deep a lot of times now," adds a third reporter. "You figure you own him?"

Mantle is now pissed. "Where do you guys come up with these questions?"

"It's just a question, Mick," says the third reporter, defensively.

"Well, this is just an answer," says Mickey. "Fuck off."

Mantle turns his back to the reporter, sips his beer, and continues unwrapping the bandages.

Photograph of Mickey Mantle from his 1951 season, which years later helped launch the baseball memorabilia craze. The Topps baseball card company colorized the picture and used it on Mantle's 1952 card, which became known as his Topps rookie card. It's the most valuable card in the business, except for a rare Honus Wagner, with a near perfect card selling at auction for $2.88 million in 2018. *Courtesy of the Mickey Mantle Museum, Cooperstown, N.Y., and Tom Catal and Andrew Vilacky.*

Among the famous personalities who wanted to meet Mickey Mantle in his remarkable rookie season was the Duke of Windsor, the former king of England. Here, Mickey listens as manager Casey Stengel talks to the duke on the steps outside the Yankees dugout. With them is Yankees shortstop Phil Rizzuto. *Courtesy of the Mickey Mantle Museum, Cooperstown, N.Y., and Tom Catal and Andrew Vilacky.*

Mickey Mantle seems deep in thought about the advice baseball legend Ty
Cobb is giving him in the dugout before the New York Yankees' Oldtimers
Game at the Stadium in 1958. "Heck, I was just hoping he was going to tell
me he was going to leave me his Coca Cola stock in his will," Mantle later
said. Cobb, who was known as the "Georgia Peach," bought a large block
of original stock in the new Coca Cola startup in his home state and ultimately became one of the game's wealthiest former ballplayers. *Courtesy of
the Mickey Mantle Museum, Cooperstown, N.Y., and Tom Catal and Andrew
Vilacky.*

New York Yankee rookie phenom Mickey Mantle greets high school sweetheart Merlyn Johnson, his younger brother Ray, and his dad and mom, Mutt and Lovell, before a 1951 exhibition game against the Boston Braves in Kansas City, Missouri. *Courtesy of the Mickey Mantle Museum, Cooperstown, N.Y., and Tom Catal and Andrew Vilacky.*

Though he was engaged to Merlyn at the time, Mickey became romantically involved with actress Holly Brooke, who virtually lived with Mantle during much of his rookie season. Here Mickey and Holly dine at Danny's Hideaway in Manhattan in 1951. *Courtesy of the Mickey Mantle Museum, Cooperstown, N.Y., and Tom Catal and Andrew Vilacky.*

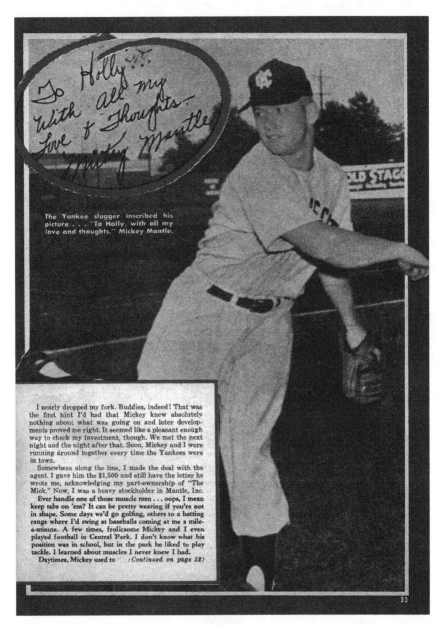

The Yankee slugger inscribed his picture . . . "To Holly, with all my love and thoughts," Mickey Mantle.

I nearly dropped my fork. Buddies, indeed! That was the first hint I'd had that Mickey knew absolutely nothing about what was going on and later developments proved me right. It seemed like a pleasant enough way to check my investment, though. We met the next night and the night after that. Soon, Mickey and I were running around together every time the Yankees were in town.

Somewhere along the line, I made the deal with the agent. I gave him the $1,500 and still have the letter he wrote me, acknowledging my part-ownership of "The Mick." Now, I was a heavy stockholder in Mantle, Inc.

Ever handle one of those muscle men . . . oops, I mean keep tabs on 'em? It can be pretty wearing if you're not in shape. Some days we'd go golfing, others to a batting range where I'd swing at baseballs coming at me a mile-a-minute. A few times, frolicsome Mickey and I even played football in Central Park. I don't know what his position was in school, but in the park he liked to play tackle. I learned about muscles I never knew I had.

Daytimes, Mickey used to (Continued on page 52)

33

Mickey inscribed one of the rare photos of him in a Kansas City Blues minor league team uniform to his girlfriend, Holly Brooke: "To Holly, with All My Love & Thoughts, Mickey Mantle." (In mid-season 1951, the Yankees demoted the slumping Mantle to their minor league affiliate in Kansas City before bringing him back to New York in August.) *Courtesy of the Mickey Mantle Museum, Cooperstown, N.Y., and Tom Catal and Andrew Vilacky.*

Mickey had the distinction of being a rookie in New York in 1951 along with future fellow Hall of Famer Willie Mays of the Giants. Before the Giants and the Dodgers left for the West Coast in 1958, a debate among New York–area fans raged each season: Who was the best center fielder? Mickey Mantle, Willie Mays, or Duke Snider? *Courtesy of the Mickey Mantle Museum, Cooperstown, N.Y., and Tom Catal and Andrew Vilacky.*

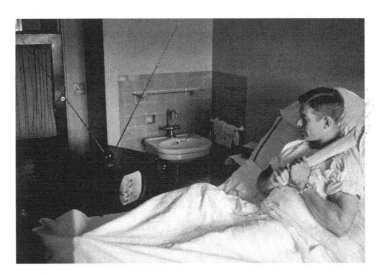

Mickey Mantle mimes holding a bat, ready to take a swing, as he watches a game of the 1951 World Series on television in his hospital room, where he ended up after tearing up his knee in Game 2 of that Subway Series against the New York Giants. *Courtesy of the Mickey Mantle Museum, Cooperstown, N.Y., and Tom Catal and Andrew Vilacky.*

This is the famous photograph of Mickey Mantle collapsing in the outfield with the knee injury that would dramatically alter his career. It occurred in the second game of the 1951 World Series as Mantle, playing right field, chased Willie Mays's short fly ball at full speed only to pull up suddenly when centerfielder Joe DiMaggio called that he was making the catch. Mantle's spikes caught on a sprinkler cover, and the Yankees rookie was never the same. *Courtesy of the Mickey Mantle Museum, Cooperstown, N.Y., and Tom Catal and Andrew Vilacky.*

Yankees scout Tom Greenwade visits Mickey Mantle, the prize signee of his career, during the Yankees' 1953 World Series championship celebration. Greenwade became like a surrogate father to Mickey after the death of his dad, Mutt, in 1952. *Courtesy of the Mickey Mantle Museum, Cooperstown, N.Y., and Tom Catal and Andrew Vilacky.*

Mickey Mantle, Merlyn, and Hank Bauer are recognizable in a photo that also includes Charlene Bauer with Stage Deli partner Hymie Asnas and his wife to the left of Mickey and restaurant co-owner Max Asnas to the right of the Bauers. Mickey and Bauer shared an apartment above the deli in the 1951 season. *Courtesy of Bobby Asnas.*

Merlyn and Mickey Mantle share wedding cake on their wedding day, December 23, 1951, in Commerce, Oklahoma. Knowing he had only a short time to live, Mutt Mantle urged his son to marry his hometown sweetheart after his rookie season. Five months later, Mickey's father was dead. *Courtesy of the Mickey Mantle Museum, Cooperstown, N.Y., and Tom Catal and Andrew Vilacky.*

PART TWO

THE BEST THERE IS

If you're betting your life on one hitter delivering for you, I wouldn't hesitate. Hurt, limping, drunk, hungover, sober, Sandy Koufax or Cy Young pitching, Mick is the guy I would send up to hit. I'd want only the greatest up there.

—YOGI BERRA

PROLOGUE

Breakfast of Champions

ACCORDING TO LOCAL FOLKLORE, THE SEEMINGLY NEVER FINISHED highway leaving Waco for Dallas in central Texas is haunted by the spirit of the Hueco Indians who were driven out of their home along the Brazos River, the vampire witches of the Seminole who stole away there from Oklahoma after the deadly Trail of Tears relocation, or the runaway Confederate slaves who brought Caribbean voodoo religion to the area. Take your pick. The karma is bad in all directions. Driving back to Dallas that night in 1971, I knew it had been a mistake to tell Mickey Mantle that kind of chilling local history.

"I'm dyin'," he kept moaning as I drove his Cadillac El Dorado onto the access road from the Old Dallas Freeway to Interstate 35, which was in the stop and go throes of construction. "I'm seeing shit. I'm seeing stikinis! It's that goddamn curse you were telling me about. I've been cursed."

Stikinis? I knew about *murcielagos* and *chupacabras* that could taunt and haunt you in your nightmares. But I'd never heard about stikinis.

"Stikinis?" I asked.

"Fuck, yes, stikinis," said Mick. "Shape-shifters. I grew up with 'em in Oklahoma. They feast on human hearts."

"Mick, we can turn back," I said. Hell, he sounded like he believed this crap more than I did.

"No, no, keep going," he said. "Fuck, I knew I was going to die before I was forty, but I didn't think it would be like this."

"Hell, Mick, you're in a brand-new Cadillac," I said. "You're not going to die, unless I crash your car."

"Fuck, don't do me any favors," he said. "I meant the woman. I think she cursed me."

"Who, my mom?" My mom was a sorceress, after all. Or at least, that's what my Uncle Roy always said, and he was deathly afraid of her. She had put a curse on him, he kept insisting up until the day he died. He once told me she was a witch. "Ask her," he urged me. When I finally did, mom just laughed and said that was just Uncle Roy talking foolishness. He had been kidnapped as a child by aliens, after all, or by the Rosicrucians. But Mickey Mantle accusing my mom of cursing him, well, that was another matter. Had my mom finally gotten her way and put a curse on my childhood hero, for all my religious blasphemies of the past?

"No, no, Goddamit! Not your mom. The other woman. What'd she do to me?"

"She blessed you, Mick." I tried to assure him. My childhood idol was just stinking drunk right now, and with a bad stomachache to boot. "That's all she did, Mick, honest." Earlier that evening, my mom's best friend Caridad, a Santeria priestess, had blessed Mickey and me. Admittedly, it was a Santeria blessing, but a blessing just the same.

"Fuck, I think she cursed me," Mickey moaned again. "My stomach's killing me!"

"Mick, I don't think she cursed you," I said. "I think it may have been that concoction you made when I left you alone in the kitchen."

"Fuck, I make that every night," he said. "Brandy, Kahlua, cream."

"Yeah, but I kept telling you, Mick, *that* wasn't cream."

"It was in a cream bottle in your mom's refrigerator," he said. "Fuck, what was it then?"

"Mexican *crema*," I said.

"Cream! Right."

"Well, not quite." I should never have left him alone in Mom's house, but how did I know he would help himself? "Mexican *crema* is crème fraîche, but it's got buttermilk as a culturing agent to thicken it up. Mick, Mexican *crema* is more like sour cream."

Those two words alone made him wretch. Me too. Mickey's concoction, which he called his breakfast of champions, would never be the same again. But he would be okay, though not before he shared his fear of stikinis. They were vampire creatures found in the folklore of the Semi-nole. They appeared human by day, but at night they turned into the form of an owl and flew through the darkness of night searching for human prey.

"They say the stikini were the curse of the Seminole," said Mick. "Their curse for being forced to leave their homes in the Southeast and relocate in Oklahoma."

"I can understand," I said. "Most people would be pretty upset if they had to go live in Oklahoma."

"Fuck you!" I had awakened Mantle's native pride. "Oklahoma's a great place."

"But you choose to live in Dallas."

"Yeah, well, growing up there wasn't so bad," he said. "Growing up in Commerce, my momma used to tell us to stay home at night because if you were outside and you heard the cry of a stikini, you would die. You wouldn't know. You don't grow up with the stikini here in Texas?"

"No, I grew up deprived of that," I said. "Here, we just have our heroes."

11

Mickey Mantle in Excelsis

Tu, tu padre y este párroco abandonado de Dios deben pensar que tu madre está loca si ella va a creer lo que dijo: que su idolátrico Mickey Mantle está sosteniendo su pedazo de madera piadosamente como Jesucristo en la cruz. ¿Qué puso tu padre alcohólico en el vino que sirvió al padre Antonio con la cena de esta noche? ¡Querido Dios! Llevé al padre Antonio a tu habitación para mostrarle cuán irrespetuoso eres de que tengas esos carteles gigantescos en las paredes de tu Mickey Mantle y de ese Joe DiMaggio que tu padre siempre está hablando, más de lo que nunca habla de mí, y de mostrarle al padre Antonio lo es tu sacrilegio porque para Dios solo tienes ese pequeño crucifijo de Jesucristo. Y nunca en mis sueños más locos pude imaginar que el padre Antonio reaccionaría así, pensé que iba a hacer una genuflexión frente a la imagen de Mickey Mantle cuando lo viera. ¡Dios mío, estaba tan avergonzada y humillada!

Y luego, para él, un sacerdote ordenado de Dios y la Iglesia, volver a la mesa del comedor y tener el valor de decirme: "Señora, creo que todas estas son solo representaciones inocentes de los modelos de rol cercanos al corazón de Tony, cada uno con sus simbólicas piezas de madera en las que han vivido y muerto sus grandes historias." ¿Quién es ese hombre que cree que es? Que Yogi Berra tiene más sentido con esa locura que me dices que dice. Piezas simbólicas de madera! Me gustaría mostrarle una verdadera pieza de madera, si él no fuera sacerdote y si no fuera una mujer religiosa. Piezas simbólicas de madera! Juro ante Dios que nunca más recibiré la Sagrada Comunión de ese sacerdote. Sé que tu padre y yo nos casamos en la iglesia San Francisco de padre Antonio, y que fuiste bautizado allí. Pero si su padre sabe lo que es mejor para él, él comenzará a acompañarme a esas reuniones para la construcción de una nueva Iglesia

Católica. Y antes de prometer un solo centavo para su construcción, exigiré la promesa de que el obispo nos asigne un párroco que nunca haya oído hablar de Mickey Mantle!

———

"You, your father, and this godforsaken parish priest of yours must think your mother is crazy if she's going to believe what he said—that your idolatrous Mickey Mantle is holding his piece of wood piously just like Jesus Christ on the cross. What did your alcoholic father put in the wine that he served Father Antonio with dinner tonight? Dear God! I took Father Antonio into your room to show him how disrespectful you are that you have those gigantic posters on the walls of your Mickey Mantle and that Joe DiMaggio your father is always talking about, more than he ever talks about me, and to show Father Antonio your sacrilege because for God you have only that tiny crucifix of Jesus Christ. And never in my wildest dreams could I ever imagine that Father Antonio would react like that— I thought he was going to genuflect in front of that picture of Mickey Mantle when he saw it. Oh my God, I was so embarrassed and humiliated!

"And then for him, an ordained priest of God and the Church, to come back to the dining table and to have the nerve to tell me, 'Señora, I think these are all just innocent representations of the role models close to Tony's heart, each with their symbolic pieces of wood on which their great stories have lived and died.' Who does that man think he is? That Yogi Berra you talk about makes more sense with that craziness you tell me he says. Symbolic pieces of wood! I'd like to show him a real piece of wood, if he weren't a priest and if I weren't a religious woman. Symbolic pieces of wood! I vow before God that I will never again take Holy Communion from that priest. I know your father and I were married at Father Antonio's St. Francis Church, and you were baptized there. But if your father knows what's best for him, he'll start going with me to those meetings for the building of a new Catholic church over on this side of town. And before I pledge a single dime for its construction, I'll demand a promise that our bishop assign us a parish priest who has never heard of Mickey Mantle!"

At some point in my young life my mom tried to exorcise Mickey Mantle from my thoughts. In coming years it would be known among my friends and family as my "Mickey Mantle exorcism." My mom thought that if she sat me down and forced me to write Mickey Mantle's name a thousand times I might become so sick of it that perhaps our lives might be rid of this idolatrous role model, that I might want to be someone else. The exorcism failed. The exercise only improved my handwritten Mickey Mantle signature, a lookalike to his early autograph. I did get sick, though. Actually I'd been running a low-grade fever that morning.

By late afternoon, it was full blown. By the evening I was delirious. I likely needed a doctor. My mother called my father's aunt, Doña Juana, a *curandera*, who from early in my childhood had often treated me for my mysterious fevers, incredible headaches, and stomach problems. I would lie on the bed with arms outstretched, my body forming a cross. Then, holding a small white handkerchief and a Mason jar of water, she would say, "Es agua santa." It was holy water. She would cover my face with the handkerchief, then dip her fingertips in the water jar and in short quick motions would sprinkle the white cloth. She would place the Mason jar on the night table and pick up two short palm leaves, yellowing and brown in the shadows of the candlelight in the room. She would make a small slit near the center of one leaf and insert the other through it, forming a cross. She would form three more crosses the same way, placing one just above each of my hands and the third below my feet. The fourth palm cross Doña Juana kissed and then used in making the sign of the cross: to the temple, near the heart, the left shoulder, then the right and to the lips again. She would ask me to uncross my legs. She would lean over me and begin sweeping the cross made of palms over my body, praying in Spanish as she swept: "Our Father, who art in heaven . . ." Still sweeping the cross of palms, Doña Juana would finish the series of prayers and would call out, "*Tony, vente. Tony, vente. No te quedes*" (Tony, come. Tony, come. Don't stay behind). That night, I was too sick and delirious to respond. But as I stared at the large photo of Mickey Mantle above my bed, I thought I heard someone answer for me. "*Hay voy*" (I'm coming). "*Hay voy.*" Thanks, Mick.

If hell hath no fury like a woman scorned, then what about heaven? And I don't think—no, I *know*—that my mom wasn't alone in wishing she could curb the obsession that gripped sons and husbands across America in the mid-1950s. It was Mickey Mantle fever, and there was no cure. My mother, who was like some incredible character Gabriel García Márquez might have created for one of his magical novels, had had her fill of Mickey Mantle from both the man she had married and the son whom they hoped would live out their American dreams. When my father returned to the United States from overseas at the end of World War II, he had stayed over an extra week in New York City just to watch the last of that season's games at Yankee Stadium. He attended four games that September of what had been a miserable season for the Yankees. It was the third straight year that they had been without the services of Joe DiMaggio, my father's favorite player, who had enlisted for military service. That alone made DiMaggio even more special in my father's eyes—he was a decorated army veteran—and he had returned home to Texas with a life-size picture of "The Yankee Clipper," as he was affectionately known by fans, that later hung in my bedroom alongside a similar large portrait of Mickey Mantle. My mom, a devout Roman Catholic, often complained that my bedroom was more a place of worship to my hero than to God. Maybe she was right. Fittingly, my nightly prayers that began with "Now I lay me down to sleep . . ." ended with a special request that God watch over Mickey, because of his bad legs. And yes, I did have a crucifix hanging over the headboard of my bed to which I prayed; however, it was dwarfed on the wall by those enormous images of Mantle and DiMaggio, yes, as Father Antonio noted, each with their own piece of wood in their hands. I don't think my mother realized that our parish priest to whom she had shown my bedroom was the coach of our CYO baseball team because he looked at the juxtaposition of the posters and the crucifix, and he said exactly what my mom had later moaned, in a ranting screed: "*Señora, I think these are all just innocent representations of the role models close to Tony's heart, each with*

114

their symbolic pieces of wood on which their great stories have lived and died."
True to her promise, Mom later became one of the founding *madrinas*
of the new Roman Catholic Church in my hometown, insisting it be
christened Sacred Heart of Jesus. In the coming years, La Iglesia del
Sagrado Corazon de Jesucristo of South Waco, Texas, would rise from
the hard caliche where nothing organic would grow across from one of
the schools I would attend, University High; it was built out of little
more than the sale of tamales, rigged bingo games at weekend *jamaicas*,
and outrageous pledges demanded by the archdiocese from working-
class faithful because the Vatican certainly didn't loosen its purse strings
to meet the needs of anyone in America or maybe elsewhere either.
Bronze plaques should have lined the church walls praising the contributions of these congregation members. The Almanzas, the Garcias,
the Silvas, the Duartes, the Jassos. The pews, the stained-glass windows,
the prized organ, the chandeliers—yes, Christ, the priest who oversaw
the construction of the eventual Spanish hacienda–styled church, had
insisted that specially made chandeliers had to light up this house of
God. Yes, a burning bush had come a long way. Wasn't Padre Antonio
looking a lot better, Mom? He only wanted to play baseball under the
sun. Father Lawrence Soler, the priest who oversaw the building of the
new parish, wanted a legacy, if not for God, then certainly for himself.

As I sometimes helped my mother form the rolls of *masa* dough at
the weekly *tamaladas*, I would joke that "Mickey Mantle ha hecho por el
haciendo de tamales lo que Noé hizo para la construcción de barcos"...
that Mickey Mantle—and her anger at Father Antonio's defense of my
religious idolatry—was doing for tamale-making what Noah had done
for shipbuilding. My line drew smiles from some of the women helping
with the tamales. How could they not laugh at my humor? I was the Castro's strange son who always wore a weather-beaten New York Yankee cap
that looked so old that the local *curandero*, the smelly, Geritol-pushing
Don Jose Arias, often said "it had been left behind by *el Baby Ruth*" when
he and the Yankees played an exhibition in Waco in 1929. Baby Ruth.
Good Lord. Even the Mexican Americans in Texas were devout Dixie-
crats disdainful of Yankees, soldiers, and ballplayers alike. But as I loved to

tell Mom after her new *iglesia* rose from nothing, Babe Ruth—whom the medical quack wrongly misnamed *el Baby Ruth*—was known for having built only a ballpark, Yankee Stadium; in the tamale-making mothers of South Waco, Mickey Mantle had inspired, if not built, a freaking church.

Mickey, of course, was heaven sent. We believed that with all our hearts. I knew this better than most in my hometown. I grew up in Waco, Texas, in the heart of the Bible Belt in mid-twentieth-century America, bilingual, bicultural, and religiously bipolar. I was both Roman Catholic and Southern Baptist. But I quoted too much Protestant scripture for a good Catholic, and I knew too many saints and too much Latin for an acceptable Baptist. So on Sundays, I prayed for Mickey in two separate denominations: with my Baptist pals like Dwain Moss and Ardie Meeker, the only one among us who could switch-hit worth a lick, and with fellow Catholics like Mikey Gonzalez, who used to go around bragging that his first name was "just like Mickey Mantle's, just without the *c*." You wanted to put a Louisville Slugger to his mug, which might have made for an improvement. I was surprised to learn that kids our age in the other parts of town were just as obsessed with Mickey Mantle and to discover later that it was a crazed fixation shared among baby boomers across the nation.

Just up a spell on U.S. Highway 84, in the West Texas town of Midland, lived a kid with whom many of us would cross paths years later. He also fancied himself the king of all things Mickey Mantle. Fifty years later, for a brief period in the 2007 season, Topps would even issue a Derek Jeter autographed baseball card in which this good ol' boy from Midland could be seen waving from the box seats behind the Yankee dugout where Mickey Mantle in his prime waited with a bat on his shoulder. By then, of course, the kid was president of the United States, though it could be argued that perhaps George W. Bush might have once traded that distinction just for a chance to have a Lone Star beer with The Mick. Wouldn't anyone? What began as a visual gag through digital manipulation within the Topps family was so hilarious that officials approved it to be printed. Perhaps it symbolized an entire generation's obsession not only with Mickey Mantle but also by the collection of his baseball cards, his signed memorabilia, and perhaps anything else that would keep his memory alive beyond his playing days and even after his death. He was Elvis, Marilyn, the Kennedys. Even their loyal followers couldn't match the Mantle faithful in boasting about their idol's memorabilia, especially trading cards, which became the centerpiece of the collectibles craze in America. Mickey Mantle, of course, could claim the Holy Grail. In 2018, Mantle's 1952 Topps card, graded a 9 on a scale of 10 by the Professional Sports Authenticator known in that trade as PSA, sold for $2.88 million. Imagine the price potential of such a card graded a perfect 10 condition, or even one rated 9.5, possibly exceeding the record $3.12 million paid for a T206 Honus Wagner card.

"Hell, if I'd known how fucking popular I'd be just from my picture on bubble gum cards, I would've invested in Topps back when they were starting out," Mantle would tell me years later. "But as a businessman I sucked. I'm sure I would've run Topps right into the toilet with my bowling alley."

It didn't matter. A nation of young boys and their fathers didn't give a plugged nickel for Mickey Mantle's net worth. His value surpassed the worldly. "Mickey often said he didn't understand it, this enduring connection and affection," Bob Costas would one day say of Mantle. He was a famous broadcaster by then, but we had shared similar childhoods, his on Long Island, that centered on a mutual obsession with Mickey Mantle. His obsession became as well known as Bob himself, with stories abounding of how he "might have the most famous Mickey Mantle card on the planet, even if it's not the most valuable." He carried a 1958 Topps Mantle card, No. 487 from that year's collection, in his wallet wherever he went on sports broadcasting assignments around the world. "People still ask me, 'Do you still have the Mickey Mantle card?'" said Costas. "It seemed like a sacrilege to throw it away, so I kept it in with my credit cards in my wallet." And he would often pull out his wallet to show it off: a special *Sport* magazine All-Star Selection card that showed Mantle swinging a bat against a red background highlighted by dozens of small white stars.

In Queens, a young Yankee fan who grew up idolizing DiMaggio and hating Mantle when he came along suddenly changed his mind when "I realized something in a cold sweat: Mickey was actually closer to me in age (ten years older) than he was to DiMaggio (nearly seventeen years younger). . . . Mickey was more like me, and I would have been scared shitless out there in center field. My heart went out to him." Stephen Jay Gould grew up loving Mickey Mantle and Tyrannosaurus Rex, eventually becoming a paleontologist at Harvard where I met him, a full-fledged baseball nerd convinced that The Mick was the best there ever was.

Mickey Mantle bonded a generation of boys and men in a way no religion, philosophy, or politician could. John F. Kennedy may have been a contemporary, but his charisma paled next to Mickey. What was it Costas also said about him? "We knew there was something poignant about Mickey Mantle before we knew what poignant meant." Absolutely.

And it wasn't just baby boomer boys who were obsessed with Mantle. When I started junior high school, I was surprised to learn that the smartest girl there—Lidia Montemayor, who would go through high school and college without ever earning anything less than an A in any course—could quote from memory Mantle's stat line for each of his seasons to date. It was also a bit annoying. I couldn't compete with her in math, English, or science, and now I was also second best to her in reciting all the baseball statistical intimacies there were to know about Mickey. Up in Roslyn, New York, there would be another young girl who was equally consumed with Mickey Mantle, her childhood hero. When she was grown up, Jane Leavy would interview Mickey as a sportswriter for the *Washington Post* and eventually author *The Last Boy: Mickey Mantle and the End of America's Childhood*. Years later, while I was signing copies of my own Mantle biography in Manhattan, I was equally surprised to see as many middle-aged women as men lined up, all reminiscing about Mickey as I met them. Many of them were in tears, not a singular experience when it came to Mantle fans, who would sometimes burst out crying when coming face-to-face with their childhood hero. In 1979, Mickey was paid an appearance fee by a New Jersey housewife to attend her husband's fortieth birthday party. The husband couldn't control his emotions when Mantle showed up, bawling so much that Mickey himself was moved, even if he couldn't understand why he affected grown men this way. When he returned home to Dallas, Mantle impulsively shipped the man the pinstriped uniform the Yankees had given him when they retired his famous number 7.

"One day I'm Mickey Mantle, a kid from Commerce, Oklahoma, that nobody outside my hometown knows," Mantle told me in one of numerous conversations in Dallas. "Soon I'm Mickey Mantle, a piece of merchandise like something you can buy at Neiman Marcus downtown. Doesn't make sense, does it?"

Quite simply, there was no other roadside attraction in America quite like Mickey Mantle, even one fading in talent. The young George W. Bush would rather have been Mickey than president of the United States. "Growing up, a fan of Mickey Mantle, all I ever wanted to be was a major league baseball player and another Mickey Mantle," Bush told me in a 1999 interview. "Ask any of my old friends from that time, and they'll likely tell you that's all I ever talked about." That's how much Mantle meant to him. Bush remembered the most memorable experience of his freshman year at Yale being the April day in 1965 when he left the campus and boarded a flight for Houston. When his mother Barbara picked him up at Hobby Airport, she could barely contain her own excitement. She was treating her son to the first game to be played at the Astrodome, the world's first domed stadium, billed as the "Eighth Wonder of the World" by the Astros' original owner, former Harris County judge Roy Hofheinz.

"I've got the best seats in the house for us," she told her son. Fittingly, some would say for the Bushes, a family with its roots in Connecticut, the Astros were playing the Yankees. The New York Yankees were the most storied team in baseball, and their aging superstar Mickey Mantle, of course, was one of George's favorite players.

"Great, Mom," said Bush, who was then eighteen. "I can't wait."

"They're called skyboxes."

Years later, Bush would shake his head when he recalled that day and arriving at one of the Astrodome's fifty-three luxurious skybox suites. "We got up in the skybox," he said. "It was the very top of the Astrodome. The players looked like ants. I said, 'Mom, these may be wonderful seats, but where are the players?'"

I can brag that my dad and I had better seats than the future governor and president, a high school graduation gift from my friends and bosses at the *Waco Tribune-Herald*, my hometown newspaper whose sports staff

I had joined that spring. We had box seats four rows behind the Yankees dugout along the third base foul line. The day was April 9, 1965, and a visibly ailing Mickey Mantle, inserted as the Yankees' lead-off hitter for the occasion, officially became the first batter in the new Astrodome. Batting left-handed against right-hander Turk Farrell, Mantle ripped the game's second pitch into center field for the first hit in Houston's wondrous new stadium.

Then, leading off the sixth inning, Mickey came to bat again against Farrell and was tempted to do something he had rarely done since learning to be a switch-hitter as a child. In the on-deck circle, Mantle assumed a stance he would have taken in the right-handed batter's box at home plate—of course, a no-no against a righty like Farrell, a lesson that had been hammered into him by his father Mutt Mantle, who once sent him home in tears from a youth game for disobeying him on this. But Mutt Mantle had been dead since 1952, and Mick was hurting badly. He was in agonizing pain not only from his right knee, which caused him to noticeably limp when he ran the bases, but also from an aggravated injury to his right shoulder. It was the old right shoulder injury Mantle first suffered in the 1957 World Series when Milwaukee Braves second baseman Red Schoendienst had fallen on him during a botched pick-off play. It was an injury that reduced the strength in Mickey's once-powerful throwing arm throughout the remainder of his career and affected his hitting as well, especially when he batted left-handed. So this being merely an exhibition, Mantle momentarily thought about finishing the game batting right-handed to rest his aching shoulder.

"I was kinda surprised no one made a big deal over me taking right-handed practice cuts while I waited for Turk to finish his warm-ups," Mickey later recalled. "I gotta admit the idea did cross my mind, but I wasn't gonna do that then. This was a game where the star really was the stadium, the Astrodome, with air-conditioning and an enclosed roof, and it was like a presidential inauguration or a Hollywood movie premiere. President Johnson and Lady Bird were there. The governor of Texas, John Connally, who had been almost killed with President Kennedy in Dallas just a couple of year earlier, was there and threw out the first pitch. This was maybe the biggest baseball event ever in Texas. Johnny Keane, who was from Houston, was our new manager, and when he tells me I'm going to bat leadoff, he says, 'Mick, you have the who's who of Texas here to see you.' I said, 'Don't fuck with me, Johnny, you know goddamn well they're here to see the Astrodome.'"

Mickey Mantle himself was partly in the Astrodome that night for the same reason. There was nothing like the Astrodome anywhere else in America, or the world, for that matter. The sensation to player and fan alike was much the same. Imagine putting a full-size baseball stadium, yes, even like Yankee Stadium, inside a facility that was big enough to accommodate it. Then imagine it all enclosed, with a roof, and air-conditioning that made it feel you were inside some gigantic modern business office. Players couldn't stop staring at the domed roof that looked like the top of a flying saucer. Late that afternoon during batting practice, Mickey and Roger Maris even tried to hit balls off the roof. They couldn't.

The capacity crowd that streamed into the Astrodome was equally fascinated, spellbound almost, and gawking. But in the sixth inning, Mantle managed to turn the attention of a crowd of 47,879 on to himself as he swung at a Farrell fastball that exploded off the sweet spot of his bat with a ferocious, rifle-shot-like crack that had never been heard indoors. *KAAHH*-WHACK! The sound reverberated and echoed throughout the Astrodome—*KAAHH*-WHACK! *KAAHH*-WHACK!—showing this to be the acoustics not of old baseball stadiums with their murky, outdated public-address systems but of the state-of-the-art concert-hall quality for an indoor stadium scheduled to soon host a Broadway-like extravaganza featuring Judy Garland. So imagine the sound of a thunderous home run smacked at Carnegie Hall, with a symphony of *KAAHH*-WHACK! *KAAHH*-WHACK! *KAAHH*-WHACK! The sound of the bat-on-ball collision had tantalized fans since the days when Babe Ruth popularized the home run, and they could never quite get enough. And it was different when it was a home run concert by Mickey Mantle. "I had never heard such an explosive sound of bat on ball as a ball I heard hit by Mickey," former Detroit Tiger pitcher Johnny James said when Mantle homered off him in 1958. "It was by far the most awesome sound I'd heard before or since, nor had I ever seen a ball leave a ballpark so quickly. It happened so fast I wasn't sure I actually saw what I thought I had seen."

That night Mantle's powerful home run off Farrell carried deep over the 406-feet sign in center field, creating a furor that might have been expected if the homer had been hit by a Houston Astros player. Almost instantly a giant electronic sign displaying the word TILT flashed on the Astrodome's monstrous scoreboard, and deafening applause, whooping, and hollering exploded in the crowd as Mickey rounded the bases in his familiar gait, even with the noticeable limp. There was no showboat standing at home watching the flight of the ball, no hot-dogging bat flip, no celebratory arm pump or hamming around the bases. Mickey had never shown up a pitcher off whom he'd just homered, and he wasn't starting now. As soon as he hit that ball, he ran hard out of the box with his head down and only started slowing up a little as he rounded second. Much of the Astrodome crowd was on its feet cheering. It took Mantle seventeen seconds to circle the bases, the same brisk home run trot he would make if he were playing at Yankee Stadium—and, living in Dallas since the 1950s, it was almost as if he were playing at home.

Some fans at the Astrodome may have also sensed that Mickey, although only thirty-three years of age, was now in the twilight of his extraordinary career. His injuries had kept him out of spring training games leading up to the Astrodome opener. He was also playing left field, having given up his familiar center field to the younger, healthier Tom Tresh. Nevertheless, the looming decline, for both Mantle and the Yankee dynasty, would be remarkably sudden, given that they had been in twelve of the fourteen World Series since Mickey's rookie year in 1951—and had won seven championships. In 1965, though, Mantle's home runs would drop off to nineteen from the previous year's thirty-five, and his runs batted in would dramatically fall from 111 to 46. Not to mention that his batting average that season of .255 would be the worst of his career to that point.

So steep a fall from so incredible a rise. Mickey couldn't have realized that he had seen his last hurrah in the 1964 World Series against the St. Louis Cardinals. It came in game three, on Saturday, October 10, in a packed Yankee Stadium. The game was tied 1–1 because of Mickey's run-scoring error in right field in the fifth inning. Leading off the bottom of the ninth, Mantle had turned to catcher Elston Howard, who was on deck, and said, "You might as well go in and start getting dressed. I'm going to hit his first pitch for a home run." Cardinals manager Johnny Keane, who brought in veteran knuckleball reliever Barney Schultz to pitch the ninth, had just sat down when he heard the dreaded blast of a bat on a ball. Having called his shot, Mickey smacked Schultz's first pitch, a knuckleball, that Cardinal catcher Tim McCarver said "dangled like bait to a big fish . . . [and] lingered in that area that was down, and Mickey was a lethal low-ball hitter left-handed. The pitch was so slow that it allowed him to turn on it and pull it." The ball shot off Mantle's bat and towered majestically deep well into the third deck of Yankee Stadium. Mickey's only World Series walk-off homer, it broke Babe Ruth's World Series home run record. It would be one of Mantle's finest World Series: three home runs, eight runs batted in, and a magnificent OPS (on base plus slugging percentage) of 1.258. But the Yankees lost in seven games in what would be Mickey's last World Series and the end of a dynasty. The Yankees would not be in the World Series again until 1976.

Mantle had not seen the swift demise of his career coming, nor the Yankees' unceremonious downfall, he later said. He thought he still had another three or four productive years ahead of him. His bad shoulder prevented him from playing center field effectively, but he thought he had already begun making a transition to Yankee Stadium's notoriously difficult left field. In the 1965 season, however, even his ability at the plate mysteriously abandoned him. It was also as if his troubles were a reflection of his team. Just as critical were a series of injuries that continued to beset Roger Maris, the man who had beaten Mantle in their remarkable 1961 duel to break Ruth's long-standing single season home run mark of sixty.

Could that have been just four years earlier? All the aches and pains made it feel as if that had been an eternity ago. In retrospect, the 1961 New York Yankees was one of the greatest teams in history, challenging the acclaim long accorded the Babe Ruth–Lou Gehrig Murderers Row legends of 1927. In some minds, the Mickey Mantle–Roger Maris team was even better. Roger Maris would win the M&M Boys competition to break Ruth's near-sacred single season home run record, but this was clearly Mantle's Yankees. New manager Ralph Houk made sure of that early in the season.

"Mickey, I want you to become the leader of this team," he told Mantle in one of their first meetings that spring. "It's your team."

Mantle had been surprised. He had never been the rah-rah type to give clubhouse speeches, but Houk told Mickey that he wanted him to lead through his example. Mantle was especially comfortable with that role because he felt he had already been doing this. He knew his teammates respected him and his unselfishness, especially in helping younger players in becoming "one of the guys" on the champion Yankees team. At the time, Mickey suspected that Houk had also asked Whitey Ford and Yogi Berra to become the leaders of the team, but he had not. He wanted Mickey and Mickey alone to lead the Yankees. This was his team.

"Mickey was such an unselfish teammate," said Merlyn, "that it's what helped Roger [Maris] deal with all the distractions and break Babe Ruth's record. Do you know what it took for someone who wanted to break that record, who was expected to break that record to watch his teammate do it? And Mickey was sincere. He was rooting for Roger. He loved Roger. I think that home run contest was a test for Mickey, a test of his character, a test that showed his character and who he was. And, you know what? I think that might have been more important than for him to break Babe's record."

The Mantle and Maris bond would deepen and last until Roger's death. They were together at this Yankee team's great moment, and they were there together as they hit its lowest. In 1965 Maris would play in only forty-six games. Still, Mickey didn't know if he could point to one single defining event that changed the Yankees' fortunes, although he did wonder if the Yankees' surprise firing of first-year manager Yogi Berra a day after losing the 1964 World Series hadn't killed an important chemistry and continuity within the Yankees dynasty. Yogi had been no ordinary manager of the Yankees. His influence on the team transcended that role. Yogi had been with the Yankees since the post–World War II 1946 season. He had won ten World Series championships as a Yankee—more than any other player in major league history. He was also a three-time American League Most Valuable Player and an eighteen-time all-star. Casey Stengel, Berra's manager during most of his playing career, once said, "I never play a game without my man." And the Yankee front office turned its back on him, for Johnny Keane, whom they fired early into his second season?

"We were never the same team again," Mickey said. "Say what you will, Yogi's firing changed everything."

If the Astrodome that April night offered any clue to the upcoming decline in the 1965 season, it may have been that, despite Mickey's historic homer, the Yankees lost 2–1 in extra innings. They would go on to finish the season with a record of 77–85, a stunning twenty-five games behind the Minnesota Twins. It marked the first season since 1925, Lou Gehrig's first season as a starter, that the Yankees failed to finish either above the .500 mark or in the first division. That disappointment, though, lay somewhere in the weeks and months to come. For that one night in Houston, Texas celebrated a new stadium's opening in unparalleled Lone Star fashion in which the Astrodome and Mickey Mantle would be forever linked in history.

Perhaps there was something providential at play as well. I wondered about that in the wee hours of the next morning when we got home from an almost four-hour drive from Houston. From the hallway leading to my bedroom, I could make out a small light flickering there and knew what it was even before I saw it. There, on a night table underneath the huge image of Mantle dwarfing everything else on the walls, was a burning votive candle that my mother had evidently lit earlier in the evening. Mickey Mantle had been swinging from the heels with a little extra help that night.

Without being indelicate, it's enough to say that my mom had become a believer. God knows, she might have even said a novena for Mickey after attending rosary around the same time Mantle came up to bat in the first inning against Turk Farrell. It was 7:48 p.m. Father Dols, the parish priest at Sacred Heart, would have been almost finished with his litany of Hail Marys in the rosary. He was Brazilian, important because his machine-gun rapid-fire Spanish with a Portuguese accent that made the repetitive *Santa Maria, Madre de Dios* sound like one lisping whine after another—*Thanta Mathria, Mathre de Dioth*—would eventually send my frustrated mother looking for God among my Aunt Mo's evangelicals as well as the Caribbean faith of her Cuban friend Caridad, a Santeria priestess herself. Completely understandable. All those *Thanta Mathria,*

Mathre de Diothes would drive even a hardened Red Sox heretic to the church of Mantle.

When I told all this, some time later, to another of my heroes, New Journalist and American studies guru Tom Wolfe, he said he understood fully. "It's Darwinian," he said with a straight face. "Think about it. We're at an age Nietzsche predicted in probably his most famous statement in modern philosophy—God is dead. He didn't mean it as an atheist manifesto. Yes, he was an atheist, but what he said was a warning. He was saying this in 1885. That the day lay ahead when once-God-fearing people would no longer believe in God. And that there would be a stumbling through—osteoporotically—what the world has to offer, looking for something to believe in, new kinds of shamans, faith peddlers, and idols. So if you're going to look for some new Christ to believe in, then I suppose why not Mickey Mantle? For people looking to place their faith in someone or something, it's certainly better than believing in nothing." Whew! *Osteoporoticly?* Did he mean we would be limping, like Mantle on the base paths, through the osteoporotic skeletons of old faiths in which we can no longer believe? This was too much, even from Pope Tom. On a down-to-earth level, couldn't a simpler explanation for my mom's newfound belief in Mantle just have been the mythical Annie Savoy's philosophy from the film *Bull Durham*? "I believe in the Church of Baseball. I've tried all the major religions and most of the minor ones. I've worshipped Buddha, Allah, Brahma, Vishnu, Siva, trees, mushrooms, and Isadora Duncan. I know things. For instance there are 108 beads in a Catholic rosary and there are 108 stitches in a baseball. When I learned that, I gave Jesus a chance."

Mickey Mantle's personal Annie Savoy, the actress Holly Brooke who stole his heart in his rookie season, might have agreed. "Mickey was the most honest person I ever knew," she said. "Behind the public Mickey Mantle that the world knew, there was a very private Mickey with a very pure heart and soul. His word was his honor, and I think that's probably why all his teammates loved him. He was truly an honorable man as well as a great ballplayer."

And his best, his greatness, lay behind him that night, somewhere in distant ballparks soon to be just memories. I don't know one among us who grew up idolizing Mickey who saw the end coming, not this way, sneaking up on us like the adulthood that ensnares us after puberty, and leaving us wondering where do we go, what do we do with all our Mickey Mantle cards, and how do we keep our faith from becoming another of those broken dreams in a landscape through which we limp osteoporotically? If we're smart like Bob Costas, we carry around our favorite Mantle Topps card, as our own personalized prayer card in our wallet.

Many years later, when I interviewed him for a magazine story on the Bush family and baseball, George W. said that after the Astrodome game he didn't pay much attention to the 1965 baseball season until an early September morning when he glanced at a newspaper sports page that shocked him. "I kinda had to shake my head," he said, "because my first thought was, man, that was some kind of party [that previous night]. I couldn't believe what I was reading. The Yankees were well out of the pennant race, and Mickey Mantle was batting like .250. These weren't the New York Yankees and the Mickey Mantle I'd grown up with. It took a moment to sink in."

Mantle himself looked back on the Astrodome home run with wistful pride. When I met him in 1970, it was one of the first memories I brought up.

"You were there?" he said, not really believing. "Fuck, half the people I meet in Texas say they were there. I bet you tell the astronauts you interview you were at the moon with Neil Armstrong last year too."

That's when I brought up him taking practice right-handed swings as righty Turk Farrell warmed up before starting the top of the sixth inning. That drew a sheepish grin. Clearly the idea had crossed his mind. "I just wanted to give the fans the best I had. I know every ballplayer feels that way. But I think Joe DiMaggio said it best. I think he once said he didn't want to play poorly in front of a fan who would be seeing him play for the first time, or the last. None of us do. But you know what. Baseball is a game of failure, for a hitter especially. A .300 hitter makes an out 70 percent of the time. You have to deal with that, and it's not always easy.

"I know that my fans, for God knows what reason, I know that my generation loves me. And it's not that they're fickle. But even I, a simple ballplayer, know that generations die, though it's reputations—it's legacies that endure, if they endure, to other generations. Look at Babe Ruth. His generation is dead and buried, but his legacy has lived on. Ruth isn't just remembered as having been great. Hell, there's no one alive who saw him play to *remember*. He's recognized by a generation who never saw him play as being great, maybe the greatest. So I have to ask myself, to ask you, when there's no one around to remember seeing me play, will that next generation recognize how great I was, if I was, and call me that? Or will they just say, fuck him, he was full of shit. He was someone who could have been great, but he was always hurting too much or too drunk on his ass to realize his potential? I hope they're not saying that. But I guess they'll say what they want to say. The time for me to have had a say, well, that time came and went before I knew it."

Perhaps not. Not if my mother and her Santeria priestess friend Caridad had a say. When Mantle died in 1995, I headed to Dallas for his memorial service not knowing that ninety miles south, in my hometown of Waco, Mom and Caridad were hosting perhaps the most unusual send-off ever given a ballplayer, at least an American ballplayer. Just a few hours after Mantle's official service at Lovers Lane United Methodist Church in Dallas, I arrived a block or so from my childhood home where a Santeria Itutu ceremony was just about to get underway. I imagined that Mickey's private burial had likely just concluded at Sparkman-Hillcrest Memorial Park. In Waco on South Twenty-Sixth Street, a stone's throw from the old Robinson highway, a purely symbolic ceremony was honoring Mantle and his passage to the afterlife. With the help of my mother, Caridad had decorated her modest home as a temporary makeshift shrine to Mickey, using many of my own belongings from my old bedroom, which had not changed since I left home. Mom had brought over the life-size poster of Mickey, my large glass-encased collection of all of Mickey's Topps and Bowman cards, a couple of autographed bats, several signed baseballs, my Mickey Mantle–signed Auto JSA Rawlings Pro Model MM5 baseball glove from my youth, and half a dozen overfilled albums of newspaper clippings collected over the years. I would have thrown a fit had we been alone. This collection had been personally valuable in my youth. In 1995, and more so in the future, its value would have been incomprehensible all those years long ago. Caridad understood my apprehension.

"Nothing will happen to your things," she assured me in Spanish. "They are important to us here tonight only because they represent the Orishas left behind now that his body has left the earth, and he is no longer here to look after them."

Orishas, I learned, were one's personal qualities and the essence of one's soul. My collection was the physical manifestations of the Orishas that made up Mickey Mantle. Soon the room was aglow with burning candles and incense, teamed with the scent from herbal potions as the dozen or so santeros and santeras taking part in the Itutu began a series of spiritual readings. No animals were sacrificed, nothing suggesting the stereotypical voodoo religion so often associated with Santeria took place.

Caridad called the ceremony "a celebration of Mickey's rite of passage to a higher world and a pantheon of greatness."

"After this, you may see him in your dreams," she said, "and even in your waking moments—he is there, he lives, he isn't immortal but the memory of him is, and the world will come to know him as those who believed in him, who cheered him, who loved him . . . the world will see him as it could not when he was with us. God throws out a halo of grace for everyone in the world. And on some, that halo sparkles. It sparkles and lights up his kingdom."

12

The Prince of America

I may not have been the best goddamn ballplayer of all time, but if I wasn't, I'd like to see who the fuck was.

—MICKEY MANTLE

IF THE 1965 SEASON THAT BEGAN WITH MICKEY MANTLE MAKING MORE history with his Astrodome dinger didn't seem as if it was his fifteenth year with the Yankees, it may have been because so many of us baby boomers who looked up to him were still in our teens. Mantle certainly didn't look much older than he had in 1961 when he and fellow Yankee Roger Maris chased Babe Ruth's home run record. He was thirty-three at the start of the 1965 season, and he still had that overgrown blonde crew cut that made him look even younger. And if he limped around the bases, well, few of us had ever seen him run any other way. We had been too young when he was fully healthy in his rookie year. We had little or no memory of what he had been like back then except for the occasional flashes such as when he legged out a drag bunt or chased down Gil Hodges's sixth inning deep blast to left center field to save Don Larsen's perfect game in the 1956 World Series.

But we were not alone. By 1965, Mickey Mantle was the prince of America. Who could have imagined a time without him in it? For almost a decade and a half, he had been the royalty of the national pastime, not only for his accomplishments on the playing field but also in large part because of the national media saturation of his exploits. Certainly Ruth, Gehrig, and DiMaggio had been equally recognized in their day, especially playing in New York, the media capital of the world. What was different for Mantle, though, was he became the heartthrob of the national pastime in the age of television. In 1946, as the baby boomer generation was beginning, there had been only 17,000 television sets in the country. By 1950, Americans had 4.4 million television sets. Then TV exploded in the country with fifteen million sets sold in 1951 alone. By 1953, two-thirds of American homes had at least one TV. If American homes now seemed like something from the futuristic George Orwell novel *1984*, replete with telescreens used for constant surveillance, well, this by now had become the age of conspiracy theories. More than fifty million television sets dotted the country in 1960. If we weren't being "watched" by Big Brother, certainly Americans were being influenced by their TVs in what they bought, wore, did, and talked about. Television was also a boon to baseball, much as radio had been in the 1920s.

In fact, you could call baseball the very first reality series of American television. Baseball was on every Saturday during the season and then Sundays and doubleheaders too. The casts were the rosters of the sixteen major league teams, though most often it was the Yankees who became what seemed like regulars on CBS's nationally televised Game of the Week. That meant that the biggest individual star of this reality series was Mickey Mantle, who was in his glory years. It so happened that television's popularity coincided with Mantle's best seven-year period, from 1953 to 1961, when he was indisputably the game's most feared hitter and arguably its best player. It also helped that Mickey played in seven of his twelve World Series during that period. Every aspect of Mantle, the ballplayer, was examined in the telecasts, down to dissecting the details of switch-hitting. It became routine for close-up camera shots even of the unique way Mickey gripped his bat from each side of the plate, with the little finger of the bottom hand curled up underneath the knob.

"I wonder why he don't just use a longer bat," broadcast announcer Dizzy Dean, a Hall of Fame Cardinals pitcher, once observed.

"Dizzy," shot back his sidekick Buddy Blattner, "that's why you were a pitcher and not a hitter."

"Yo're right, pahd'ner," answered Dean. "Yo're right!"

Lucy, the Lone Ranger, and the Beaver. Those had been America's television pop culture heroes of the 1950s. By the end of the 1950s,

Mickey Mantle was arguably more popular thanks to his exposure via millions of television sets. Viewers celebrated in their living rooms for each home run they saw Mantle slug, or they grimaced and felt for him if he struck out, swinging with that famous uncoiling that seemed to spring from his legs and then explode in an energy of sheer power as if he had just swung from his soul. Only Mickey Mantle swung like that.

The Columbia Broadcasting System wanted more than Game of the Week rights. The network had its eye on the Yankees and on Mickey Mantle. Television and baseball, after all, were already in business together, but CBS didn't want to share the best team and best player in sports. At the time, baseball was still America's national pastime, and the World Series the highest-priced sports event carried by television. The National Broadcasting Company, CBS's primary competitor, had telecast the World Series for several years, but that contract was open for bids between the networks. So after the 1964 World Series, when baseball and the Yankees were still riding high, CBS bought itself a ball club. Dan Topping and Del Webb, who had owned the Yankees for twenty years with brilliant success, sold 80 percent of their team to CBS for the then unheard of price of $11.2 million.

"When they bought the Yankees, the network suits thought they had hit the mother lode and gotten the key to Fort Knox—they owned the greatest team in sports and Mickey Mantle, the greatest baseball star of all time, on its payroll, and they could start printing money," Blackie Sherrod, the legendary sports columnist of the *Dallas Times Herald* and *Morning News*, told me in an interview years later. "They didn't realize—who would?—that they had just bought themselves a ticket on the *Titanic*, a front row seat to Black Tuesday. Hell, it was the Sixties. America was hit with cultural, political, and technological change. So why should baseball have been exempt? On January 15, 1967, a little over two years after buying the Yankees, CBS would realize just what a horrible deal it had made. It wasn't just that the great Yankee dynasty was over. It was that America had dumped baseball as its national pastime. The first Super Bowl, on January 15, 1967, was the changing of the guard. I remember talking to one CBS executive not long after that game, and he was shaking his head. 'We shoulda bought the Dallas Cowboys,' he kept saying. 'We shoulda bought the Dallas Cowboys.'"

Baseball would never again hold the same place in America's heart. It may have not had anything to do with who owned the Yankees or whether Mantle had played—and played well—another four or five years. The Yankees didn't have any ballplayers coming along with the skills of a Mantle, or close to them, and that is important to consider. When Babe Ruth reached his end in 1934, the Yankees had Lou Gehrig still around and then added Joe DiMaggio in 1936. The end of DiMaggio's reign saw Yogi Berra in the Yankee fold and Mickey Mantle arriving in 1951. In the mid-1960s, baseball also added the amateur draft system, which meant that the teams with deep pockets like the Yankees could no longer outbid other teams for the best young players—though remember that they got Mantle at the rock bottom price of $1,500.

By the time CBS owned the Yankees and Mickey, $1,500 might not even have been enough money to buy a ticket to the Super Bowl. A little more than three months before Mantle and the Yankees opened the Astrodome, a twenty-two-year-old college quarterback—Joe Namath—had received a mind-boggling $400,000 contract to play for the New York Jets. Four hundred grand. They'd given this untested rookie quarterback Rockefeller money and half of Manhattan, it seemed to Mickey and a lot of other pro athletes. "I remember reading that and quickly sobering up," Mantle said in one of our interviews. "And I remember thinking, 'What cheap-ass sport have I been playing all these years?' Goddammit! I couldn't even buy a car with the bonus I got. And no one in baseball got that kind of money. Four hundred thousand dollars! Fuck! I don't know if I'd made that much in the fourteen years I'd been with the Yankees. On top of that Dan Topping and Del Webb had just sold us for eleven million. Mind you, I wasn't against Joe [Namath] or any other athlete getting the best deal and bonus they can. What pissed me off was that this proved that those motherfuckers [owners] had the money to pay us all what we were worth—and we made that money for them!—but they weren't going to pay it out unless they absolutely had to."

Mantle was pissed. Other Yankees were pissed. A whole industry of athletes was pissed. But the owners continued to plead that they were on the verge of going broke. With the Yankees' ownership change, a cold corporate shield seemed to instantly envelop the team. In one of CBS's first moves, the new owners fired broadcaster Mel Allen, the Voice of the Yankees since 1939, supposedly because of cost-cutting demanded by longtime broadcast sponsor Ballantine Beer. Perhaps it's only a coincidence that while Topping and Webb had owned the Yankees, the team missed getting to the World Series only five times and won ten championships. The CBS-owned teams never went to the World Series, and the network finally sold the Yankees—at a $3 million loss—to George Steinbrenner in 1973.

Who could have imagined that we had seen the best of Mickey or that he would be history in three more years? He began the year with 454 career home runs, and who hadn't thought that he would soon be nearing the magic 500? But by June, Mantle himself thought his career was over. His nagging injuries had worsened, and he was batting an un–Mickey Mantle .240. By then, the Yankees also had reluctantly concluded that this might be Mantle's final season. Forget ever coming close to Babe Ruth's career 714 home runs, 659 as a Yankee. It looked as if Mickey might not even catch up to Lou Gehrig's career mark of 496 homers. Fittingly, the Yankees decided to give Mickey a special day at the stadium, an honor that had been bestowed on only four other players—Babe Ruth, Lou Gehrig, Joe DiMaggio, and Yogi Berra.

"Mantle's Misery," *Life* magazine called the season in its July 30, 1965, issue. What underscored the frustration of Mantle and the Yankees hitting rock bottom was photojournalist John Dominis's memorable photograph of Mickey flinging his batting helmet away in disgust, apparently shot during the first-ever "Bat Day" at Yankee Stadium, packed with 72,244 fans for a June 20 doubleheader. "It isn't any fun when things are like this," Mickey is quoted in the story. "I'm only 33, but I feel like 40."

Writer John R. McDermott's portrait of Mantle is sympathetic but telling:

"All season long it has been this way, or worse. There was a night, for instance, when he stood in left field at Yankee Stadium, shackled to his two luckless legs, tensing his body for the next play. The pain had already started in his thighs and was throbbing through his elaborately bandaged knees. There was no longer enough cartilage in his knees to absorb the shock of running—and the pain would be almost unbearable if he suddenly had to change direction. He glanced behind him at the four-foot fence that borders left field and circles out toward center. A ball caroming off that concrete arc could make a fool of him. Left field, a new position for him, was full of hard and soft spots, subtle depressions and holes that could catch a spike and wrench his leg. There was a crackling and a ball arching up toward him. He forced himself to run in and to his right. But a younger player rushed out from the infield, screamed and waved him off and pocketed the ball in his glove for the third out. Mantle jerked himself to a wincing stop. Then he jogged toward the dugout, taking small steps, running like a toy whose spring has wound down, his arms and elbows flopping as if to help take the weight off those legs."

Still, to fall so low after such a great height. Did the Yankees tank the 1965 season? No, it's unlikely, though the rhetorical question begs asking. Those Yankees had seven of the same everyday players as the 1964 Yankees, except for Roger Maris, whose injury limited him to thirty games. These Yankees had four-fifths of the previous season's starting rotation and, in essence, the same team back that had won ninety-nine games in 1964 then lost the World Series to the Cardinals in seven games. But these Yankees were also plagued by age and being overconfidently full of themselves. Perhaps it took someone coming in from the outside to see the Yankees for how they really were. In 1965, that role belonged to journeyman catcher Howard Rodney Edwards, known as Doc Edwards, who was traded by the Kansas City Athletics to the Yankees to back up the aging Elston Howard. Edwards was in for a shock when he soon realized this was no longer the World Series team of recent memory.

"They were not the Mickey Mantle and the Whitey Ford and the Roger Maris that we knew," Edwards recalled. "They had reached a point in their lives where they were all hurt. You just don't take that many thoroughbreds and replace them with ponies—and, in my case, a draft horse—and win races. You just don't do it."

Enough also can't be said of how these were different times. America was breathing heavily on the neck of the seventies, the alchemically dreamy age that American author Tom Wolfe, the stylish sage of the New

Journalism literary movement, had christened the "Me Decade." The Yankees' face on this age of varnished dandyism and self-promotion, of course, was Joe Pepitone. He was a respected three-time all-star at first base who may be remembered as much for being the first major league ballplayer to bring a hair dryer into the locker room as for carrying a bag of hair products to control his rapidly balding head and, not one, but two toupees. He had squandered his $25,000 bonus, enjoyed acting as the team clown, and had a reputation for partying as if *he* were Mickey Mantle. In his 1975 autobiography, *Joe, You Coulda Made Us Proud*, Pepitone famously claimed to having smoked marijuana and gotten stoned during the season in the sixties with the proverbial last boy himself, Mickey Mantle.

"He didn't like that too much," Pepitone said in a *Rolling Stone* interview. "In front of people, he'd tell them, 'That was bullshit, that would never happen!' But it was true! He came to my room, him and Whitey [Ford], and they could smell the shit in the room. They said, 'We heard you do that shit. What's it like?' 'Well, try it!' 'Oh, no no no!' 'C'mon, take a hit!' They each took a hit. Next thing I know, they're talking to me about all kinds of shit, and they're laughing at anything I said. I could have had them jumping up and down on the bed, if I'd wanted to!"

In 1965, though, a clubhouse exchange between Mantle and the then twenty-four-year-old Pepitone cut to the heart of one of the internal problems that may have led to the demise of the Yankee dynasty that season. In that incident Pepitone walked into the clubhouse bragging about the balls he had slugged in batting practice when Mickey turned to him.

"You think that if everyone on this club is batting .195 and you're batting .200 that's all right, huh?" Mantle asked.

"Sure," said Pepitone, "I got to think about myself—it's the only way I'm going to make my money."

"Well, you keep batting .200," said Mantle, "and you'll make a lot of money Jody."

Pepitone immediately shut up.

By this time, the Yankees were shell-shocked in a season gone wrong. Almost every major publication had picked the Yankees to win a sixth straight pennant. It shows what they knew—or, more accurately, what they didn't know. When heroes fade, it isn't with the drama of Achilles being killed by an arrow destined by the gods to the only mortal weakness in an otherwise immortal. Mortals, be they athletes or teams, just whimper quietly and go away. The Yankees in their history had witnessed this and relished it. Gehrig slid from superstar to spastic. Ruth was put out to pasture with a bankrupt team in Boston. DiMaggio, barely able to hobble, bore the stings of Casey Stengel's insults, a clown's folly. And Yogi Berra was ingloriously fired. Mickey Mantle? Perhaps the Yankees didn't know what to do with him. This might explain why in the coming years he would become the most honored player in Yankee Stadium history.

"I was the most honored player at the stadium," Mantle would later tell me, "because our teams in the mid- and late sixties were goddamn awful, and so was attendance. So they'd say, 'Hey Mick, we honor you with a Mickey Mantle Day?' Sure. What they weren't saying, which was true, was, 'Hey, Mick, attendance is down. We need a sellout. How 'bout we honor you with a Mickey Mantle Day?'"

Mickey was right, of course. The Yankees honored him with four Mickey Mantle Days. Three of them came during the Yankees worst seasons when attendance had tumbled to near record lows. The fourth Mickey Mantle Day was held in 1997, two years after his death. The first was held near the end of that disappointing 1965 season, commemorating Mantle's two thousandth game on September 18 against the Detroit Tigers. Just as Mickey knew would happen, the Yankees sold out the stadium that day, selling more hot dogs, popcorn, and beer, especially beer, than at any time that season. The Yankees made a killing out of their aging star, salvaging what they could out of a horrendously disappointing season. Mantle's cut of the take was more gifts than he knew what to do with: a new car; two quarter horses; vacation trips to Rome, Nassau, and Puerto Rico; a mink coat for Merlyn; a six-foot, hundred-pound Hebrew National salami; and a Winchester rifle. Yankee Stadium was dressed up in the bunting normally used for Opening Days and World Series. Fans brought large banners reading "Don't Quit, Mick" and "We Love the Mick." It was a celebration that even the archbishop of New York, Francis Cardinal Spellman, had helped promote, "an almost holy day for the believers who had crammed the grandstands early to witness the canonization of a new stadium saint," author Gay Talese wrote in his *Esquire* profile of Joe DiMaggio.

It would be DiMaggio who would give the celebration the behind-the-scenes drama that would overshadow the event in the memories of many. And it had nothing to do with his supposed feud with Mickey. Knowing the importance of the event in Yankee lore, Joe flew to New York to personally introduce Mantle on his special day. The two men had never been friends, but they were friendly with one another and not the bitter enemies that the news media and others sought to portray. They were around each other at the annual Yankee Old-Timers' Day games as well as almost every spring because DiMaggio attended the Yankees' training camps as a special instructor. They were also a photographer's dream, and they were routinely photographed together. In 1961, famed photographer Ozzie Sweet worked with the two Yankee legends in a photo session that he said dispelled any feud between them. Sweet recalled that Mantle appeared "relaxed and confident" around DiMaggio who seemed "antsy and uncomfortable." So much so that Sweet said he carefully watched his step. "With anyone else, I might say, 'Adjust your cap,'" said Sweet. "But with Joe, I didn't dare. I just wanted to quickly get some images of the two of them together." In one photograph from that session, Joe looks as if he is awkwardly straining his neck as he tried to move his head closer to Mantle's. "I didn't know what the heck he was doing there," said Sweet. "But with Joe, I didn't want to fool around for long. I didn't want to say, 'Mr. DiMaggio, could you please change the angle of your neck so you don't look like a turtle?' I think he might have walked away!"

DiMaggio was famous for brooding over even perceived insignificant slights. For instance, DiMaggio always insisted on being the last player to be introduced at Old-Timers Games, basking in the loudest applause produced when the fans' energy and enthusiasm reached a fever's pitch. But there was one time when the public address announcer unintentionally introduced the great Yankee Clipper before Mantle instead of last. That meant it was Mantle who received the biggest and loudest ovation. "I heard Joe was pissed off about it," Mickey later remarked with obvious satisfaction. Of course, there were times when Mantle himself seethed at playing second fiddle to Joe, such as over the 1960s classic song "Mrs. Robinson." Amid the social and political upheaval of the 1960s, songwriter Paul Simon wrote the song's most memorable lyric, "Where have you gone, Joe DiMaggio? Our nation turns its lonely eyes to you." Simon later told author David Halberstam that a disappointed Mickey Mantle once asked why he'd used DiMaggio in the song and not him. Simon chose not to get into the complex idea of the simpler times of DiMaggio, so he said to Mantle, "It was syllables, Mickey. The syllables were all wrong."

At that first Mickey Mantle Day, with the Yankee franchise in decline and Mickey already talking about retirement, DiMaggio's presence seemed a reminder of Yankee pride even in bad times. He was, after all, the image of quintessential New York Yankee grace, tall and regal as if a national aristocrat in exquisitely tailored pinstriped suit. With all eyes on him, DiMaggio waved to the fans as he walked with his customary grace from the dugout on to the field after he was introduced. It was then that he noticed Mickey's mother Lovell standing off alone to one side. DiMaggio was first a gentleman, so he went to Mantle's mom and, cupping her elbow in his hand, escorted her to where all the players and dignitaries were lined up along the infield grass. There, at home plate, DiMaggio glanced at Mantle, who was in the Yankee dugout with Merlyn and their boys. Then, Joe's thin smile froze and for a split second changed into a dark scowl.

Senator Robert F. Kennedy was walking back and forth in the dugout, anticipating his own introduction. DiMaggio bitterly hated both Bobby Kennedy and his brother, the late president, for their romantic involvement with Marilyn Monroe. He blamed them, among others, for her personal decline and death. The Joe DiMaggio–Marilyn Monroe romance, of course, is one of America's most famous love stories. His love and devotion to her lived long past their nine-month marriage of 1954. He also believed a reconciliation might be possible and was devastated when Marilyn was found dead of an overdose in 1962. Since then, DiMaggio had avoided having anything to do with the Kennedys, but now that seemed unavoidable. In November 1964, Bobby Kennedy had been elected to the U.S. Senate from New York and now was perhaps even more important than DiMaggio to the honor being bestowed on Mickey Mantle. What was Joe intending to do? For the moment, he turned his attention to Mickey and his special day. "I'm proud," he announced to the fans at Yankee Stadium, "to introduce the man who succeeded me in center field here in 1951. He lived up to all expectations and there is no doubt in my mind that he will one day be in the Hall of Fame."

Mickey and his family walked on to the field amid a wild, thunderous standing ovation that was sustained for several minutes. Mantle waved and smiled at the adoring crowd, and then posed with his wife and sons for the photographers kneeling in front of them. His speech was typically short. "I think just to have the greatest baseball player I ever saw introduce me is tribute enough for me in one day," he said. "To have any kind of success in life I think you have someone behind you to push you ahead and to share it with you.... And I certainly have that," he said, acknowledging his wife Merlyn, his four boys, and his mother. It was especially important to Mickey to know that donations made by the fans and the Yankees would be going to the Hodgkin's Disease Fund that had been founded in memory of Mantle's father Mutt. "I wish he could have been here today," Mickey said. "I know he would be just as proud and happy at what you all have done here as we are.

"There's been a lot written in the last few years about the pain that I've played with. But I want you to know that when one of you fans, whether it's in New York or anywhere in the country, say 'Hi Mick! How you feeling?' or 'How's your legs?' it certainly makes it all worth it. All the people in New York, since I've been here, have been tremendous with me. Mr. Topping, all of my teammates, the press and the radio and the TV, have just been wonderful. I just wish I had 15 more years with you."

Mickey's eyes welled with tears as he turned and shook hands with the dignitaries and officials standing nearby. The DiMaggio-Kennedy drama, what there was of it, was about to unfold.

"Among them now," wrote Talese, "was Senator Kennedy, who had been spotted in the dugout five minutes before by [Yankee broadcaster] Red Barber, and had been called out and introduced. Kennedy posed with Mantle for a photographer, then shook hands with the Mantle children, and with Toots Shor and [New York political leader] James Farley and others.

"DiMaggio saw him coming down the line and at the last second he backed away, casually, hardly anybody noticing it, and Kennedy seemed not to notice it either, and just swept past, shaking more hands."

"Mickey Mantle Day" in September 1965.... As the scheduled game got underway that day, the pitcher for the Detroit Tigers was a right-hander named Joe Sparma.

When Mickey came up to bat in the bottom of the first inning that day, he received another thunderous ovation from the crowd. Then Sparma did an unbelievably classy thing. Stepping off the mound, he walked to home plate and extended his hand to offer Mantle his personal congratulations.

"You know, I've never had a chance to meet you in person," said Sparma, "and I've always admired you."

Mickey was so moved that it took him a moment to settle into the left-handed batters box. The crowd had applauded again, and Mantle once more tipped his batting helmet to acknowledge his fans. But had the mercurially unpredictable Sparma, who had quarterbacked Ohio State to a Big Ten championship in 1961 only to quit the team two years later over differences with Coach Woody Hayes, just played Mickey like those street hustlers in his rookie year? He returned to the mound and wasted little time in striking out Mantle to end the inning and put an early damper on Mantle's day.

A smirk crossed Mickey's face, and he looked at Tigers catcher Bill Freehan who later recounted the meeting in his memoir *Behind the Mask*.

"They have a day for me and your manager's got to put some hard-throwing kid out there," Mantle said. "Couldn't he have put in some soft-tossing left-hander for me to hit off of, so I could look like a hero in front of all those people?"

13

Now Teeing Off . . . Mickey Mantle

He who has the fastest golf cart never has a bad lie.
—Mickey Mantle

Mickey Mantle's rise to fame was so improbable that he saw it as divinely ordained: the friend who suggested that maybe he could become a great ballplayer but nothing more; the doctor who intervened and saved his leg from amputation with a miracle drug; and the actress he met his rookie season and regretted not having married and who told him he reminded her of King Arthur. Recalling the leaps of faith that turned him from another clichéd young ballplayer into a prince of the city in New York with the Yankees, Mickey Mantle talked about what he now needed to prove.

When I met him, Mantle wanted to show me how to hit a driver. You can tell a lot about men by the way they approach golf—not just how they teach you to hit any golf shot but also how they approach a driver, that most macho of golf clubs. I had played a round of golf with Mickey the day before, and he didn't think it was very manly of me that I had used a three-wood on all but one shot on holes that weren't par threes. On that hole, I had hooked a drive into a fairway bunker in an adjoining fairway and taken a seven on the hole. I had played six over par over the rest of course for a respectable 79, extremely respectable considering I had been playing with my childhood baseball idol. It might as well have been an 89 or a 99 as far as Mantle was concerned. And he didn't think it was much because I'd been afraid to use my driver.

For someone who had been the home run hitter of his day, it must have been like playing with a singles hitter. Years later, I would read a quote attributed to Mickey, in which he said, "If I had played my career hitting singles like Pete [Rose], I'd wear a dress." That's how he felt about those things, and so I imagine he must have seen my use of a three-wood instead of a driver as a golfer in a pinafore. Mickey would have none of this. He was only two years into his retirement from baseball, and he would be back with the Yankees that summer coaching first base for a while. As he showed then, he looked as if he could still be playing—and perhaps would have still been playing had the designated hitter rule been in place in 1970. The designated hitter rule is the common name for major league baseball rule 5.11, adopted by the American League in 1973, that allows teams to have one player, known as the designated hitter, to bat in place of the pitcher. No telling how long Mickey might have extended his career if all he'd had to do was hit four times each game without the wear and tear on his knees of chasing fly balls in the outfield. He had retired two years earlier, having hit 536 home runs. Perhaps he could have come close to 600 home runs playing as the designated hitter (DH) and conserving strength in those legs. Who's to say he couldn't have inched that lifetime .298 batting average over the .300 line, which he said was one of the things he regretted—not having finished as a .300 hitter. Ah, but there was no DH in 1968, and the pain in the legs had been almost unbearable any longer, not to mention that his limited mobility made him too much of a liability no matter where the Yankees might try to play him.

"Playing the outfield in major league baseball is a young man's profession," he had said to me the afternoon we met. "As I look back, I gotta admire Joe [DiMaggio] and how he was able to persevere out there his last couple of seasons. And playing first base. . . . It wasn't a switch I couldn't make, had my legs been there."

His voice trailed off, as if his mind had stopped working in midthought. We could think of it all we wanted. We would anyhow, wouldn't we? With Mickey and what might have been, it always seemed to come back to the legs and the injuries. Not just the famous one, when he blew out his right knee trying to avoid crashing into DiMaggio in the second game of the 1951 World Series. But all the injuries that cumulatively took a toll during a career in which the legs came to symbolize the Achilles' heel of a baseball immortal. All Mickey Mantle accomplished, and he did it playing on one leg. That would be like a mantra coming out of the mouths of former teammates, writers, commentators—anyone, it seemed, talking about Mantle and what might have been. But Mickey, you sensed, wanted no part of that lamentation. Feeling oppressed, sad-assed, and sorry for himself was not a sport he wanted any part of. And yet, who among those who followed him could help thinking of him as what he might have been and that awful curse of expectations that Casey Stengel had placed on his head—of being the next Ruth and DiMaggio or even greater.

It was a Thursday. Mantle seemed relaxed and laid back, probably because he had just played eighteen holes of golf. Actually he was drunk, but then he was always drunk. Blackie Sherrod, the sports editor at my newspaper, had warned me that spending any time with Mickey was an exercise in futility. I would be disappointed, he said. Everyone who thought they would tap into something more positive in Mickey was always disappointed. Mantle's drinking was as legendary as his home run hitting had once been. He had famously slugged home runs while sloshed. So hitting a golf ball sitting perfectly still on a tee? Mantle could have put it out of the stadium, and he drove several balls far past the three-hundred-yard sign on the driving range. We were at a driving range on Preston Road well beyond Mickey's home course, the Preston Trail Golf Club of which he had been a founding member when it was built in 1965. Mickey hadn't wanted to hit on their range that day, and I could understand. Even there, among Dallas Cowboys–loving wealthy golfers, he couldn't escape their awestruck gazes and attention from the clubhouse to the putting practice green and the range. He told me he got so tired of the stares that he made a habit from time to time of stripping naked in the locker room after a round of golf and then heading straight to the clubhouse bar in his birthday suit to order a drink. Even at snooty Preston Trail, or maybe especially at men-only Preston Trail, which was home to the Byron Nelson Golf Tournament each year, this was just too much. The club soon instituted what was unofficially known as the Mickey Mantle Rule, dictating that members had to be fully dressed before entering the clubhouse bar.

"Fuck 'em if they can't take a joke," Mickey said. "We ain't got no women members who would be insulted anyway."

So there we were halfway to Oklahoma it seemed, in an old driving range, amid mesquite where perhaps only armadillos roamed, with Mickey giving my graduation gift Ben Hogan clubs a power test they were never meant to have. The ear-piercing sound of Mickey striking a golf ball was unlike anything I would ever hear on a golf course. KAH-WHAAACK! It was reminiscent of the sounds at batting practice in cavernous major league ballparks where hard-hit balls resonate and echo like a distant rifle shot. Good lord, how the man could hit—and loved to. Each time Mantle teed off I glanced at the driver. How the driver head withstood the long hissing whish and explosion—KAH-WHAACK!—and not broken in half or even cracked was almost as stunning as the drive itself. A thought crossed my mind. What would I do if the driver cracked? Did I return it to the Ridgewood Country Club pro shop in Waco and demand a replacement? Or did I keep it and frame it as a souvenir over the fireplace mantel—the Ben Hogan driver that Mickey Mantle broke?

"So you said you interviewed Orville Moody?" Mickey asked.

"Yeah, my senior year I was working in Temple," I said.

"Imagine being in the army, qualifying for the U.S. Open, and then winning that motherfucker," Mickey said with a chuckle of admiration. "That's something you would expect Mickey Mantle to do, ain't it?"

I had learned in just a few days that Mantle sometimes could drift into speaking about himself in the third person with surprising ease, as if he were talking about Mickey Mouse. I would understand later that it was his way of dealing with that incredible fame that possibly could be a burden with the crushing weight most of us would never understand. *Now batting . . . number seven . . . Mickey Mantle.* Bob Sheppard, the longtime Yankee Stadium public address announcer, once said that Mickey Mantle had been his favorite name to announce—how could it not be? *The center fielder . . . Mickey Mantle* is how Sheppard would announce him during each succeeding at-bat. "I knew he was talking about me," Mantle told me when I brought it up, "but I couldn't put myself there, you know?" How was it he later put it in another interview? "When I was playing, I used to feel like everything was happening to some other guy named Mickey Mantle, like I was just me and this guy called Mickey Mantle was another person."

Orville Moody was the toast of the golf world in 1970. Like Mickey, he was an Oklahoma guy two years younger than Mantle who had astounded America in 1969 by coming out of nowhere to win the U.S. Open championship. A career soldier, he had given up the military to chase his golf dream. Living near Fort Hood, Texas, where he was last stationed before his retirement, Moody had done the near impossible. He had gone through the demanding task of qualifying at local and sectional tournaments just to get into the U.S. Open, held that year at the Cypress Creek Course of the Champions Golf Club in Houston. Then he had played magnificently to overcome incredible odds in beating the best golfers in the world to win the Open by one stroke. It would be the only title he would ever win in a PGA tour career in which his glory was as brief as Mantle's was long: twenty all-star teams, eighteen seasons with the Yankees, seven World Series championships, baseball's Triple Crown winner in 1956, and three Most Valuable Player awards. But the way Mickey talked about Moody winning the U.S. Open every time the topic had come up, well, it made me wonder if that wasn't something that he would have traded everything to have had. He had once confided to his friend and personal teaching pro Marshall Smith, "I wish I had become a pro golfer instead of a pro baseball player. [Why?] I'd still be cashing paychecks, and my knees wouldn't hurt so goddamn bad." Yogi Berra, Mantle's old teammate and frequent golf buddy, would recall years later, "Baseball was Mickey's first love, and then he fell in love with golf. . . . He never felt pressure [playing golf] like the way he did as a Yankee." So how serious had he been? Would he really have traded places with U.S. Open champ Orville Moody?

"Nah, nothing like that," he said. "But it makes you wonder. Fuck, I don't have the putting game for something like that."

As it turned out, neither did Moody. Plagued by poor putting, he would not win another tournament until turning fifty when he captured eleven Senior PGA Tour titles.

"Golf can be crueler than baseball," Mickey said. "Out there all alone."

The apparent attempt at self-pity was getting to be a bit much.

"Yeah, no third base coach," I said, hoping he could take the jibe. "No Casey. No Whitey. No Yogi. No Billy."

"Well, fuck you too," he said in feigned anger. "Did you ever see me play? Besides from a fucking color TV?"

"Yeah, when you christened the Astrodome," I said. "Sixth inning. Center field, past the 406-foot sign. Remember the pitcher?"

He thought for a moment but was puzzled.

"Turk Farrell," I said.

Mickey's brow suggested he was still puzzled.

"In the on deck circle, you were taking practice cuts as if you were about to hit right-handed," I said.

"Aw fuck, I think I did."

Mantle let out a roar. He was wearing a canary yellow polo shirt and navy slacks, and he had a couple of days of stubble on his face. He wore white golf shoes, the kind Jack Nicklaus made famous. He looked like a bigger guy than he actually was. Was he six feet tall, as later biographical pages would say? Just under that, most likely. But he had the shoulders of a linebacker, a massive nineteen-and-a-half-inch neck, and body-builder chiseled arms like Popeye. No one would suspect that Mickey couldn't play another season, but then we didn't have to do any of the running.

"I can still hit, and I could always catch a ball, but now you'd have to hit it right at me," he told me. "But the good Lord only gives you one pair of legs. There was a time, though, when I could run all day."

There was still the possibility of coaching—serious coaching, not the ceremonial crowd draw the Yankees would soon give him. Or managing. He had been known as a great teammate, but could he work himself into becoming a player's manager? Could he get enough self-control of his drinking so that the Yankees might gamble on grooming him by managing in the minors or coaching under someone like Billy Martin? Could their friendship handle the ups and downs of a long major league season trying to manage and coach a team? Billy knew the intricacies and psychology of the game better than most, and could outmanage the likes of Casey Stengel. But he was complicated and conflicted. Would Mickey spend his time as Billy's keeper, dragging him off umpires and opponents, flailing and thrashing like a madman, as he was sometimes prone to do? Who could forget that during Martin's playing days in 1960 he was at the center of a mauling of Chicago Cubs pitcher Jim Brewer, who required two surgeries to repair a fractured orbital bone near his eye?

Mantle's decision not to seriously consider himself an ideal coaching or managing candidate had been made on the advice Billy gave him when they both played with the Yankees.

"We didn't talk too much baseball away from the field," Mantle recalled. "The only time we did was if I messed up. Then the first thing he'd do before we got to having too much to drink was to say, 'You know, Mick, I got to tell you something. On that ball you caught in right center, the one you threw over my head? From now on you better be sure you hit the cutoff man.' Hell, he'd tell me stuff like that any time. It was like he was my big brother. . . . See, I was never known for being very smart as a baseball player. Like people ask me if I'd ever want to manage? Well, there's no way I could manage. I didn't know when to bunt or steal or hit-and-run or squeeze or take a pitcher out. I was just . . . I could run and throw and hit. That was it. But I didn't know the game. He did. He taught me a lot about baseball, yeah. He'd even tell me when to steal sometimes, like if Casey didn't give the signal to steal second. I hardly ever got thrown out. . . . If it was like the eighth or ninth inning and we were one run behind or tied or something, I'd look in to the bench and Billy'd give me the go-ahead. He'd tell me to go ahead and steal and I would."

I had to wonder, though, if Mantle wasn't having second thoughts about being able to teach, which is essentially what a good coach does. This intention of his in insisting I could master the driver, for instance. We had played our first round of golf Tuesday at the Prestonwood Country Club just south of Preston Trail. I happened to live at one of their apartment complexes that offered golf privileges, and I had met Mickey a day earlier. Prestonwood was a shorter course than Preston Trail, and Mantle had actually driven from tee to green of a par-four hole that was just under four hundred yards. I must have been 160 yards behind him using a three-wood. Mickey was immediately on my case, insisting I was losing twenty-five to thirty yards by not using the driver. True, but where would the ball be? When I tried to compensate for a mean hook using the driver, I usually wound up with a wicked slice and the ball lost somewhere in the woods.

That afternoon on the driving range, though, I got an idea of what it would be like to have Mickey Mantle as a batting instructor in spring training. For what he was teaching wasn't so much how to hit a driver as much as how to hit a changeup up the middle. Seriously. As a kid growing up in the 1950s, I had been obsessed with baseball. My family owned a semipro baseball team in Waco, a fact that only reinforced the game in my young life. Mantle's driving lesson that afternoon reminded me especially of summer camp at the Big State Baseball Camp in Meridian, Texas, where you were taught to focus on hitting against your left side, as a right-handed hitter, transferring your weight and swinging inside out. Mantle now took me back to those days. Forget about trying to drive a ball like Nicklaus or Arnold Palmer. Do what came more naturally: hitting like a baseball player swinging at a ball a couple of inches off the ground. When he started teaching Mantle the game in 1954, golf pro Marshall Smith intentionally groomed Mickey's golf game after his baseball swing—and had him play right-handed since most golf courses are designed for right-handers. Not surprisingly, in Mickey this produced a follow-through similar to his right-handed baseball swing. By 1970, Mantle's left knee was so bad that he couldn't rotate the way most golfers turn on a golf swing. Instead, he would push off his right foot and power his torso like a tennis player on a forehand. It had the beauty of his right-handed home run swing with a speed that produced the violence of a wrecking ball: KAH-WHAACK!

"Mickey was a lot of things to a lot of people," fellow Oklahoman Smith remembered of Mantle. "But he hated the attention. Golf rejuvenated him. It's crazy to hear this, but he got as much satisfaction hitting a big drive as he did hitting a home run."

In just a few days of knowing him personally, I could tell that was true.

In 1970, I was a young newspaperman in Dallas, doing what all cub reporters at big-city papers do, hustling for stories while working long hours, often on the lonely night shift in the newsroom where there is little to do but hope and wait. There was a giant Rolodex on the city desk, and one night I found myself flipping through it and stopping at the name and phone number of my childhood idol. Over the coming days I must have called a dozen times trying to talk to him in hopes of setting up an

interview, though neither the sports nor city editors showed much interest in a story on my hero in retirement. Gay Talese's incredible *Esquire*
magazine profile of Joe DiMaggio in 1966—*The Silent Season of a Hero*—
remained the standard for that kind of story, and I had hoped to model
mine about Mantle in a similar fashion, the silent season of DiMaggio's
successor.

Dallas in this period was like a baseball purgatory for Mickey Mantle. It was a big city in America without a major league baseball team.
As the country finally exited the troubled sixties and entered the seventies, Dallas was also a city still in mourning for the most defining event
of the recently completed decade, or of the century for that matter. The
Kennedy assassination had left Dallas not only with a civic black eye
but also at a loss for a national identity beyond the Dallas Cowboys, the
city's National Football League franchise. That alone said volumes. Dallas was a big enough city to have its own professional football franchise,
two of them, in fact, when the Dallas Texans of the old American Football League had been around before their move to Kansas City where
they became the Chiefs. However, it wasn't a big enough city to have its
own major league baseball franchise. When big-league baseball did come
to the area in 1972 with the move of the Washington Senators, Dallas
would share the franchise with Fort Worth, and the games would be
played in Arlington, midway between the two big cities. Mantle, though,
was hardly a newcomer to Dallas. He had lived there since the 1950s
and in that time had irked local sportswriters more than any other sports
figure in town. His drinking and carousing in the heart of the Bible Belt,
a sports star's bad boy exploits that were then rarely reported in newspapers or television, had already become legendary in Dallas, where he had
also earned a reputation for boorish behavior, especially toward members
of the news media. So acclimating to retirement was difficult for Mickey,
especially in Dallas, which was so different than New York. That is to
say, nightlife was dramatically different. Toots Shor's and bars like it in
Manhattan, now that was what Mantle knew and loved. You couldn't
find anything like those in the Bible Belt. There, when you mentioned
nightlife and clubs, everyone knew you were talking about strip joints,
though in 1970 that began including new discos and private clubs with

dance floors and small bars with backgammon games. Actually, though, by nighttime, there wasn't much Mickey could really do. Later, when I'd gotten to know him, I tried to get Mickey to appear on the Dallas PBS television affiliate's early evening live feature show *Newsroom* that Jim Lehrer had originated in 1970. We wanted Mantle on the show to talk about the Washington Senators, who were relocating to Dallas–Fort Worth after the 1971 season. He would have been the perfect guest as the biggest baseball name in Dallas and someone whose name was being talked about as a possible manager. But Mickey balked. At first I thought it had to do with demanding an appearance fee, which the show wouldn't pay. Later Merlyn told me the real reason.

"Mickey could do a taped show in the morning," she said. "But you've seen how he is. But midafternoon he looks like he's been drinking all day because he's been drinking since eleven in the morning. So by early evening, he looks and talks like he's been drinking all day. It's been a problem when he's been invited to speak somewhere. He embarrasses everyone: himself, me, and the people who invited him. I think he's afraid of doing that on television, even local television. I think it's a blessing that he wouldn't do the show."

When we finally met, it was at one of those quaint restaurants of that time littered with peanut shells on the floor in the trendy Turtle Creek area of the city. It took all my willpower to stop staring at him. I was nervous and didn't know if I could actually talk to him until Mantle gave me a handshake worthy of a lumberjack. He was also sloshed and slurring his words. What broke the ice was golf. He played almost every day, and I had been a golfer growing up in Waco, Texas. I also now lived with my wife in a townhouse community in North Dallas with a golf course off it that Mickey said he knew.

Mickey Mantle was drunk. Just how drunk I didn't realize. He was trying to balance peanuts, still in their shells, on his nose. He would perfectly balance a peanut on his nose, snap his head upward so as to pop the peanut in the air, and then catch it between his teeth. Mickey had wanted to bet $10 that he could catch ten peanuts in a row that way, but so far he hadn't been able to make it past six. It was amazing he could even get that far given his condition. I had heard stories of Mickey having slugged prodigious home runs while hungover, so perhaps catching half a dozen peanuts in a row between his teeth shouldn't have been so amazing, but it was. We had also attracted the attention of the patrons sitting at the tables around us, and they were all now engrossed in watching a grown man behaving like a drunken adolescent. Worse, a couple of the men looking on appeared to recognize him.

"Is that Mickey Mantle?" one of the men whispered to me as Mickey began making another run of peanuts.

I ignored him and could hear him and his lunch partner whispering as to whether it was.

"That's Mickey Mantle?" the other man said, disbelieving.

"Yeah, it's gotta be him. Look at his arms."

"Nah, I don't think it is. What would he be doin' here?"

It was a late spring lunch at which I was supposed to be meeting my childhood hero. Instead it felt like what I imagined having lunch with my father would be like when he was on one of his drunken binges, which had been often when I was growing up. The restaurant served its beer in sixteen-ounce Mason jars, and Mickey had insisted each of his beers be served in a fresh jar and that the jars be left at our table, as if some marker of what we had drunk.

"What the fuck!" Mickey finally gave up trying to make it to ten peanuts in a row. "I feel like I'm in some god-awful dream where the peanut man at Yankee Stadium's been using me as a fuckin' dart board." I had to be drunk myself, I thought, to be sitting here watching Mickey Mantle play a silly peanut-catching game and listening to him talk about some baseball peanut vendor in a nightmare. "What the fuck!"

The afternoon had been full of What the Fucks. What the fuck came out of Mickey's mouth the way other people use you-know, as in "What the fuck, this has been the shittiest year. What the fuck, how long's it fuckin' gonna take to get these fuckin' burgers?"

Mickey said the words flowingly, though, not like an angry piece of off-color language but as if it were the name of a Willie Nelson country tune on some imaginary jukebox that the restaurant didn't have. He said it a decibel or two just above a whisper. What the fuck. Half wonderment and half frustration. I could imagine not even paying attention to him saying it after a while. This was Mickey *Fuckin'* Mantle, after all, easily recognizable, even out of uniform, in a football town at that, and no one seemed to mind it—least of all the waitresses, who likely assumed that a star this big and with people sending notes to our table, was tipping big.

Actually, I left the tip that afternoon after Mickey had insisted on paying and snagged the check from my hand. "Let's see how you tip," he said. Mickey noticed a photograph of a woman behind a plastic covering in my wallet and motioned to look at it.

"What the fuck, who's that knockout?" he demanded.

"That's my wife, Mickey." I pulled the photograph out of the wallet so that he could get a better look.

"What the fuck, she looks like a movie star, Waco," he said. I had told him I was from Waco, south of Dallas, and that had been a mistake because he started calling me "Waco" after that. "Talk about marrying the hell up! Tell me about it."

"We got married two years ago," I said. "Secretly."

"You eloped?"

"Yeah, and no."

"What the fuck, you did or you didn't."

"We did," I said. "We'd been dating secretly for a year. Then got married and kept it a secret for almost another year."

Mickey let out an unexpected laugh and lost the gulp of his last beer. I began telling him my crazy story of being twenty, in college, falling in love with a high school cheerleader who was only sixteen, and whose parents objected to her dating me.

"I would, too, Waco. You're lucky her old man didn't shoot your fuckin' ass off."

"That's why we decided to get married," I said. "So if they found out we were dating, we could say, 'Hey, we're married. Fuck off. You can't do shit about it.'"

"What the fuck, Waco, you fucker, you're fuckin' lucky her old man still didn't shoot you!"

Then, for what seemed like an eternity, Mickey Mantle continued to give the photograph a cross-eyed stare. He turned it around and studied the picture as if it were a puzzle he had to decipher. A smile darted across his eyes, as endearing as the crooked grin that had been locked on his face for much of the afternoon.

"She's awfully purty," he said, his words growing more slurred every time he spoke. "She reminds me of my first."

"Merlyn?" I asked, thinking he was talking about his wife.

"Naw, Merlyn wasn't my first," he said. "I'm talking about a girl I met in New York my rookie year. Her name was Holly. Holly Brooke. She was a redhead like your wife."

If there was any doubt that Mickey was drunk, this was a dead giveaway. My wife was a blonde, and the color picture I had shown Mickey had actually made her hair look even lighter than it was. So there was no reason for mistaking her for a redhead unless you considered that Mickey was seeing what he wanted to see.

"Mick," and, as I said the name, I mentally pinched myself. I was sitting here talking to Mickey Mantle, calling him "Mick" as if I had known him for years, and talking about women in a way I had never spoken to anyone. I'm not sure how the interview, whatever there was of an interview, had taken a turn in which Mickey had begun quizzing me about being new to Dallas, about having recently graduated from college, and about my wife. He had noticed my wedding ring, and he had wondered why I had married so young. He should talk. I reminded him he had gotten married after his rookie season, when he had barely turned twenty.

"I know, but that was a long time ago," he said. "We were kids. We were foolish. I don't know if we woulda done that today."

Then he went back to looking at the photograph of my better half. I wouldn't understand until years later when I finally saw a picture of Mickey with Holly Brooke in that year when he was young, in love, and happy.

14

Holly Brooke

*Just looking out at [New York] City. It's some city, and that son of a
bitch used to be all mine.*

—MICKEY MANTLE

IF ONLY THE YANKEES HAD KNOWN IN HIS ROOKIE YEAR WHAT THEY
realized in the coming seasons—that despite the country boy appearance,
their switch-hitting kid from Oklahoma with a guileless grin was a party
animal with a penchant for alcohol and a recklessness no one could have
foreseen—the story of Mickey Mantle might have been different. There
were clues, but the Yankees and almost everyone else mistook them for
the innocent signs of adolescence, especially since on the field Mantle
appeared to be the prodigy the team expected after his spectacular spring
training. However, those incredible talents carried with them monstrous
appetites for the kind of life Mickey couldn't have found in the back-
woods of Oklahoma but that were readily available all around him in New
York. And Mickey didn't waste time connecting. When veteran Yankee
outfielder Hank Bauer took him under his wing early in the season, he
found Mickey moving into an apartment they shared above the Stage
Delicatessen at Fifty-Fourth Street and Seventh Avenue carrying a bottle
of Jack Daniels.

"I had drunk some in Oklahoma with some of my pals back in high
school when someone would sneak us a bottle," Mantle told me in 1970.
"But it wasn't something I was about to do much with my dad always
looking out for what I was doing. But in New York, once we got there that
[1951] season, it didn't take long for me to find what I liked, and it didn't

seem to matter that I was underage. There was always someone willing to buy it, even though I don't think I would have had any problem buying it myself. But there was usually someone there, and it had nothing to do with Billy Martin. I know everyone likes to blame Billy for my drinking, and the Yankees even ran his ass off thinking that would be the fix. But, hell, I was drinking long before Billy and I started hanging around. He just made it more fun!"

Was it Holly Brooke who got Mickey drinking? Years later, she would wonder and feel partly responsible, though there were many others to share the blame, if blame were to be assigned. Just how Mickey began drinking his rookie season was never clear, or maybe he just didn't want to say. He remembered that one night, while having a meal with some teammates, drinks were brought to their table. "I think it might have been a fan or someone who knew us who sent over drinks," Mickey recalled. "We had a good time, and the next day I wake up hungover and with an awful headache, and we had a game that afternoon."

This would become typical for Mickey in the years to come. In that rookie season, the drinking was like a baptism under fire into big-city life, for which he seemed totally unprepared, but then what nineteen-year-old would be? He was a kid in a man's body believing he could do things other men did, and perhaps be just as foolish.

Mickey's favorite hangout quickly became Danny's Hideaway at 151 East Forty-Fifth Street. It was a place that Clay Cole, a popular New York disc jockey from that time, described as "a restaurant for stand-up guys: Boxing champs, . . . actors, teamster bosses, well-heeled merchants and well-mannered mobsters." It was the place to be seen, and Mickey was. Holly Brooke was invariably always with him, expanding her own networking, hoping it could further her own career.

"Mickey may have been that hillbilly hick everyone loves to say he was when he first came to New York," Holly said in an interview. "But it didn't take him long to fit in. Alan Savitt taught him a big lesson about fast-talkers in New York; and before you knew it, it was the other way around. He may have been a rookie and only nineteen, but in those first weeks in New York he quickly became a star. And people treated him that way. He rarely had to pay for anything. Not just drinks. People would pick up the check for dinner as well, especially at Danny's. They wanted to be in that circle of people who could say they bought the new Yankee star dinner and drinks. Men who owned clothing stores who would be in Danny's—and there were a lot of them—would come up, give Mickey their cards, and tell him to stop by and they'd take care of him. Mickey was one of the lowest-paid players on the Yankees that year, but you'd never know it from looking at him because he was soon dressing like he was making the kind of money Joe was being paid."

It wasn't long before Mickey and Holly were being ushered out of sight, to the VIP Room at Danny's. By 1951, Danny's was no longer the one-room bistro seating six that it had been at its beginning. It had expanded to a four-story building, with eleven dining rooms, with two separate kitchens and two completely stocked bars on each floor. Mickey got to know the layout as well as the Yankee Stadium outfield, Holly said, and on any given night when the Yankees were home, Mantle would be there for hours before he would emerge, slightly inebriated. He would sign a few autographs and leave.

Mickey didn't even realize that Joe DiMaggio was also an occasional guest at Danny's until the night when Mantle and Holly were arriving and found a horde of men and a few women packing the front of the restaurant, not moving or allowing anyone to enter or leave but instead straining curiously to move closer to the center of the commotion. Holly thought someone might have had a heart attack or fainted. She had seen that happen there in the past. However, that night there were no signs of anyone panicking or needing help. As men slowly moved away, Mickey and Holly saw what everyone had wanted a glimpse of.

It was DiMaggio. He was surrounded by well-wishers enthralled at just being near the great Yankee Clipper who had become even more popular, if that were possible, in New York in the weeks since his announcement that 1951 would be his final season. Everyone seemed to be lobbying for him to play at least another year: "Joe, you're still the man"..."Joe, please don't retire"..."Joe, you're still the best." DiMaggio had a reputation of rarely going out for dinner, ordering room service instead, but that had changed since the breakup of his first marriage. He had often been seen the past year at Toots Shor's restaurant and at

Danny's where he loved the manicotti. Usually he was quickly escorted past the adoring fans, many with their jaws dropped at the surprise of personally seeing DiMaggio just feet away. He was always impeccably dressed, trim, and looking taller than most imagined him to be, and nodding at anyone he personally recognized. Of course, there was always one diner who, not wishing to miss the opportunity, would stop Joe by extending a handshake that he would quickly firmly acknowledge and slide past.

"Joe, are the Yanks gonna take it again this year?" asked a man who stood up and patted his arm.

"We're going to try," DiMaggio said.

"Joe, you look like you could play another five years," said another well-wisher.

"I'm just looking to play this year," said DiMaggio, who was already ailing in the young season.

"Joe, are you thinking of managing?" asked a third man.

"No, the Yankees have a manager."

Mickey was frozen taking in the scene, Holly recalled. He watched as DiMaggio weaved through the people milling around him, totally in command. Mantle felt awkward even in small crowds, never knowing what to say and now seeing that all he had to do was to converse in the simplest manner, the way DiMaggio was doing, and to remain cordial.

DiMaggio seemed surprised to see Mickey arriving, and he was especially pleased to see the pretty redhead at his side. Mantle introduced Holly to his teammate, and Joe made an innocent mistake.

"Good to meet you," he said. "You're from Oklahoma, too, I understand."

Joe saw Holly and Mickey exchange nervous looks and quickly realized he had said something wrong.

"No, Joe, I'm from Jersey," Holly said, smiling and putting DiMaggio at ease.

"I'm terribly sorry," said Joe. "Please accept my apologies. Mickey, I'm sorry . . ."

"Don't be silly, Joe," said Mickey. "I met Holly here. She's an actress."

"Anything I might have seen?" Joe asked.

"A couple of things," said Holly.

Then, as Holly mentioned a couple of recent off-Broadway shows in which she had parts, DiMaggio asked if he could buy them dinner. Mickey was shocked. He had heard clubhouse stories of how DiMaggio could be distant and how few players could say they ever dined with the legendary Yankee. That night DiMaggio not only dined with his rookie teammate and his date but also recounted a story about his mishap in his own rookie season in 1936 that got him off to a late start.

In spring training his rookie year, DiMaggio told them, he burned his foot in a diathermy machine, a device commonly used in sports medicine. Joe said he was so shy that he didn't dare ask anyone why it was that his foot was getting so hot in the treatment machine. When the treatment ended, the trainers discovered that Joe's foot was red and blistered so badly that he had to sit out the Yankees' season opener against the Washington Senators at Griffith Stadium where President Franklin D. Roosevelt threw out the ceremonial first ball. DiMaggio not only sat on the bench but also was unable to play for several weeks, not making his Yankee debut until May 3 when he singled twice and tripled in six at-bats in a come-from-behind 14–5 win over the St Louis Browns. DiMaggio went on to have a brilliant season—batting .323 with forty-four doubles, fifteen triples and twenty-nine home runs—and would have undoubtedly won Rookie of the Year honors if the award had been given out. It wasn't instituted until 1947, when Jackie Robinson won it.

"I've heard stories over the years about how Joe DiMaggio was standoffish, unfriendly, and not a very nice person," Holly said years later. "And I don't know who they could be talking about because it wasn't the Joe DiMaggio that I knew. I wasn't a close personal friend, and the only time I was around him was when Mickey and I ran into him or the times we had dinner with him—and once later when he was with Marilyn in New York. But the Joe DiMaggio I got to know was a sweetheart. That first night at Danny's, I think that went a long way in making Mickey feel comfortable around him. I remember Mickey later saying that Joe seemed to be all business when he was in the clubhouse and at the stadium. 'He acts like the president of a bank, all serious all the time,' Mickey told me. And I said to him, 'Well, Mickey, the Yankees are like a bank aren't they?

All those salaries, all that responsibility, and if Joe is who everyone says he is—Mr. Yankee—then he is like the president of the bank, isn't he? Hasn't Joe been that for as long as he's been a Yankee? Hasn't Joe been the reason that the Yankees have remained the greatest team in America after Babe Ruth was gone and after Lou Gehrig was gone? Mickey, who could ever know the pressure that Joe DiMaggio's been under to keep the Yankees from being anything less than the New York Yankees?'"

Mantle came to that realization thanks to Holly, and perhaps that is what Mickey meant when he told me that she had been the best business-woman he had ever known.

"If she hadn't been there," he said, "I don't think I would have made it that first year. She made me understand that I was no longer just a base-ball player. I was a *professional* baseball player. I tried to live up to that. Sometimes I didn't do too good a job of it, but I kept tryin'."

Until Holly, Mickey had never fallen head over heels for any woman, but Holly was unlike anyone he had ever known, he would tell her often, especially in their first days together, though he might have said that about any beauty he could have gotten to know then. Holly lived in an all-women housing complex near the theater district, but it wasn't unusual for men to be snuck in, as she often did with Mantle. Soon, though, she found her own apartment where Mickey began spending as much time as he did at the Concourse Hotel in the Bronx or the place he later shared with teammates above the Stage Deli. Bauer and fellow Yankee Johnny Hopp each had their own bedroom in that place, and Mantle would sleep on a cot in the living room. "I don't think they knew when I wasn't there," Mickey said of his roommates. "I was always there when it came time to leave for the stadium or to get to the train station, and I think that's what they figured was important."

Mickey Mantle, the most prized rookie in Yankee history, was barely a couple of months into his career in 1951 and already steeped in the city's cultural fabric. He just didn't realize or understand how deeply interwoven with it he had become.

Another New Yorker whose life often intersected with Mickey that year was an unusually devout Yankee fan, an Italian American who had closely followed Joe DiMaggio's fabulous career and now wanted to see as much as he could of what would be The Yankee Clipper's final season. Matthew Ianniello was a thirty-year-old decorated World War II veteran who had received a Purple Heart and Bronze Star for combat as an army artillery gunner in the Philippines. Two years earlier he had become partners with his uncle in his own restaurant, Matty's Towncrest Restaurant in Midtown. Ianniello himself had once been a young ballplayer with some promise as a hitter and had earned an unforgettable nickname, Matty "The Horse." However, it wasn't for his swing with a bat. In a youth baseball game, an opposing pitcher threw a high fastball that struck a teammate of Ianniello's squarely in the face. The teams' benches cleared, and Ianniello charged the mound knocking down the pitcher, surprising because the youngster was older and taller than Matty. Someone who witnessed the brawl couldn't help but say about Ianniello, "That boy is as strong as a horse."

Matty "The Horse" Ianniello would become one of New York's most notorious mobsters, a made man in the Vito Genovese crime family whose sponsor was future mob boss Frank Tieri. Years later, he would be convicted of skimming $2 million from an assortment of Manhattan restaurants and food suppliers—including one that provided the hot dogs for Yankee Stadium. In 1951, however, Matty "The Horse," the former kid ballplayer from Manhattan's Little Italy, was just a fan who wanted to catch the start of the farewell season of the Favorite Son of all Italian Americans. As a fan he was especially drawn to Italian ballplayers, particularly DiMaggio and Yankee catcher Yogi Berra. He often sent invitations to the Yankee clubhouse, hoping he could get DiMaggio or any of his teammates to stop by his restaurant. Occasionally some of the Yankees did go eat at Matty's place, but their loyalty was to the Stage Deli. When Ianniello learned this, he started dropping in at the Stage Deli as well as Danny's Hideaway where he knew Mafiosi often hung out. It was through those connections that Ianniello had met Alan Savitt, who tried to interest him in buying an interest he had in a deal to represent the Yankees' hot rookie, Mickey Mantle.

"He was a hustler and not a very good one," Ianniello said in a rare interview years later. "It was a long time ago. Who wouldn't know who Mickey Mantle was even then. That's all the papers wrote about. And this hustler was claiming he had his claws into Mantle. Maybe he did. Maybe he conned the kid. But it wasn't gonna go anywhere. And Savitt . . . how could you believe anything coming out of that man's mouth? There's an Italian expression: *Bocca di miele, cuore di fiele.* A tongue of honey, a heart of gall."

Could there have been more, though, to an old rumor among mobsters that in 1951, Matty "The Horse" Ianniello had quietly owned a part of the young Mickey Mantle through that ill-fated scam of Alan Savitt's, even though there reportedly hadn't been any takers besides Holly Brooke? Ianniello's former partner in the mob's silent underworld ownership of several New York bars thought so.

"Matty used to brag that he had owned a piece of Mickey Mantle back in the early 1950s, before he was a big star," said Paul Gelb, a survivor of World War II Nazi concentration camps who for years was the king of organized crime's strip joint operations in New York. "I don't know if he ever got any money from Mickey. He just said he had bought a piece of him from a guy he knew, and, of course, Matty knew a lot of people and he had a way of worming his way into a piece of any action he wanted. That's what he did with me."

In the mid-1960s, Gelb took his savings built from almost twenty years in the garment and jewelry businesses and bought a Manhattan Midtown topless bar from a man named Philly whom Paul knew had organized crime connections.

"What I didn't know," Gelb told me in a series of interviews, "was that Philly had been selling this club over and over again to people who would give Philly a down-payment, pay a few months' rent, then have to give him back the club when they went broke. Philly'd done this dozens of times. This was Philly's scam, until his sold it to me."

Gelb quickly turned his new topless bar into a surprising moneymaker. Impressed, Philly became Gelb's new close pal. Gelb's success, however, quickly angered a competing topless bar impresario, none other than Matty "The Horse" Ianniello, who according to Gelb, retaliated with several unsuccessful attempts to run Paul out of business.

"He tried muscling me out," said Gelb, "but by this time Philly was my best friend and Philly was 'connected,' too. I said to Philly, 'Matty the

Horse is trying to put me out of business. What am I gonna do?' Philly made a call, and the next thing I know Matty is now trying to become my new good friend."

It didn't happen overnight, but by the late 1970s, Gelb and Ianniello were as thick as thieves. Gelb said that during baseball seasons Ianniello would often pine for the days of the great Yankee teams of DiMaggio and Mantle and on more than one occasion how he had for a brief period owned a piece of the great switch-hitting slugger. Gelb, according to government prosecutors, became a front man for both Ianniello and partner and fellow wiseguy Benjamin Cohen. Their operations included numerous topless bars and restaurants in Manhattan that by the early 1980s had attracted the attention of federal investigators. Gelb, according to court documents, became the mob's mole through whom ownership in these bars and restaurants was hidden from federal and state authorities. A lengthy federal investigation that included extensive wire taps and surveillance conclusively linked Gelb to an organized criminal conspiracy involving skimming bar and restaurant earnings, mail fraud, racketeering, and tax evasion. In 1985, Gelb was convicted on all twenty-seven counts filed against him, as was Ianniello the following year. Both received six-year prison sentences.

In an interview, Ianniello, who died in 2012, said that he sometimes hung out at Danny's Hideaway in the 1950s, part of the group of mobsters who blended in with the nightly scene, and he said he often did see both Mantle and DiMaggio, usually separately, as they came to dine there. "You have to understand New York, the culture of New York, especially in that day," said Ianniello. "You could be sitting down to dinner with a princess, a real princess on one side of you, the mayor on the other side, and, yeah, DiMaggio or Mickey Mantle a table down. Whadaya make of that? Nothing, people eat, drink, live, and let live. Did I ever lay a bet after seeing them there? I can't say I didn't. DiMaggio? He was book. You could count on him in his day. Mickey Mantle? There were times, even when he was young and in his prime, you'd see him having a good time, maybe too good of a good time, and you'd think, 'No way. No way he can help the Yankees win tomorrow.' Then the next day, he goes 3-for-3 with a homer. Can you believe that, 3-for-3 and an upper deck jolt, and he's drunk on his ass, or pretty close to it cause it's a day game, and you saw him at one in the morning, and you knew you couldn't have even made it to work the next day in the condition he was in. I can't say I didn't lay a bet against the Yanks when I'd seen him that way, and hell if I didn't get burned."

Gelb said that on a handful of occasions, he had picked up the checks at Danny's and the Stage Deli for both DiMaggio and Mantle. "I would have done it more often except most times when you would tell a waiter that you wanted to pick up Mickey's tab, they'd say, 'Thanks, but it's taken care of.' I'm sure if he had wanted to, he could've had his tabs picked up by someone the rest of his life. Whadaya gonna say?

"It was Mickey Goddamn Mantle."

15

Down the Rabbit Hole

Being sent down to the minors was the lowest point of my life. I felt like they might as well have castrated me. I had to go through shit to find my confidence.

—MICKEY MANTLE

DIMAGGIO, RUTH, GEHRIG—NONE OF THE YANKEE GREATS AND FEW of the legends of baseball—have been humbled in such a way as to have had their worthiness of being in the major leagues challenged by being demoted to the minor leagues. For Mickey Mantle, who was sent down to the Yankees' Triple-A minor league team in Kansas City midway through his rookie year, the degradation of the experience almost put him out of baseball. By the time the Yankees shipped him out, Mickey wasn't just in the midst of a horrendous batting slump that no one could explain or seemingly correct. He was in free fall professionally and personally. He was experiencing mood swings of anxiety, euphoria, guilt, and loneliness. He was nauseous at times and throwing up almost every day. There is a good reason that Mickey was showing these obvious signs of alcohol abuse. He was drunk most of the time when he wasn't on the field. Few teammates were aware that he had quickly become addicted to the high lifestyle of going out every night and drinking heavily. Mantle's famous drinking, which was later blamed on his association with teammates Billy Martin and Whitey Ford, had actually begun before he started going out on the town with them. As Holly Brooke confirmed half a century later, "Mickey's alcoholism I regret to say began when we began seeing each other early in the 1951 season. That's awful to admit, I know, but I didn't realize the extent to which the drinking was affecting him. Looking back, I feel terrible about it. And I guess, you're right. His troubles playing baseball that rookie season, after such a terrific beginning in spring training and the early weeks in April and May of that year . . . those troubles and the slump began around the time that we started going out. It's a terrible thing to have to admit that I might have contributed to making Mickey Mantle an alcoholic. That's the last thing I would have wanted to do to someone I cared so much about. You know that. I hope it's not true. But if that's true, I have to live with that."

Mantle's turnaround from super rookie to apparent bust was dramatic. He was doing so amazingly well through the first few weeks of the season that at one point he matter-of-factly boasted to pitcher Allie Reynolds, "Do you know that I'm leading the league in average, RBI and home runs?"

A nineteen-year-old rookie, Mickey was leading the American League in its Triple Crown categories. He was doing so well that *Collier's* magazine profiled him in its June 2 issue. But his offensive productivity swooned, and the falloff was heightened by Mantle's growing number of strikeouts and his explosive temperament. At the same time, the Yankees were struggling. No one felt the pressure more than Casey Stengel, whose early proclamation of Mantle as the next Ruth seemed increasingly foolish. It didn't matter that on July 12 Mantle broke up Bob Feller's bid for a second no-hitter in two weeks with a sixth inning double. Three days later, his once-league-leading batting average having dropped to .260, Mickey was stripped of his major league status. Whether deserved or not, Mickey Mantle had become the Yankees' fall guy.

Mantle was called aside by the clubhouse man at Briggs Stadium in Detroit, who told him Stengel wanted to see him. Mickey knew what was coming and walked into the manager's office to find Casey with tears in his eyes.

"This is gonna hurt me more than you," Stengel told Mantle when he broke the news.

"No, skip, it's my fault." Mickey struggled to hold back his own tears.

"Aww . . . it ain't nobody's fault," said Stengel. "You're nineteen, that's all. Mickey, you're getting a little nervous and tight at the plate, swinging at too many bad pitches. You're going to develop into a big-league star one of these years. But maybe a change of scenery might do you a lot of good. I want you to get your confidence back, so I'm shipping you down to Kansas City."

Mantle was crushed. Stengel later said that it was one of the most difficult things he ever had to do in his life.

"It's not the end of the world, Mickey," the Yankee manager said. "In a couple of weeks you'll start hitting and then we'll bring you right back up again. I promise."

Understandably, Mantle took Stengel's assurance of returning to the Yankees as what he later described as "no more than a crude effort to take the curse off of the sentence he had just passed."

"Casey probably assumed that, as I had been ready to go to Beaumont in Double-A ball, it would be no serious jolt to find myself in Kansas City, which was Triple-A then," Mickey said years later. "But he might as well have told me he was shipping me back to [Class D minor league] Independence. I had been a Yankee, and now I was nothing. I was always one of those guys who took all the bad luck doubly hard, who saw disaster when there was just everyday trouble, and who took every slump as if it were a downhill slide to oblivion."

The *New York Times* the following day called Mantle's demotion "startling."

Mantle couldn't stop crying. Hours later, he was still in tears in the lobby of the Cadillac Hotel where he was waiting for a taxi to the airport. "Kind of like it was the end of his career," recalled Joe Gallagher, a young golfer who was also broadcaster Mel Allen's assistant. "All I could say to him was 'You'll be back.'"

There was another complication as well. Manager Casey Stengel and George Weiss, the general manager, apparently were not aware of just how far Mantle's self-confidence had sunk. If they had been, they might have sent him down to the Yankees' Class AA team in Beaumont where Mantle might have felt more comfortable playing for Harry Craft, who had coached him his previous year in the minors. The Yankees, however, thought they were doing their best by sending Mantle to learn patience at the plate from Kansas City Blues manager George Selkirk, a former

Yankee outfielder. In 1935 Selkirk had replaced Babe Ruth in right field and was even issued Ruth's uniform number, the famous number 3 that eventually would be retired on Babe Ruth Day in 1948, just weeks before he died. While he could not come close to Ruth's home run output—he hit twenty-one homers at his best in 1939—Selkirk batted better than .300 in five of his first six seasons. A patient hitter, Selkirk had the distinction of having drawn two walks in an inning four different times, and he walked 103 times in 1939. In 1935, Selkirk had been the first to suggest that a cinder path six feet wide be installed in the outfield so that a player knew when he was nearing the wall—the modern-day warning track. In Selkirk, someone who had played with Ruth, Gehrig, and DiMaggio, the Yankees also thought he might impart some badly needed wisdom to their presumed heir. In addition, Stengel had a fondness for Kansas City and thought Mantle would be better off there than in an outpost of Texas. Stengel had been born and raised in Kansas City, and he had quit high school in 1910 just short of graduating to play baseball professionally with the Kansas City Blues.

In the coming years, when Kansas City became a major league baseball city with the arrival of the Athletics, this would be one of Mickey's favorite stops on the Yankees' American League schedule. He had some extremely well-heeled friends by then, friends who were trustworthy and discreet. It also helped that Kansas City was home to some of the most beautiful women in America. But in 1951, Mantle thought he was going to die there. It wasn't that he couldn't look anyone else in the face after his demotion. Mickey couldn't even look himself in the mirror. He didn't know how he would ever make it back to the majors, nor if he could. He was learning about the hard life of the minor leagues the toughest way possible—from the perspective of someone who has just been to the majors and failed. There was also this disturbing fact: only one of fourteen minor leaguers ever makes it to the major leagues. Mantle quickly learned that the minors are a collection of underpaid, overworked players and coaches, none of whom are impressed by squandered talent and overblown press clippings. It would only be later that Mickey would also describe the Blues in particular as a group of "malcontents" whose pitchers "carried pints of whiskey in their back pockets." And most of them didn't like or care much for Mickey Mantle, who in their minds was the big team's privileged character sent down to the minors for some practice and refinement, not to mention special treatment. It was hard to deny that, especially when he was immediately put into the Blues lineup with the designation of being a promising hot prospect. Mickey, though, didn't help his case. He beat out a drag bunt on his first at-bat and got yelled at by the manager.

"What's the matter with you?" he screamed at Mantle. "They didn't send you here to bunt. You're here to get some hits and get your confidence back."

"That finished me," said Mickey. "I felt like hell when I went out to my position, I could feel the tears of self-pity stinging my eyes. 'What did a guy have to do?' I asked myself."

Mantle became his own worst enemy by being down on himself. He lost his confidence, and he looked bad trying to hit American Association pitching, going hitless in his next nineteen at-bats. He had no friends on the team, and he was getting hate mail, much of it over his draft status. None of his critics seemed to care that Mickey had twice been classified 4-F by pre-induction doctors who concluded that the osteomyelitis that had hospitalized him as a youth posed too great a risk of returning if he were pressed into military service.

For Mantle, however, the personal war he was now fighting was no longer against opposing pitchers. It was instead against his own fear and foreboding at the prospect of failure. The real slump wasn't on the baseball diamond—it was in his head. Years later, a therapist working with Mantle and Merlyn had concluded that "Mickey is totally controlled by fear. He is filled with fear about everything." At the height of his slump, each time Mantle came to bat, he was overcome by sudden surges of overwhelming fear that came without warning and without any obvious reason. It was more intense than the feeling of being "stressed out" that most people experience.

Baseball slumps, according to Kevin Elko, adjunct professor to the sports medicine fellows at the University of Pittsburgh School of Medicine, are largely fueled by panic. "The panic," said Elko, a consultant to several professional sports teams, "has become a condition. More than any other variable, panic is the malady." Selkirk and some of the other Blues coaches had begun to suspect that Mantle's problem was a case of nerves—that maybe Mantle just didn't have it. However, it may have been something far more serious: a hint of possible panic disorder.

Later in his life, Mantle would exhibit similar symptoms that were perhaps too easily and prematurely attributed to his drinking. These panic or anxiety attacks became more frequent as Mantle traveled around the country for card shows. Mantle was nationally famous, so these incidents received news coverage. One of the most publicized attacks occurred on a flight back to Dallas when Mickey was feared to have suffered a heart attack. Emergency paramedics who met the plane at Dallas' Love Field diagnosed Mantle as having had a panic attack. "Depression was a regular part of my life," Mickey admitted in a 1993 interview with sports broadcaster Roy Firestone. "At times, I thought about killing myself." So what was happening with Mickey back in 1951? His condition was never diagnosed at that time, but it appears that at age nineteen his symptoms fit the profile for someone suffering with panic disorder. Mickey was suffering from stress, his self-worth and confidence having taken a serious jolt from his demotion to the minors. "When Mick retired," Merlyn later said of Mickey, "a big chunk of his self-esteem went out the window. I question whether he ever had much to begin with."

The only thing Mickey felt he had going for him that summer was Holly Brooke with whom he was talking by long-distance telephone calls almost daily.

"I was calling him 'Mickey Mouse,' a pet name only his mother had used before," Holly said, almost word for word to what had appeared in a 1957 *Confidential* magazine exposé. "More than once, Mickey would ask me how I felt about marrying him, owning him 100 percent . . . permanently. But he always answered his own question. 'No, I guess not,' he'd say. 'You'd never be happy in a little town like Commerce.' And he was right on that. Other towns were different though. For instance, I remember flying to Columbus [Ohio] to see him and buck up his spirits. I'd planned to stay one night but wound up staying three days. That was in 1951 when the big blow fell and the Yankees shipped him off to their Kansas City farm club. When he heard the news, Mickey broke down and bawled like a baby. He often called me from there and other minor league towns, asking me to fly out and spend a few days with him because he was so lonesome." Brooke also wound up with one of the few existing photos of Mantle in a Kansas City uniform, which he inscribed, "To Holly, with all my love and thoughts."

Soon, however, Holly was concerned enough to put her life in New York on hold and immediately join Mickey in Kansas City. "He called me and said he needed me," she told me. "But this was different than when-ever he had said that before. He sounded desperate and helpless. When I got to Kansas City, he looked terrible. He had been drinking too much and sleeping too little. All I could really do was console him and to try assuring him things would get better. But he was at the lowest period of his life to that point and feeling sorry for himself."

It was the lowest point of Mickey life so far. He was spending time on the phone with Holly, who visited him in Kansas City. No amount of loving, however, could restore his confidence on the ball field. He gave up and called his father to tell him their dream was over. He was no minor league ballplayer, much less a big league one. Mutt had been reading about his son's troubles in the newspapers and shared Mickey's agony. But it was the desperation in Mickey's voice that concerned Mutt most. He thought that maybe a visit from his family might help, or at least ease Mickey's anxiety. Almost immediately he packed Lovell, son Larry, daughter Barbara, and Merlyn into the car for the five-hour drive from Commerce to Kansas City. Mickey was staying at the Alad-din Hotel. But Mutt, the family, and Merlyn hadn't expected to find a woman staying in the same hotel room with Mickey, who didn't even try to explain Holly Brooke to his mom, dad, and fiancée. When I asked him about this years later Mickey just shook his head, his mouth half open as if still disbelieving the scene and the looks that Merlyn and Holly exchanged.

"I was living there, and boy, was I glad to see him," Mantle said, stress-ing just that he focused on his father who was left alone with his son. "I wanted him to pat me on the back and cheer me up and tell me how badly the Yankees had treated me and all that sort of stuff. I guess I was like a little boy, and I wanted him to comfort me."

"How are things going?" Mutt asked Mickey.

"Awful. The Yankees sent me down to learn not to strike out, but now I can't even hit."

"That so?"

"I'm not good enough to play in the major leagues," Mickey said. "And I'm not good enough to play here. I'll never make it. I think I'll quit and go home with you."

"I guess I wanted him to say, 'Oh, don't be silly, you're just in a little slump, you'll be all right, you're great,'" Mantle later said. "But he just looked at me for a second and then in a quiet voice that cut me in two he said, 'Well, Mick, if that's all the guts you have, I think you better quit. You might as well come home right now.'"

Mickey wanted to tell him that he had tried, but he knew better than to argue with his father when he was in the mood he now found him in.

"Mickey, you can't have it easy all your life. Baseball is no different than any other job. Things get tough once in a while, and you must learn how to take it—the sooner the better. It takes guts, not moaning, to make it. And if that's all the guts you have, I agree with you. You don't belong in baseball. Come on back to Commerce and grub out a living in the mines for the rest of your life."

Then Mutt said the words that tore into Mantle's heart:

"I thought I raised a man, not a coward!"

After saying hello to Mutt, whom she had met in New York, Holly had retreated to the bathroom while Mickey's mother, his brother and sister, and Merlyn had gone back out into the hallway. Merlyn later said she heard much of what Mutt had said to Mickey through the door, as did Holly in the bathroom. As for Holly and Merlyn, Holly said they exchange tentative glances but didn't speak to one another.

Mickey would later say that Mutt's lecture that night "had been the greatest thing my father ever did for me. All the encouragement he had given me when I was small, all the sacrifices he made so I could play ball when other boys were working in the mines, all the painstaking instruction he had provided—all of these would have been thrown away if he had not been there that night to put the iron into my spine when it was needed most.

"I never felt as ashamed as I did then, to hear my father sound disappointed in me, ashamed of me," Mantle said. "I have wondered sometimes exactly what it was. I know that I wanted my father to comfort me. He didn't. He didn't give me any advice. He didn't show me how to swing the bat any different. He didn't give me any inspiring speeches. I think that what happened was that he had so much plain ordinary courage that it spilled over, and I could feel it. All he did was show me that I was acting scared, and that you can't live scared."

Indeed, throughout both his childhood and adult life, fear was the one emotion that ruled him and motivated him as both a boy and a man, as both a player and a husband. It began as a mixture of fear and respect for his father, much as it is for many youngsters who are pushed to succeed in any endeavor that is as meaningful to a parent as to the youngster, if not more so. But Mutt's influence over Mickey—Mutt's ability to motivate his son by the fear of disappointing him—would extend far beyond Mickey's childhood as well as beyond baseball. Mickey's marriage to Merlyn during the Christmas holidays that year would be an act possibly more out of love and fear of disappointing Mutt than out of love for Merlyn. In later years, Mickey would measure himself as a husband and father to his own father and, of course, pale in the comparison because anything short of perfection would have failed his father.

Mutt, the family, and Merlyn stayed around to watch that night's game, which perhaps was all that Mickey needed. He slugged two monstrous home runs, as if this was his great spring training season all over again. Mantle's horrible slump was over, and his bat let everyone know it, especially the doubters on the Blues. He hit eleven home runs, three triples, nine doubles, drove in fifty runs, and batted .361 over the next forty-one games, putting the Blues in the middle of their own American Association title race. But that ended when the Yankees recalled Mantle. Kansas City native Calvin Trillin would later lament his own frustration with baseball, blaming the Yankees for stripping his beloved Blues of their power-hitting young star. "I hate the Yankees," he wrote. "They called Mickey Mantle up from Kansas City right in the middle of a hot pennant race with the Indianapolis Indians." As I wrote in *Prodigal Son*, if

Mantle could do this for the intelligentsia of Kansas City, imagine what impact he must have had on the fans in the cheap seats.

In mid-August, Stengel and the Yankees decided to bring Mantle back to the majors, only to learn that they would have to stand in line. In what had become an ongoing soap opera lasting much of the year, the Selective Service had called Mantle back for yet another physical examination.

No one at the time dared boast that their son was classified 4-F, a military reject. However, the draft board in Mantle's Oklahoma county had already rejected Mickey for service because of the osteomyelitis when he was called for his pre-induction physical examination. Mickey's medical records bore out that he had been hospitalized for extensive treatment of osteomyelitis in 1946 and again for a flare-up in 1947. Osteomyelitis happened to be one of the medical conditions that the government had decided was automatic grounds for denying entry into any of the branches of the military. Although the disease had been arrested, it could recur at any time. If that were to happen while in the service, the government would be liable for paying a disability pension for life—conceivably hundreds of thousands of dollars in pension payments and medical bills.

However, after his fabulous spring training, Mickey Mantle found that he was no longer simply the unassuming youngster from Oklahoma. At the end of Mantle's triumphant showing on the Yankees' exhibition swing to the West Coast, Mickey had returned to the team's spring training facility in Phoenix to find a letter from his father and learn that his draft board wanted him to take another physical examination.

"My dad wrote . . . that a lot of people were asking why I wasn't soldiering in Korea," Mantle recalled years later. "To be candid, the war was the furthest thing from my mind. Certainly I knew about the mounting casualties, the talk going around that General MacArthur was planning an all-out fight against Communism, even thinking of dropping an atomic bomb on China. Well, I could understand how some people felt, especially those who resented seeing young, apparently healthy guys hitting baseballs while their own sons and husbands were being killed in battle."

In his biography of Casey Stengel, author Robert W. Creamer claims that the Yankee organization, seeking to quell growing criticism about

Mickey's 4-F status, went so far as to ask the Oklahoma draft board to reexamine Mantle's case. Indeed, no one was more aware of the potential public backlash and harm over Mickey's draft status than the Yankee brass, especially General Manager George Weiss, who soon enough would begin developing a protective attitude toward Mantle. Weiss had an aristocratic gentility about him, and he saw Mickey as a naïve, vulnerable country boy completely out of place in the big city. Unfortunately for Mantle in 1951, as the hailed successor to Ruth and DiMaggio and with the spring training exploits to prove it, he had become virtually a walking expression of the American culture's irrationality, as he would be throughout his career and even beyond. He was loved for what America thought he should be—a personification of the country's own aspirations; he was vilified for his human vulnerability that kept him from realizing those expectations.

Despite being rejected a second time for military service, Mantle continued receiving criticism questioning his courage for not fulfilling his "military obligation." In fact, it seemed that the hate mail and public taunts increased the more that the legitimacy of his draft exemption was mentioned, even throughout the rest of the decade. "Mantle began to receive vituperative hate mail and as the debate raged around him, the shy, uncommunicative boy shrunk deeper and deeper into his shell of silence," Yankee historian Peter Golenbock wrote in *Dynasty: The New York Yankees, 1949–1964*. So on August 23, 1951, Mickey underwent a third physical by army doctors at Fort Sill, Oklahoma, and was once again classified 4-F because of the osteomyelitis.

The next day, the Yankees recalled Mantle to the majors.

When Mantle returned to New York, one of the first people he went to see was Yankee Stadium clubhouse man Pete Sheehy, to get his uniform. For years, the traditional story had been that Sheehy decided to give Mantle number 7 on the chance that perhaps his former number 6 might bring back bad memories of how Mickey's hot start had so stunningly gone bad.

"To be honest," Mickey later said, "I didn't put any stock in whether I was wearing number six or number seven. But after I had number seven on for a while, no one was gonna take it off my back."

Years later, however, Holly Brooke would disclose the story of how Mantle truly switched to what would become his famous number.

In 2014, in one of our numerous conversations in recent years, I visited with Holly and found her unusually emotional as she discussed Mickey's return to New York after his minor league exile to Kansas City.

"Above Grand Central Station, there used to be this incredibly fabulously opulent apartment that looked like a palace that the original architect built as part of the original design, and in 1951 I knew someone—I knew a lot of people even then—who arranged for me, for us, to stay there one night that summer," Holly recalled. "And so Mickey and I spent one of the greatest nights of our lives there. It was a romantic, magical evening. We made love all night. We were both young and in love, and he wanted to marry me and spend the rest of our lives together."

Her eyes welled up, and Holly cleared her throat. She was recovering from a bad cold that came on over the holidays and hadn't retreated much, and her face slackened, making her voice parched and masking the gentle lilt of earlier conversations about days now more than six decades ago. Although small and fine-boned, any hint of frailty was deceptive. She was a hard-edged New Yorker at heart and, from her tenth-floor apartment just off Central Park near Trump Tower, had the view of Manhattan to match. As she sipped her afternoon tea, it was evident that her mind remained wit sharp, unbothered by her age. Holly would be ninety-one that coming June—June 7, she emphasized because the number had always been special. So special, she said, that in that late summer of 1951, when she was in Kansas City living with the love of her life, she had begged that when he returned to New York from his minor league demotion, that he ask the Yankees to change his uniform, to take back the jersey with the number 6 on the back and to give him the jersey with the numeral 7.

"It will bring you luck," she told me she said to Mickey. "I promise."

Mickey Mantle would do just that when the Yankees called him back to the majors that August, after tearing up Triple-A pitching with a vengeance in only forty games with the Blues. Some skeptics feared that Mantle, who would not turn twenty until the end of October, was washed up for good when he went into a slump after a magnificent start to his rookie season. However, Casey Stengel had dismissed that kind of talk, telling reporters who asked if Mickey was finished playing, "You wish you were through like that kid's through."

On August 22, 1951, the Yankees' new prodigal son returned to New York, arriving with Holly on the Super Chief at Grand Central Station and passing through what was then known as the "Kissing Room," where travelers once embraced their sweethearts, friends, and family, and offering cozy access to the Biltmore Hotel above. That was where Zelda and F. Scott Fitzgerald had honeymooned, she whispered to Mickey as they snuggled arm and arm with the crowd.

"I don't know if Mickey knew who F. Scott Fitzgerald was," said Holly, smiling as she dreamily remembered that day. "I shouldn't say that. He was a very smart man. He just didn't like to show it, but his mind was like a steel trap. Once he heard or saw something, he knew it by heart. I suspect that's what helped make him such a great hitter and ballplayer. But I think he enjoyed being seen as that good ol' country boy.

"We had a drink at the Kissing Room. We had come in a day early, and Mickey didn't have to report back to the team until the next day. He didn't want to go to the Concourse Plaza where they had a room for him. That was all the way out in the Bronx, and we were in Manhattan and at Grand Central Station, and we had the day to ourselves, and I had come to think that we would have the rest of our lives together as well.

"'Holly, I want you to marry me,' Mickey said to me that night. He had said it earlier, but I think, returning to New York, he knew he now had it together. The Yankees wanted him back in the majors, and this time he knew he was going to stick with the team for good, and that he would live up to all they were expecting of him. We had talked about marriage. *He* had talked about marriage. He had talked about wanting to marry me and about adopting my son. But this time was different. He was so insistent. And when he asked me to marry him this time, it wasn't like the other times. He knew the only person who could stand in our way was his father. But Mutt had seen us together in Kansas City, just as he had seen us together here in New York before Mickey was sent down. And in Kansas City, I think he saw in Mickey's face his determination to be with me. There in front of me, Mickey said to his father, 'Dad, so what if she's older than me? She's seven years older than me. Mom was ten years older than you when you married her, and she had been married before as well. If it can work out for you and Mom, why couldn't it work out for Holly and me?' I thought Mutt was going to cry. He left our room, and I wouldn't be surprised if he did shed a tear later. You could tell that Mickey had hit a soft spot. So that night back in New York, Mickey says to me, 'Dad won't like it. You saw what he's like. He wants me to marry Merlyn, but I can't. I'm not in love with her. I'm in love with you. So I'll bring him around.' And, of course, I said, 'Yes, Mickey, I'll marry you. I love you.' And he told me he loved me, too. 'You're the love of my life, Holly.' And that's how we left it. Mickey was going to talk to his father—'Come hell or high water,' I think is how he said it—and we were going to get married as soon as the season ended. Mickey said the only thing that would be more perfect was if the Yankees won the World Series as well."

16

Svengali

People used to ask Billy and me if we were related, and he would tell them that no, we'd met at an orphanage. I think that tells you what he thought of the Yankees!

—Mickey Mantle

Mickey's return to New York that summer marked the beginning of his friendship with Billy Martin, the Yankees second baseman who would become a central figure throughout his life. If Casey Stengel saw in Mantle the son he never had, Billy Martin found in him the little brother of his dreams. Mickey was the adoring kid brother who would go along with anything Billy proposed doing, and who would never dare to talk back. Mickey also marveled at Martin's unique friendship with Joe DiMaggio, of which Mickey could only be admiring and envious. Few Yankee players could boast of anything but a passing acquaintance with the team's star center fielder, who often could sit in the clubhouse for hours without speaking to anyone. Martin, however, had managed to endear himself to DiMaggio with his clubhouse pranks and joking manner that amused the stoic Yankee Clipper.

Somehow Martin, who was twenty-three and had only joined the Yankees in 1950, had quickly become among the few who could break through DiMaggio's aloof exterior. Billy and Joe had lockers next to one another, and Martin would sometimes surprise his teammates by walking into the clubhouse a step or two behind DiMaggio without Joe realizing he was imitating his distinctive walk. A natural comic, Billy would then continue mirroring DiMaggio mannerisms in what became a Marx brothers routine:

how he ordered his coffee, how he took off his pants, and how he hung up his shirt and coat. "You fresh little bastard," DiMaggio would say.

"I think the reason they became friends," said Phil Rizzuto, "was because Billy would do anything DiMaggio wanted, any time. You had to want to do anything Joe wanted to do and, you know, that's hard to do. But Billy was the type who wasn't bothered by that, and Billy loved Joe. He idolized him."

Both DiMaggio and Martin were Italians, which seemed like the only explanation to Joe taking to Billy. Martin also had a way of putting Joe at ease with his frank, unpretentious manner. DiMaggio also had a history of opening up to players who were Italian. Joe and Billy spent hours together, sometimes having dinner together or nursing a beer and talking baseball after a game. Billy also always treated Joe not like a star but like any other teammate. "Billy would say to me, 'He's just like anyone else,'" Whitey Ford said. "'All you have to do is open up when you're around him.' I'd tell him, 'I can't do that.'"

Mantle remembered the DiMaggio-Martin relationship from the 1951 season. "Joe DiMaggio was my hero," Mickey recalled, "but Billy used to play jokes on him and hang around with him. Billy wasn't afraid of Joe, maybe because they both came from San Francisco. Besides, Billy was a fresh kid, and he even pulled some stunts on Joe. There was one in particular I'll never forget. Billy had one of those pens with disappearing ink. Well, Joe would always come to the ballpark in a shirt and tie and these expensive suits. Anyway, I just couldn't believe that Billy would do this, but he goes up to Joe and asks him for an autograph for a friend. And as he hands him the pen, he shoots ink all over Joe's nice-looking suit. Joe started getting angry, telling Billy, 'Damn it, how could you do that?' Well, Billy got a laugh and quickly explained that the ink would disappear. Billy could get away doing things like that with Joe and then going out to eat with him. I used to watch and ask Billy what Joe was like. And he'd say, 'Shit, he's just like anyone else. All you have to do is open up when you're around him.' And I'd say, 'Shit, I couldn't do that.'"

In the days after his return from the minors, Mickey hung especially close to Billy, seeing him almost as a big brother—his personal Svengali. They became roommates on road trips. In New York, they were carefree bachelors, notwithstanding the fact that Billy was married and Mickey was engaged to Merlyn and virtually living with Holly. Mickey and Billy were also becoming big-time drinking buddies, hanging out after games with teammates Hank Bauer and Charlie Silvera. One of their regular spots was the Harwyn Club on the East Side, where on any night Mantle and his pals were rubbing elbows with celebrities and other sports stars. In 1951 that included future heavyweight boxing champion Rocky Marciano. Just as life on the town could be high, through pranks and hijinks it could also sink to lows. Once, at the same Harwyn Club, Mickey and Billy sneaked in a whoopee cushion that they slipped under the seat of a contractor friend as a practical joke that succeeded in erupting their side of the club into an uproar of laughter.

"That place—I was like a kid in a candy store," said Martin friend Jack Setzer, who had grown up with Billy in West Berkeley, California. "I met Joe DiMaggio, Leo Durocher, Charlie Dressen, some umpires—I don't know who—and I met Sid Caesar, Jo Stafford and her husband, Paul Whiting, Imogen Coca, Carl Reiner—the whole 'Show of Shows' cast. . . . And then the other nights on my trip . . . I'm having dinner with Yogi Berra and Mickey Mantle and Billy."

Anyone looking inside the Yankees' clubhouse or in their dugout might not have believed the sight of Mickey and Billy as two merry pranksters, beginning late in the 1951 season and continuing for several years. They bought water pistols that they squirted each other with in the clubhouse. They sneaked Polaroid camera shots of one another on the toilet. They wrestled on the trains when the team traveled on road trips. Mickey had never known that baseball could be such fun.

For Mantle, the world had completely turned around in the less than six weeks' time he had spent in the minors. A day after his return to the Yankees, Mantle slugged a home run off Mike Garcia that helped New York beat the Indians, 7–3. A week later, against the Browns in St. Louis, with his family looking on, Mickey slugged another home run and drove in four runs. In the thirty-seven games after his return to the majors, Mantle hit .283 and drove in twenty runs to help the Yankees win their third straight American League pennant. His strong comeback against American League pitching in the homestretch of the pennant race had reaffirmed the Yankees' faith in him, and he was already looking ahead to the next year with anticipation.

Mutt had been pleased with the courage his son had shown in Kansas City and then with the Yankees after he had been recalled—so much so that he arranged to take time off at the mine to drive to New York to watch Mickey play in the subway series against the Giants. Mickey couldn't wait to show the New York he now knew to his father, or at least the New York he knew Mutt would approve of. Mutt was driving up from Commerce with two of his friends, which was going to make the series a little easier for Mickey. He didn't know what he would have done had the entire Mantle family decided to come to New York and brought Merlyn with them, as they had to St. Louis earlier in the season, especially since Holly would be at all the World Series games at Yankee Stadium.

All summer long Mickey had been vacillating in his emotions, torn between his feelings for Merlyn and the duty he felt to keep his promise to marry her and his newfound love for Holly. Mickey was engaged to Merlyn, but he was sleeping with Holly. He didn't know how he would ever explain Holly to Merlyn and was hoping he wouldn't have to. In fact, after seeing Holly in Mantle's hotel room in Kansas City, Merlyn had come to the realization of impending heartbreak and had decided not to pin her hopes on a future with Mickey, no matter how many assurances she kept getting from Mutt. At the end of September, as the baseball season was winding down, Merlyn had quit her job at a local bank in Commerce and relocated to Albuquerque, New Mexico, presumably to get a fresh start on life. She continued to wear the engagement ring Mickey had given her, though how much sentiment Mantle had invested was questionable. Merlyn's ring had been bought by Theodore Mantle, Mickey's half brother, who had used most of his army discharge pay to help pay for it. Additionally, the fact that no wedding date had been set may have said even more about the solidity of Merlyn and Mickey's relationship.

Meanwhile, Holly had Mickey all to herself in Manhattan. She had helped him adjust to life in the big city, which had been part of the problem that had doomed Mantle midway through the season. However, he now felt he knew how to balance his life off the field with his responsibilities as a Yankee. Mickey was both in love and indebted to Holly and uncertain of what to do next. He wanted his father to get to know her better, and he was hoping that if he did, he would understand that he needed her in his life.

Mantle, however, couldn't effectively stand up to his father. Mutt went to his grave with a domineering father's hold over his son, who would have done anything to please him. Mickey's notion that his father would come around to approving of Holly was a childlike dream. He sensed that the moment Mutt met Holly, and so did Holly.

"Mickey, you do the right thing and marry your own kind," Mutt said to Mickey after pulling his son aside.

Mantle tried to explain his relationship.

"Merlyn's a sweet girl," Mutt said, cutting him off, "and she's in love with you."

"Yeah, I know."

"The point is, she's good for you," said Mutt. "She's what you need to keep your head straight."

"I know."

"Well, then after the series, you ought get on home and marry her."

However, Holly said that as the 1951 regular season drew to a close, the issue of Mickey's future with either Merlyn or her was far from decided. When Mutt was nearby, his influence over his son was extraordinary, beyond the usual father-son relationship. New York, though, had already changed Mickey, who had come to realize that the provincialism of Oklahoma had dated his father's beliefs and that they were each part of separate generations. Holly was also symbolic of that growing divide between father and son and their two generations.

"We didn't talk that much," Mickey said, talking about his father in an interview years later. "First of all, we didn't have a phone in Whitebird, Oklahoma, and that's where we was living at that time. We didn't talk a lot, but I knew he was watching the papers to see what I was doing or listening to the radio if he ever had the chance. I knew he was paying attention and watching what I was doing and everything, and I know it made him really proud that after he left [Kansas City] that I started doing a lot better."

Holly told me that at the height of the pennant chase, she was surprised by Mickey again talking about them marrying at the end of the season. Mantle figured that once the World Series was over and his father was on his way back to Oklahoma, he and Holly would elope, possibly to Niagara Falls, which at the time was the place for honeymooners.

"Mickey said to me, 'I don't suppose you want to marry me?' That was his proposal," Holly remembered. "He really didn't want to marry [Merlyn]. He never, ever, really loved Merlyn, never."

Mickey Mantle's career took a dramatic slide in the 1960s because of mounting injuries and his notorious drinking. But when he was sober, The Mick still sported that golden-boy look that made him a 1950s symbol of the proverbial All-American kid next door. *Courtesy of the Mickey Mantle Museum, Cooperstown, N.Y., and Tom Catal and Andrew Vilacky.*

Roger Maris and Mickey Mantle were christened the M&M Boys during the ·
1961 season when they made their separate runs at Babe Ruth's single-season
home-run record of 60, which had stood since 1927. Maris eventually broke
the record, hitting his 61st home run on the final day of the season. Mantle hit
54 before he was sidelined in September because of an abscessed hip. Mantle
and Maris still hold the single-season record for combined home runs by a pair
of teammates, with 115. *Courtesy of the Mickey Mantle Museum, Cooperstown,
N.Y., and Tom Catal and Andrew Vilacky.*

Mickey Mantle and Hank Aaron played against each other in the 1957 and 1958 World Series, with the Milwaukee Braves winning the first matchup and the Yankees the second. Aaron would go on to break Babe Ruth's career home-run record. The always humble Mantle said of Aaron in 1970, "As far as I'm concerned, Aaron is the best ball player of my era. He is to baseball of the last fifteen years what Joe DiMaggio was before him. He's never received the credit he's due." *Courtesy of the Mickey Mantle Museum, Cooperstown, N.Y., and Tom Catal and Andrew Vilacky.*

Mickey Mantle and Whitey Ford were the best of friends on the greatest of teams, with Mickey the switch-hitting slugging sensation and Whitey the team's best pitcher. A story not well known that Mantle loved to tell was that Whitey had actually tried out for the Yankees as a first baseman. Fortunately, one of the coaches at the tryout noticed that Ford had a strong arm and asked him if he had ever pitched. *Courtesy of the Mickey Mantle Museum, Cooperstown, N.Y., and Tom Catal and Andrew Vilacky.*

Manager Casey Stengel places the crown emblematic of baseball's Triple Crown, which Mantle won in 1956 when he led the American League in home runs, RBIs, and batting average, on Mickey's head. Mickey chased Babe Ruth's single-season home-run record of 60 and had 47 at the end of August, but he hit only five homers in September. *Courtesy of the Mickey Mantle Museum, Cooperstown, N.Y., and Tom Catal and Andrew Vilacky.*

After Babe Ruth's death in 1948, his widow, Claire Ruth, became the keeper of Babe's flame, regularly attending Opening Day and other special events at Yankee Stadium. In 1961 she took special interest in the pursuit of Ruth's single-season home-run record by Roger Maris and Mickey Mantle. Maris won their titanic contest, breaking Ruth's record when he hit home run no. 61 on the final day of the season. *Courtesy of the Mickey Mantle Museum, Cooperstown, N.Y., and Tom Catal and Andrew Vilacky.*

With Casey Stengel looking over his shoulder, Mickey Mantle uses his favorite bat from his 1956 Triple Crown season to point at the incomparable Babe Ruth, the immortal whom Mick's manager predicted his young slugger would surpass. *Courtesy of the Mickey Mantle Museum, Cooperstown, N.Y., and Tom Catal and Andrew Vilacky.*

A frustrated Mickey Mantle tosses his batting helmet in disgust after striking out in a famous photograph that symbolized the Yankees' disastrous 1965 season when the historic run that included seven World Series championships and a dozen American League pennants ended. *Courtesy of the Mickey Mantle Museum, Cooperstown, N.Y., and Tom Catal and Andrew Vilacky.*

After their 1961 chase of Babe Ruth's home-run record, Mickey Mantle and Roger Maris made the film Safe at Home! and then made a cameo appearance in Doris Day's and Cary Grant's romantic comedy That Touch of Mink. Mantle later boasted that Doris Day had been one of his sexual conquests. Day would make no comment on the claim. Safe at Home! producer Mike Hamilburg, who befriended Mantle during their filming and maintained that friendship until his death, said that Mantle told him he had made the claim as a joke, which some gullible writers had taken seriously. *Courtesy of the Mickey Mantle Museum, Cooperstown, N.Y., and Tom Catal and Andrew Vilacky.*

Retired legend Joe DiMaggio and Mickey Mantle accompany Mick's mom, Mrs. Lovell Mantle, at ceremonies for Mickey Mantle Day at Yankee Stadium near the end of the 1965 season. *Courtesy of the Mickey Mantle Museum, Cooperstown, N.Y., and Tom Catal and Andrew Vilacky.*

Merlyn Mantle remained the loyal, dedicated wife to her husband from their days as high school sweethearts through a storybook baseball romance with troubling times that tested her love and devotion. *Courtesy of the Mickey Mantle Museum, Cooperstown, N.Y., and Tom Catal and Andrew Vilacky.*

Looking as if he was destined to be there himself, Mickey Mantle stands next to the monuments of baseball legends Lou Gehrig, Miller Huggins, and Babe Ruth that used to be part of the playing field in deep center of the original Yankee Stadium. Since then, the monuments—plus others honoring Mantle and Joe DiMaggio—have been moved to the new Yankee Stadium Monument Park beyond the outfield fence. *Courtesy of the Mickey Mantle Museum, Cooperstown, N.Y., and Tom Catal and Andrew Vilacky.*

PART THREE

THE BEST THERE EVER WILL BE

The nicest thing anyone ever said to me was the lady who came up to me one day when things were going bad, and she says, "Don't feel like you're doomed. That's just being human. You'll never be stronger than you are now."

—MICKEY MANTLE

Prologue

"I Gave You Such a Good Start . . ."

Mickey Mantle once told me that as he approached the age of forty—an age by which time he used to think he would be dead—he sometimes looked back on his life and wished he could have had a conversation with himself as a boy.

"What would you have said to him?" I asked. Didn't we all have thoughts about what advice we would share with our younger selves? But Mickey startled me.

"I think the important thing," he said, "is what he might have said to me."

Mickey was sober, which perhaps might have explained the unexpected profundity of what he had just said. He hadn't had a drink since late morning, and he was sober now only because we had been on the road from North Dallas to Waco to play a round of golf at the Lake Waco Golf Course, public links on which I had learned the game. That summer, the summer of 1971, we had been playing at Mickey's club, Preston Trails, as well as on public courses around Dallas. I'd been complaining about those golf courses because they were mostly open grassy plains with few of the country club charms of Lake Waco, like its oak tree-lined fairways resembling those of Augusta National, home of the Masters Tournament. With that kind of buildup, Lake Waco was a course Mickey insisted we had to play. So here we were on the southbound part of the still-to-be-completed Interstate 35, me driving his new El Dorado because Mickey thought he would catch up on his sleep, though he remained wide awake.

"So what is it you think your younger self would have said?" I asked.

Mickey squirmed for a moment. He seemed to know the answer, as if this might have been a conversation he had imagined having with himself on more than one occasion. "Well, maybe he would have said, 'Why are you in such a bad place right now when I gave you such a good start?'"

I couldn't believe I was hearing those words, repeating them to myself, hoping I would not forget them. The child within Mickey saw him now being in a "bad place" in his life, which must have meant that this was how Mantle viewed himself just a few months shy of his fortieth birthday. How could he feel himself to be in a "bad place." When he retired before the 1969 season, he was third on the all-time home run list with 536. In three years, when he would become eligible, he was virtually assured of being elected to baseball's Hall of Fame. His knees were bad. They had been bad for more than a decade now, but otherwise he seemed to possibly be one of the healthiest forty-year-old men in America and arguably its most famous. So why this negativity?

He gave me one of what I came to call his "Mantle ahs," half-grunt verbal shrugs kissing off the topic of conversation. We had broached it a couple of other times: retirement. Mickey didn't know what to do with it. Do any of us? In Mickey's case, though, he actually hadn't counted on living this long and being this healthy at this age. It was a topic of amusement among his chroniclers: Mickey Mantle surviving the family curse in which many of the clan's men had perished by the age of forty, his father Mutt among them. What it meant for Mickey was middle age, married to a teenage sweetheart he barely knew, and having no skill beyond being a baseball player, a washed-up one now, like one of those prize fighters who would come into the public consciousness again every time he entered the ring at an introduction for a title bout among new fighters. How did Rocky Marciano, Carmen Basilio, and Sugar Ray Robinson handle life as has-beens, and was it any easier being a little too punch-drunk to care? Mickey wasn't punch-drunk, and he didn't want to rest on an introduction on past laurels.

"Oh, man, maybe it would be so much easier if I still didn't so easily remember," he said at last.

"Remember? Remember how great it was?"

"Yeah, that. And how much greater it could have been. You don't realize it, until it's no longer there."

17

Best in the Game

A lot's been made of how I was a favorite of my teammates. Well, Case was responsible for making me that. He was such a horse's ass to play-ers that someone had to stand up to him, and I was the only one he couldn't fuck with.

—Mickey Mantle

In a sparsely populated section of the Park Lawn Memorial Park in the Los Angeles suburb of Commerce lies the grave of Califor-nia transplant John Alton Benton, interred with his wife of thirty-four years Moneta. The inscription on their joint gravestone lovingly reads "Together Forever." It is an epitaph that could serve for his two-decade career in professional baseball where he is remembered in the game's his-tory as the only pitcher to have faced both Yankee slugging legends Babe Ruth and Mickey Mantle. There, too, they are together forever.

Perhaps it speaks for Benton's pitching prowess that neither Ruth nor Mantle, who together hit 1,250 home runs, homered against him.

Benton made his major league debut for the Philadelphia Athletics in the game in which he pitched to Ruth on April 18, 1934, the second game of what would be The Babe's final season with the Yankees. At the time Mickey Mantle was a two-and-a-half-year-old toddler in Spavinaw, Oklahoma. Benton relieved the Athletics' starter in the third inning and pitched four and two-thirds innings, facing Ruth twice and retiring him both times. The Babe did slug his first home run of the season, an eighth-inning solo shot off Tim McKeithan.

Benton closed out an eighteen-year career with the Boston Red Sox where on July 2, 1952, he relieved in the seventh inning, pitched two and a third hitless innings, and earned a save in a 5–4 win over the Yankees. Among the Yankees he faced and retired was the twenty-year-old Mantle who was in his second season, a season in which he would establish himself. He helped lead the Yankees to their fourth straight pennant with a .311 batting average, twenty-three home runs, and eighty-seven RBIs, good enough to make a run at the Most Valuable Player award in which he finished third in the balloting.

It was in the World Series, however, where Mickey made his name—where Mickey Mantle became Mickey Mantle. He batted .345 and decided the seventh game with a tie-breaking home run off Joe Black as well as driving in an insurance run in the Yankees' 4–2 victory over Brooklyn.

The National League champion Dodgers were suitably impressed, especially their star Jackie Robinson. Mantle's hustle outplayed even that of the fabled racial trailblazer. Mickey made a spectacular defensive play off a line drive Robinson hit into right center field. Casey Stengel had tipped Mickey that on a hit like that, Jackie would be on the lookout for his throw. The Yankees' scouting report on the Dodgers noted that it was ever-aggressive Robinson's tendency to take a big turn around first base and to immediately try to take second base if the outfielder threw the ball behind him. So when Mantle fielded the single on the third hop, he looked toward Yankee first baseman Johnny Mize and began his throwing motion to first base. Seeing this, Robinson, who had made his anticipated big turn around first base, quickly took off for second base. Mickey, though, had faked the throw to first base and fired instead to Billy Martin covering second base. Jackie Robinson was easily thrown out.

"I'll never forget the sight," Mantle recalled. "Jackie getting up, dusting himself off, and giving me a little tip of the hat, his eyes saying, 'I'll get you next time.'"

After the Yankees won the seventh game, Robinson swallowed his disappointment long enough to go into the Yankee clubhouse to personally congratulate Mantle. "You're a helluva ballplayer," he told Mickey.

"Man, what a classy guy," Mantle said years later. "I never could have done that, not in a million years. I'm a really bad loser."

"Mantle beat us," Robinson told reporters after the game. "He was the difference between the two clubs. They didn't miss Joe DiMaggio. It was Mickey Mantle who killed us."

Later, reflecting on his early years with the Yankees in an interview after his retirement, Mantle would credit Jackie Robinson for raising his consciousness on race, equality, and civil rights. "I don't know if until the series in '52, if there'd ever been another player I played against who praised me the way Jackie did then," he said. "On top of winning the series, there he was in our clubhouse, not just congratulating me but saying, 'You're gonna be a great player, kid. You're gonna be a great player, kid.' That meant a lot, especially after the year I'd been through, with my father dying that May and all. I can't tell you how thrilled he would've been to hear Jackie Robinson say that about his son."

Meanwhile, Mickey's growing friendship with Billy Martin began to infuriate Stengel, who would never be able to communicate with Mantle in the way he so desperately wanted to. Was Stengel jealous that the young player whom he thought would be his Mel Ott had chosen not to pursue that kind of relationship with him? Had the childless Casey Stengel, after Mutt Mantle's death during the 1952 season, expected to fill the role of Mickey's surrogate father? Did Stengel sense that the one player he saw as his personal athletic creation had a mind of his own and a world in which Casey figured only as his manager? Those are serious questions that Stengel's own biographer, Robert W. Creamer, believed had legitimate credibility. He found that the Yankee manager was bitter and unforgiving about one player, "almost irrationally so." That player, of course, was Mickey Mantle. Stengel's feelings only intensified in the coming years.

"He's gotta change a lot," Casey said after the disappointing 1954 season when the Indians ended the Yankees' five-year hold on the American League pennant. "He's gotta change his attitude and stop sulking and doing things he's told not to do. He'll have to grow up and become the great player he should be when he reports next spring."

Near the top of the list of Stengel's frustrations with Mantle were the injuries that plagued Mickey after the knee injury from the 1951

World Series. There were so many that Casey couldn't keep up with them, from season to season, from month to month, and from one body part to another. Casey should have called it Mantle-itis. Muscles, ligaments, cartilage. Pitcher Tommy John would suffer one injury to his arm and eventually have a surgery to repair the injury named after him. That being the case, an argument could be made for Mickey Mantle's name to be attached to much of a ballplayer's anatomy. "I never saw Mickey when he wasn't in pain from some injury he had suffered," Whitey Ford told me in an interview. "I'm surprised he didn't leave his body for sports medicine to study."

Much would be made of how Mantle would be only a shadow of the player he was after his 1951 World Series knee injury. After that, rarely a season went by when he didn't sustain a serious injury that would keep him out for weeks, though often he usually played through them. It is questionable, however, that Mickey ever fully recovered from any of the injuries, as he was a careless patient who usually failed to follow strict rehabilitation programs designed to strengthen the injured muscles and tendons. In the off-seasons he paid little attention to Merlyn's urging that he follow doctors' orders, and Billy Martin was useless in keeping his best friend on the training and rehab routines he needed for full recovery. Later in Mickey's career, *Sports Illustrated*'s Jack Mann would write that "Mantle, the one-man orthopedic ward, is even more a symbol of the Yankees in crisis than he was in their predominance. He plays on, on agonized legs that would keep a clerk in bed, and the opposition wonders how."

No one was more aware of Mantle's dedication to play while injured than Stengel, who often played head games with Mickey when he had no business being on the field. Knowing Mantle was hurting from the pain in his legs, Stengel would sometimes approach his ailing star in the clubhouse.

"Well," Stengel would say, approaching Mantle when he was clearly in pain, "I guess I better keep you out today."

Mantle never wanted anyone feeling sorry for him, so his pride would well up.

"Goddamn it, Case," he would tell his manager, "put me in."

Mickey didn't realize that Stengel already had his lineup card made out with his ailing star's name on it.

Stengel was also not above using Mickey's high tolerance for pain as an example for motivating his injured players to play despite the pain. To some, Mantle's locker in the clubhouse took on being a kind of religious alcove within the cathedral that was Yankee Stadium. There, before every game, Mickey could be seen going through his ritual of bandaging his legs from his thighs to his ankles, even when he was healthy, for preventive purposes. Awestruck teammates couldn't help but be inspired by Saint Mickey. Over the years they spoke of how he courageously endured the endless pain from all his injuries. Word spread through the league, and opposing players were moved by his dedication and inspiration, feeling the same way, and some recognized what Mantle was accomplishing despite the injuries. "On two legs," said White Sox second baseman Nellie Fox, "Mickey Mantle would have been the greatest ball player who ever lived."

In Stengel's mind, though, the problem all stemmed from Mickey's 1951 World Series injury and his failure to rehabilitate properly. Casey traced Mantle's future physical problems and his unavailability for development instruction in subsequent spring training camps to that one moment.

"If he did what he was told after the first operation," Stengel later said, "he would be able to play now. This kid—you can't ever teach him nothing in the spring because he's always hurt. You want to work with him batting left-handed and you can't. You want to do something for him and he don't let you. What's the good of telling him what to do? No matter what you tell him, he'll do what he wants. He's got it here and here." Casey touched his arm and his body; then, tapping the side of his head, "But he ain't got it here."

Stengel's biographer Robert Creamer wrote that it was "doubtful that [Casey would] have had much luck teaching Mantle. Once when Mickey was having trouble with his bunting, Stengel arranged for Frank Crosetti, the coach, who had been a skillful bunter, to work with Mantle each day before practice. Crosetti showed up for the sessions, but Mantle didn't. After three fruitless days the lessons were abandoned. . . . Stengel was never able to teach Mantle because he was never able to reach him. It was a genuine father-son relationship, but it was an angry father and a stubborn son."

Tragically, Stengel even became physically abusive with Mantle, according to Billy Martin. "Once I saw the old man grab Mickey by the back of the neck and shake him hard when he did something the old man didn't like," Martin recalled. "He said, 'Don't let me see you do that again, you little bastard!' Can you imagine him doing that to Mickey?"

Of course, this occurred at a time when managers and coaches could get away with that kind of abuse, especially since neither the public nor the sportswriters ever saw this private, petty side of Stengel. Stengel was also riding a phenomenal winning streak that included World Series titles in 1952 and 1953 as Casey topped Joe McCarthy's record of four consecutive championships. Even after that incredible run of five straight titles ended in 1954, it was difficult for the Yankee management, writers, or fans to put the blame on Stengel—even if he had boldly declared that spring that "if the Yankees don't win the pennant, the owners should discharge me." The Yankees won 103 games, beaten by the Cleveland Indians who set an American League record by winning a phenomenal 111 games. Stengel wasn't fired.

By this time, too, Casey had fully established himself as the darling of the writers covering the top sports team in America. Nobody called them America's Team, the designation eventually claimed by the Dallas Cowboys in the 1960s, but they could have. Those writers did as much in creating a mythology around Stengel as they did around Mantle. But with Mickey, it was his exploits on the field that spoke for him. For Stengel, it was his mouth, colorful language, and the accessibility for quotes. Casey exploited this role as few managers or coaches ever have. He had used the writers to build up Mickey and the Mantle myth, and he used them as well to detail the flaws and shortcomings of the New York hero. It added to the animosity between Mantle and the press that turned mean and petty. "His anger, his ability to look right through men he dealt with every day, men whose reporting had in general helped build the myth of Mantle as the greatest ballplayer of his era, could be shattering," observed author David Halberstam. "Once when Maury Allen, the beat writer on the *Post*, was standing near the batting cage and Mantle was taking batting practice, Mantle turned to him and said, 'You piss me off just standing there.'

That became something of a motto in the Allen household when one member of the Allen family was irritated with another."

But there was no way anything Casey now said could derail the Mantle myth. It survived Mickey's own early struggles. It survived his increasingly bad behavior and water-cooler-demolishing temper tantrums. It even survived the fans who booed him for any number of reasons: his replacement of DiMaggio in center field, his draft deferment status, his failure to immediately be the super baseball hero everyone was talking about in 1951. Even if some of the writers bought the knocks laid on Mickey by his manager, how could anyone ignore the greatest home run hitter anyone had seen in the game since, well, since Babe Ruth?

The very foundation for the growing Mantle myth was his incredible power, unknown in the game until his arrival. Early in his third season, on April 17, 1953, Mickey slugged what was then believed to be the longest home run ever hit in major league baseball. He drove a pitch from Senators' southpaw Chuck Stobbs over the fifty-five-foot-high wall behind the left field bleachers in Washington's old Griffith Stadium. The ball Mickey hit cleared the park's 391-foot mark, clipped a sixty-foot-high beer sign on the stadium's football scoreboard estimated to be 460 feet from home plate. Then it stayed on its course until landing in a resident's yard. A ten-year-old Donald Dunaway found the ball there, and soon Yankee publicity director Red Patterson added his spin to the phenomenal feat. Patterson produced the story of how he had immediately bolted from his press box seat, tracking down the baseball, and measured that the Yankee's twenty-one-year-old star had hit the ball an unbelievable 565 feet. Mickey Mantle had just given baseball the tape-measure home run. Of course Ruth and Gehrig had hit prodigious blasts of their own. Gehrig once hit an exhibition home run that reportedly traveled 611 feet. But their dingers didn't become part of the pop culture lore the way that Mantle's tape-measure homers did in the 1950s.

Mantle and his historic home run in Washington dominated the sports pages for days. It was not yet the era of fabricated accounts, so no one would take issue with what Yankee officialdom had decreed. That would come later. Mantle eventually said that Patterson told him he had never left the stadium but had been given the ball by the youngster who found it and then guessed at the distance and came up with 565 feet. The exact distance was irrelevant then or later. Nobody in the major leagues or in the Negro leagues, whose teams also played at Griffith Stadium, had ever hit a ball over the bleachers there. The wind was blowing that day in Washington, but Senators owner Clark Griffith said it hadn't made any difference. "I don't care about that," he said. "That wind has been blowing for 100 years, and nobody else ever hit one out of this ballpark like that."

That distinction would be Mickey Mantle's alone, and his home run became a baseball equivalent of a religious miracle. Mickey's home run ball and Mantle's bat were soon placed on display at the National Baseball Hall of Fame in Cooperstown, New York. Go match that, Lourdes.

Nothing baseball put in Mantle's path could stop the forces of Mantle destiny, not even the fabled 1953 Dodgers team that would come to be immortalized as the "Boys of Summer." They won the National League pennant by thirteen games over the Milwaukee Braves, and what a team they were. Could they finally win the World Series championship that had eluded the Dodgers in six previous fall classics? Their leader was a fabulous hitting catcher who had become a myth of his own. Roy Campanella won the league's Most Valuable Player award, hitting forty-one homers and driving in 142 runs. He was supported by center fielder Duke Snider who slugged forty-two home runs and drove in 126 runs, and first baseman Gil Hodges who hit thirty-one homers and knocked in 122 runs. Then there were right fielder Carl Furillo who won the National League batting championship with a .344 average and Jackie Robinson who batted .329. Not to be left out of the acclaim was Dodgers second baseman Jim Gilliam who won the league's Rookie of the Year award. But even the Boys of Summer were no match for the Yankees, who won the series in six games. Mickey helped win game 2 with a two-run homer and then belted a grand slam in the game 5 triumph that put the Yankees ahead.

With this championship, Casey Stengel also cemented his legacy as being on the same level as his hero John McGraw. No team had even won five consecutive World Series championships. Stengel, however, still wasn't completely satisfied with the development of his Mel Ott. His ongoing pet peeve with Mickey—which would continue for as long as he managed the Yankees—was his high number of strikeouts, in which he led the American League five times. The Yankee manager wanted Mantle to cut down on his powerful swing, especially on a two-strike count. In fact, Stengel wanted Mickey to change much of his approach to hitting. He specifically wanted him to curb his uppercut swing and instead to "hit down on the ball," the approach to hitting that was popular at the time. Mantle would put more balls in play, Stengel believed, and still hit with power. Mickey, though, was not about to change the one thing that still linked him to his father. It was as if Mutt Mantle's teachings on hitting were sacred scrolls to his son. Mantle also wasn't convinced that Casey Stengel could teach him anything about hitting.

In the 1953 World Series, Stengel would at least reach an accommodation with his hard-headed star. Casey's solution to curbing Mickey's strikeouts had been to keep him on a strict regimen of looking to the third base coach whenever he had a two-balls, no-strikes count. Too often, Stengel figured, the opposition was pitching around Mantle, willing to walk him, or trying to lure him into swinging at pitches outside the strike zone. Usually on a 2–0 count, Stengel would flash the Yankees' third-base coach the "take" sign to signal to Mickey. But in game 2, with the score tied 2–2 in the bottom of the eighth inning, Mantle came to bat right-handed against left-hander Preacher Roe, who faced him with Hank Bauer on first and two outs. When Mickey went up on the count to 2–0, he expected to get the "take" sign. Instead, Stengel flashed the "hit" sign. Mantle parked Roe's next pitch to the left field stands to give the Yankees a 4–2 lead. The strategy made Stengel look like a genius.

"One bad pitch," Stengel boasted to reporters after the game, "can decide any game in this Series, and maybe the Series."

Mickey recalled that game with a particular sense of irony in one of our 1970 conversations.

"I hit the home run, and Case considers himself a genius," Mantle said. "Casey was an okay hitter when he played, but let's be serious here. I once asked Billy to check for me, and it turned out that in his entire career Casey hit sixty home runs. Babe Ruth hit sixty home runs in one season. Christ, fuck, I'd listen to Babe Ruth if he said, 'Mick, let me give you a tip or two about hitting.' But I sure as hell wasn't going to take advice from a goddamn fungo hitter!"

18

Angels and Demons

If I thought praying would help me hit home runs, I would have been in church every day.

—MICKEY MANTLE

THE FIRST TIME MICKEY MANTLE ATTENDED MASS IN HIS LIFE WAS April 20, 1956, a Friday, the day of the Yankees' season home opener against the Boston Red Sox. Mickey wasn't a Roman Catholic, but his teammate and best friend Billy Martin was. Billy had crashed at Mantle's room at the St. Moritz to finish a Thursday night of heavy partying after returning to New York from Washington, D.C., and insisted that Mick and his longtime girlfriend Holly Brooke join him in attending services at St. Patrick's Cathedral. Mantle initially resisted the idea. Hungover and with a game to play that afternoon, Mantle wanted no part of attending an early morning Mass, nor any other church service for that matter.

"I don't go to church, Billy," Mantle said to his teammate, Holly Brooke would recall years later. "I can't remember the last time I went to church."

"It'll be good for you," Billy said. "DiMaggio went to Mass before every home opener. Every time I went to Mass with him, I'd get a big hit."

Mickey hurried to get dressed. He had vowed to avenge the way he had finished the 1955 season. Mantle had been the American League's top slugger in 1955, leading in home runs, slugging, on base percentage, and extra base hits, while batting .306. However, he had not been healthy for the World Series, unable to run, and had not played in the deciding seventh game in which the Yankees lost the series to the

Brooklyn Dodgers. Only three games into the 1956 season, Mantle was looking for any edge he could get, physical or spiritual, for the long year ahead.

Holly also convinced him he would enjoy seeing the architecture at St. Patrick's Cathedral, one of the notable landmarks in his adopted city, which he was still exploring in his sixth season with the Yankees. St. Patrick's, she told him, was also the largest decorated neo-Gothic-style Catholic cathedral in North America.

"They held Babe Ruth's funeral there," Holly said. "I remember reading that the cathedral was packed. People couldn't get in, and they had 50,000 mourners waiting outside in the rain."

"Fifty thousand?" said Mantle. "That's almost as many as what Yankee Stadium holds."

Actually the number of mourners had been estimated at 75,000—bigger than the capacity of Yankee Stadium—who weathered intermittent heavy rain outside St. Patrick's that August day in 1948. Cardinal Francis Spellman officiated the Funeral Mass in his role as the sixth archbishop of the Archdiocese of New York, as well as the leading clerical fan of the New York Yankees. In the 1940s, the cardinal, with a familiar and towering presence in the city, often hosted Joe DiMaggio for private dinners at the archdiocese. It had been on one of those occasions where DiMaggio had asked his eminence if his teammate, fellow Italian, and fellow Roman Catholic Billy Martin could join them. Spellman had readily agreed. No Roman Catholic in America typified clerical association with power more than Spellman, who had been a confidante of President Franklin D. Roosevelt, a friend of Joseph P. Kennedy Sr., and so influential in national affairs that his official residence around the corner from St. Patrick's Cathedral had been nicknamed "The Powerhouse."

Late for the early weekday service, Billy assured Mickey and Holly that they didn't need to fret. They were there to see someone after Mass, when they were soon greeted by a familiar figure. Mantle had seen Cardinal Spellman on several occasions at Yankee Stadium, but he had never met him.

"Billy, I am so glad you came," Spellman said. "I wanted to ask you about Joe. Now that he's not playing, I rarely ever see him."

"Me neither, your grace," Martin said. "He's living in San Francisco, and I don't think he keeps the apartment here in New York anymore."

"He hasn't returned any of my messages," the cardinal said. "Is he here for today's home opener?"

Mantle and Holly looked on, uncertain what to say, if anything at all, as Billy looked at the cathedral floor a long time. "I don't know if Joe is here for today's game, your eminence," Martin finally said. "But if he's here, I'll ask him to call you."

Then Billy surprised Mickey with an introduction to the cardinal.

"Your grace, I don't know if you recognize who I have with me. It's the fella who replaced Joe in center field. Your grace, it's my honor to present Mickey Mantle and his friend, Holly Brooke."

The cardinal's blush was that of a fan. "Mickey, I thought that was you," he said. "And Miss Brooke?"

Holly wasn't sure what the protocol was. She half curtsied and bowed her head. Mickey extended his right hand to shake the cardinal's hand.

"My, this is a special day," the cardinal said. "Mickey, will we be seeing you here with Billy?"

Mantle didn't know what to say. "Well, Cardinal Spellman, I have to confess that I don't know a lot about religion. I don't think God hears me."

"I can't believe that," said the cardinal. "You're one of God's children. Put no stock in religion for religion's sake. Place your faith in God. He hears you. He will answer your prayers. And by everything I read about what a gifted ballplayer you are, he's been answering someone's prayers. Mickey, your talents are a gift from God."

Spellman smiled broadly and made the sign of the cross, blessing Holly along with the two Yankee players. Holly would remember every word of the meeting and recount them years later. Then the cardinal walked them out.

"Billy, it would be nice to see you at Mass more often," Holly recalled the cardinal telling Martin.

"I come when I can," said Billy, who could hardly plead a case for not needing religion. In his career as a player for the Yankees, as well as his time as a manager years later, Martin had been a poster child of self-destruction. He got drunk, insulted umpires and Yankees team owners, kicked dirt at umpires, flaunted his mistress at the ballpark, and got into barroom brawls. But Billy had an infectious charm that had made him Joe DiMaggio's closest friend on the team, that drew people to him, and that led them to forgive his sins.

"Yes, but I see you only a couple of times a year," said Spellman. "Billy, I know you were a soldier defending your country. Now I wish I could recruit you into the army of God."

Mantle snickered under his breath, and Holly was forced to gently elbow him.

"Well, your eminence, I am already in God's army," Billy said.

The cardinal stopped and looked at him curiously. "Really?"

"Yes, eminence," said Martin. "You just don't see me because Mick and I are in God's secret service."

The cardinal let loose an unexpected, long laugh that broke the solemnity of the majestic cathedral and seemed to multiply and combine into a soft, rollicking echo that reverberated along the rows of carved stone pillars rising in graceful arches supporting the massive stone vaulted ceiling high overhead.

That afternoon, Billy Martin got two hits and scored two runs. Mickey Mantle slugged his third home run of that young season and drove in four runs. He had been blessed. It was going to be a great year.

19

The Last American Hero

I was supposed to break Babe Ruth's records. To be real honest, I can't help but have wished that it had been the other way around.
—MICKEY MANTLE

MICKEY MANTLE USED TO SAY THAT SOMETIMES HE DIDN'T KNOW WHAT part of his life was real and what was a dream, which perhaps is understandable when you have come to a place in your existence after the cheering and the sun, the brandy and Kahlua champions' breakfasts, and all the vodka and the golden blondes and brunettes who too often had kept you in bed until 5:00 a.m., with thoughts surfing on the suicidal if you'd indulged in enough of the uppers they secretly fed you to need three Tuinals to reduce agitation. When you reached that point, did it really matter what was real and what wasn't? In the early 1960s, this was what he had asked his longtime girlfriend Holly Brooke. They were only occasional lovers by then, she told me, but still good friends. They'd had a tremendous friendship during the past decade.

"I saw the rise and creation of Mickey Mantle," she said. "I guess on some level I didn't understand then I'd seen the slow self-destruction of Mickey Mantle as well."

Sometimes she bore witness from close quarters even when Mickey didn't immediately know she was around. She distinctly remembered one summer night during the height of Mickey's reign as crown prince of the city in great seasons of the mid-1950s. This wasn't a dream but a recollection of a wild and wonderful time of her great love's escapades in the city.

Holly remembered one special rainy, slick, wet, miserable midsummer night in Manhattan's theater district:

Taxi and umbrellas are congested everywhere as well-dressed pedestrians push, run, and wave down cabs. The unremitting sounds of honking and shouting play against the dull pitter-patter of rain. The glare of yellow, red, and green lights reflects off the pavement and cars. Near Times Square the rain falls on the street bums and aged poor. Junkies stand around on rainy street corners; hookers still prowl rainy sidewalks. There is a sense of a deflowering element of New York in myth and society: lost innocence, lost souls, and the damaging effects of the city.

A cab pulls up in front of Toot Shor's. The rain has let up. Three men step out of the cab, all dressed in suits . . . all three carrying a can of beer. It's Mickey, Billy Martin, and Whitey Ford. They have one last swig. Whitey spots a trash can some twenty feet away and, setting up like a free-throw shooter, sinks his shot. Then, mixing up his games, he does an umpire's imitation.

"Steeee-rrike!" shouts Ford.

Mickey and Billy eye each other.

"Okay, slick," says Martin to Mantle. "Fifty says I make mine and you don't."

"You realize I was the Oklahoma state free-throw champ?" says Mickey.

"Yeah?" says Martin. "Well, then I go first."

Without waiting for an answer, Martin hits his shot. Mickey then sets up, and just as he shoots, Billy jumps in front of him as if to block the shot. Mantle's beer can hits the lip of the trash can and falls onto the street.

"You little shit!"

Martin dashes into the bar with Mantle giving chase.

Inside Toots Shor's, the restaurant and lounge are crowded with a lively mix of couples, bachelors, important people and some not so important, showgirls and starlets, and writers and producers. An oversized circular bar dominates the lounge.

Mickey, Billy, and Whitey are drinking hard at a table with teammates Yogi Berra and Hank Bauer, with Toots himself entertaining them. Toots is sitting between Mickey and Yogi. He checks Mantle's drink and sees he needs another.

"Toots," says Mickey, "if only your food was as good as your liquor . . ."

"Whadaya sayin'?" asks Toots, feigning hurt and surprise as he waves a waiter over to the table. "Give us another round here."

"Mick, you're lucky," Toots continues. "I let ballplayers get away with runnin' down my food, but not actors. Lemme tell you what I once did with Chaplin when he complained about my food. Next time he came in, I made 'im wait in line, and I told 'im, 'Let's see you be funny for the people in line for the next twenty minutes.' That fixed his ass!"

Mantle and the others all laugh, as Toots's attention is drawn to someone waiting in line.

"Be right back," he tells the players. "Mick, drink your dinner."

Toots leaves the table, but the guys keep talking.

"Henrich says he brought Eileen here the other night," says Bauer, talking about their coach and former player, "and she hated it. Told Tommy it was a man's bar. Tommy says she said . . ." Bauer then imitates a woman's voice: "Can't we please go to Sardi's? They treat me as well as they treat you there."

The guys have a good laugh just as Toots returns with a tall, husky guy who looks like Ernest Hemingway because he is Ernest Hemingway.

"Guys," says Toots, "want you to meet an important writer who wanted to meet ya. Ernest Hemingway. Ernest, you've probably heard of Mickey Mantle, Billy Martin, Yogi Berra, and Hank Bauer.

"'Course," says Hemingway, who is sweating heavily. "The great Yankees."

The guys all greet Hemingway at the same time. Toots offers him his chair at the table. "Ernest, why don'tcha have a seat while you wait for your party?"

Yogi makes room by scooting over his chair.

"Yeah, have a seat," says Berra. "What paper you with, Ernie?"

Hemingway does a double take.

Minutes later, the players are regaling Hemingway with some of their wildest, craziest stories in what has become a loud, boisterous night of serious drinking. Billy wants Mantle to tell the famous writer his best story, but Mickey is resisting.

"Come on," Billy urges him. "Tell 'im about the cow."

Mickey tries to shoo off the story.

"What cow?" Hemingway is curious.

"Tell 'im the cow story," Billy says again.

Mickey appears hesitant.

"We went huntin' early one morning in Texas . . ." says Billy.

Mickey finally bites. "I knew a guy who had a ranch near Austin, and Billy and me drove down there early one morning," he begins. "I went up to his front door and asked 'im if it was okay, and he said, 'Sure, Mick, but could you do me one big favor? I got an old mule behind the barn that needs puttin' down, and I don't have the heart for it. So if you could, I'd really appreciate it.'

Mantle's face is suddenly lit up as he visibly enjoys telling the story. Everyone around him in the bar is attentively listening.

"So I went back to the car thinking I'd play one on Billy and said, 'That damn sonofabitch won't let us on to hunt, so I'm gonna teach him a lesson.' Then I got my rifle, walked behind the barn, and shot the old mule. I turned to see Billy's face, but he's run off. Next thing I hear are two gunshots. So I go to see what's happened, and Billy says, 'Well, just to make sure he gets the message, I just shot two of his cows.'"

Mickey, Billy, and everyone around them all but roll on the floor with laughter. Mantle is so drunk that he is having trouble sitting upright.

"Slick," says Whitey, "I gotta go hunting with you guys next time."

—◦—

Later that night, Mantle and Martin step out of a cab outside the St. Moritz Hotel, looking drunk but still carrying on. Each is holding a drink glass and leaning on each other for support. Ahead of them a couple has also gotten out of a cab. The man recognizes Mickey.

"It's Mickey Mantle," the man whispers to his wife. He walks over to Mickey, pulling out a pen and a theater program, with his wife trailing behind.

"Hey, Mickey," says the man. "Could you sign this for my kid?"

"No," says Mantle. "Fuck off."

Stunned, the man and his wife retreat toward the hotel entrance, staring at Mantle in disbelief. Mickey and Billy walk away from the couple, look up, and stop dead in their tracks—coming face-to-face with Casey Stengel, who has been watching them from just a few feet away. In his surprise, Mickey drops his drink and the glass shatters on the sidewalk.

"Son," begins Stengel, showing his disapproval, "why is it you somehow manage to disappoint everyone who tries to love ya?"

Stengel walks into the hotel.

Mickey enters the hotel with Billy, and they pass the reception desk when the desk clerk's voice calls out.

"Mr. Mantle . . ." Mickey stops and looks.

"You have a phone call, sir," says the desk clerk, directing him to a phone booth. "You can take it over there."

"Catch you later, Mick," says Billy, walking to the bank of elevators.

Mickey shrugs and heads for a phone booth on the other side of the lobby. It is in semidarkness. Mickey pulls on the cabin door when suddenly a naked, braceleted arm reaches out and pulls him inside.

Inside, Mickey finds himself in the arms of a beautiful redhead. She is in a sexy, off-the-shoulder blouse that reveals a brilliant ivory coloring. Her face and arms glow lusciously. Before Mickey can react, her hands are all over him, wandering playfully, groping him.

"Tell me what you want me to do?" she asks Mantle.

Mickey flashes her an amused grin. It's apparent he knows her—that she could be any woman he's been with in New York. Of course, she is. It's Holly Brooke. There's no room to move so he rests his arms on her shoulders.

"Thought you'd know by now . . ." says Mantle.

"I just like to hear you ask . . ." she says.

Without giving him a chance to answer, she brings an arm up out of Mickey's coat pocket and kisses him hungrily. A room key dangles from her hand.

The next afternoon is one of the dog days of summer. The scoreboard shows that the Yankees are trailing the Orioles late in the game. In the Yankees dugout, Stengel paces up and down the bench. At the far end of the bench, Mantle and Ford are sitting together. Both look beyond hungover. Mickey has a towel over his head and an ice pack nearby. The Yankees are in the field, so Mantle obviously is not in the lineup. Stengel comes up to Mickey, who looks up.

"This flu's the worst," he says.

Stengel scratches his ear and dismisses the comment. "Well, I guess you can't pinch-hit?"

"Nah, nah, Case," says Mantle. "Pencil me in. I can hit."

Stengel considers it, then walks away.

Minutes later the Yankees' Gil McDougald lays down a perfect bunt single. Stengel claps his hands, encouraged his team may be rallying. "Awright! We got it goin' again," he says before looking toward Mickey, whose head is again covered by a towel, and walks in his direction.

Ford nudges Mickey awake.

"Mickey, you're up," says Stengel.

Mantle starts to wobble up, a bit disoriented. He then whispers to Ford, "My cap?"

"You're sittin' on it," Ford tells him.

"Fuck, I can barely focus," Mickey mutters.

"Slick," says Ford, "just hit the first pitch you see."

Mickey smiles crookedly, sticks a badly rumpled cap on his head, and shuffles over to the bat rack to pick out a bat. As he steps out of the dugout, even before he is introduced, the crowd begins to energize with a growing chorus of boos, cheers, and jeers, as the voice of Yankee Stadium announcer Bob Sheppard says, "Pinch-hitting . . . number 7 . . . Mick-ey Man-tle."

Just then, the Orioles manager calls time and walks quickly to the mound to talk to his pitcher.

"He's just another guy," the manager tells his pitcher.

"And leadin' the league in everything," says the pitcher.

"Yeah," says the manager, "includin' hangovers. He smells of booze and pussy, and he ain't never goin' to get around on a fastball."

As Mantle settles in at the plate, we can hear the voice of Yankees radio broadcaster Mel Allen: "Tying run's on first, and Mantle is batting for the first time today. Mick was under the weather with the flu . . ."

No sooner does the pitcher wind and deliver before Mickey strides and unloads.

"Mantle swings at the first pitch . . . ," says Allen.

And the ball explodes off Mickey's bat . . .

"This ball is going, going . . . gone!" yells an excited Allen. "With one swing, Mantle has put the Yanks out in front! How 'bout that!"

The stadium erupts in celebration. Mantle circles the bases, shakes hands with McDougald waiting for him at home, and continues to the dugout where he gets slaps on the back and the rump as he makes his way back to where he had been sitting with Ford, who is visibly amused and shaking his head.

"Great hit, Slick," he tells Mickey. "I dunno how you hit that."

"Fuck, hittin' the ball was easy . . ." says Mantle. "Runnin' around the bases was the tough part."

It is funny. It is poignant. He is our hero larger than life.

"Oh, how I loved that man," Holly said. "Oh, how we all loved him. I wanted him all to my own. I guess we all did."

20

The Triple Crown

I could have ended up buried in a hole in the ground, and I ended up being Mickey Mantle. There must be a god somewhere.
—MICKEY MANTLE

MICKEY MANTLE SOMETIMES HAD NO REAL RECOLLECTION OF HIS FIRST five years in New York. When he looked back, it all was blurry and unclear, as if it had been someone else playing in Yankee Stadium and living his life. Perhaps it was that the excessive booze, which destroyed his career far too early, had damaged his brain as well. Maybe Mickey just didn't want to remember. After all, his rookie year in 1951 had ended chaotically. He had been hurt in the second game of the World Series, and at the hospital he had learned that his father was dying. Then, to please his father, he had married his hometown sweetheart, Merlyn Johnson, during the Christmas holidays, for what would be a long, unhappy union.

When his second season began, he was still limping and hobbling from his knee injury in the World Series. Barely two months into the 1952 season, Mickey's father died of Hodgkin's disease. He had only recently turned forty. That fall, after the Yankees repeated again as World Series champs, Mickey had broken down in tears, crying because his father hadn't been there to celebrate with him. It was the same in 1953. He couldn't even remember his statistics, maybe because they were good but not great—and the expectations still hung like a pinstriped albatross around his neck. In 1954, he reached a baseball milestone, breaking the 100 RBI number in a season, but it seemed like a wasted year: the Yankees lost the pennant to the Cleveland Indians. Finally in 1955, Mickey had slugged thirty-seven home runs and driven in ninety-nine runs. They were all-star numbers, and he was named to his fourth straight American League all-star team. But then the Yankees lost the World Series to the cross-town Dodgers, and the fact of the matter is that Mantle still wasn't the bona fide star of the team. That title belonged to Yogi Berra, who won his third Most Valuable Player award to go with the trophies from 1951 and 1954.

"I was an All-Star, but, fuck, let's face it—other than some moments here and there, I had some pretty shitty seasons on the whole," Mantle said in an interview a couple of years after his retirement. "The whole fucking world was waiting for me to do great things, to carry on the legacy of Ruth, Gehrig, and DiMaggio, and here's Mickey Mantle, the next great Yankee not even hitting forty home runs. Fuck, not even thirty home runs in those first four seasons. Who the fuck was I kidding?"

A harsh assessment? Of course. No one could be or would be as hard on himself as Mickey Mantle, and not because the writers were disappointed that he hadn't met those lofty expectations or because Casey Stengel had predicted so much greatness. Mickey was being hard on himself because he knew his father would have been, had he been around to watch his son in those first five seasons. That was the hell that Mantle was having to live with and live through.

Ah, but 1956. Almost two decades later, even in the haze of a long day of hard drinking, Mickey could look back and see 1956 as clearly as if it had been yesterday. The effect was sobering, as if memories of 1956 were an antidote to all the booze in his system.

"I was seeing the ball all season long like it was the size of a fucking grapefruit," Mickey told me in a coffee shop off the Central Expressway in North Dallas. "And I mean *all* fucking season long, like I had fucking binoculars on, and I could read fucking [American League president] William Harridge's signature on the fucking ball as if it were three inches high. When I could see a pitch that well, there's no way I wasn't going to hit the shit out of it. Hell, Opening Day [Washington Senators pitcher] Camilo Pascual threw me two curveballs down and in, and I could read the writing on those balls like they were standing still on a [batting] tee. And whop! I planted each of them five hundred feet. I knew then this was going to be a fucking great season like no other."

As he was talking, a man carrying his toddler daughter while holding the small hand of his young son approached our booth, and Mickey straightened himself as he usually did when he met young fans.

"Mr. Mantle, excuse me for intruding on you like this," the man said, "but I wanted my son to meet you, if that would be all right with you."

"Of course," said Mantle, fixing that familiar grin on his face and holding out his right hand to the boy. "Good to meet you. My name's Mickey."

"Mine is, too, sir," said the boy.

Mickey's eyes lit up. "I like the name, son," he said.

"He's named after you, Mr. Mantle," the man said. "The greatest Yankee of them all."

Mantle appeared speechless as he signed his autograph for the boy on the back of an empty receipt stub a passing waitress gave him. He wrote, "To another Mickey. Your friend, Mickey Mantle, Triple Crown, 1956."

Mickey would come alive when he talked about 1956. Who could blame him? At the time, he was only the twelfth player to win baseball's elusive Triple Crown—leading the league in batting average, home runs, and runs batted in. Only a handful have accomplished that in the true modern era, since the integration of the once all-white game in 1947, and Mantle's numbers that season are truly astounding: the .353 batting average, 130 RBIs, and fifty-two homers, including a chase for most of the season of Babe Ruth's home run record. Mickey had at last fulfilled expectations. He was the king of New York. "Mickey who?" teased a song by Teresa Brewer, who popped to the top of the 1950s hit parade with perky, relentlessly cheerful tunes. "The fella with the celebrated swing."

It seemed, in listening to him talk, that Mickey knew that 1956 season by heart. In less than a month that April, he batted .415, slugged four home runs, drove in fifteen runs, and scored ten runs. May turned into an even better month, beginning with home runs in three straight games. Then came May 5, his second multi-homer game of the season, with his second homer ricocheting high off the right field facade as he almost became the first player to hit a ball out of Yankee Stadium. Mickey's May onslaught didn't let up: four more home runs in the next dozen games, followed by multiple homer outings, four-for-four and five-for-five showings, home runs from both sides of the plate, and finishing the month by belting homers in three straight games. The last of those, on May 30, came within eighteen inches of clearing Yankee Stadium. While he had almost done that on May 5, this one had been an even more prodigious blast, still on an upward trajectory when it hit the facade in right field. Had it not, according to Yankee publicists at the time, it would have traveled more than six hundred feet.

"Mantle's got more power than any hitter I ever saw—including the Babe," Yankee Coach Bill Dickey said on Opening Day and repeated again.

Ah, *The Babe*. Always, it seemed, The Babe loomed over any discussion of Mickey, his potential, and the expectations. Even in his rookie season, Ruth's widow Claire wanted to meet the young rookie who was being mentioned as another Babe Ruth. She invited Mickey to her home where she treated him to milk and cookies while she showed him all of The Babe's memorabilia. Mantle took particular interest in one of Ruth's famous bats, surprised by its extraordinarily heaviness and holding it much of that afternoon. Claire Ruth would make an effort to briefly visit with Mickey during each of her yearly visits to Yankee Stadium. She seemed to sense that there was something unique in Mantle for all the fuss that was made of him each spring and an anticipated new assault on Ruth's single season home run record. The oversized expectations that Casey Stengel placed on Mickey as a rookie—and the inevitable disappointment—may have been best summed up by sportswriter Milton Gross, who wrote, "Mantle was to be the monument the old gent wanted to leave behind. Casey wanted his own name written in the record books as manager, but he also wanted a creation that was completely his own on the field every day, doing things no other ballplayer ever did, rewriting all the records."

In 1955, those following Mantle and the Yankees got a glimpse that a special season like 1956 was just waiting to explode. Mickey won the first of his four home run championships, and on May 13, he'd had the only three-homer game in his career and first switch-hit homer game—one righty and two lefty. He also hit the first of his only two All-Star Game home runs, tagging the Phillies' Robin Roberts for a three-run shot. By

September, Mickey seemed certain to become the first Yankee to hit forty home runs since DiMaggio in 1937. But in mid-September, while trying to bunt for a hit, Mickey tore a muscle in his right thigh. It was an injury that may have cost the Yankees the World Series championship when they met the Dodgers. Mantle missed the first two games. He homered in a Yankees' loss in game three but could play in only two of the final four games, appearing once as a pinch-hitter.

Then came the Triple Crown season. For Mantle, the year 1956 would mark the time of his life when promise and potential would be fulfilled with a season that, in its own way, only raised expectations even higher. There were no signs, though, early in the season to suggest that this would be the year that Mantle would emerge as the Yankee superstar to finally make many fans forget the great DiMaggio. The season didn't begin easily. In spring training, Mantle reinjured the hamstring that had spoiled the homestretch of 1955. But the previous season had been a learning experience for Mantle. He hadn't understood how he could have led the Yankees in most offensive categories but how teammate Yogi Berra wound up being named the American League's Most Valuable Player. Mickey had outhit Yogi by thirty-four points, had slugged ten more home runs, and driven in just nine fewer runs than the Yankee catcher. Mantle wasn't sure what to make of that until just weeks before the start of spring training when he asked the Yankees' assistant general manager, Bill DeWitt.

"Look, I was glad to see Yogi got the Most Valuable Player award," he told DeWitt. "There's no better guy in the world than Yogi. But I'm just wondering: What's a guy have to do to be considered Most Valuable?"

"Well, Mickey, I'm glad you asked me this," DeWitt said. "You may not know this, Mickey, but when the baseball writers are deciding who's been most valuable, they take other things into account. Maybe a ballplayer has to do more than have a good season on the field. Maybe he has to win a little personal popularity. Maybe he has to put out a little effort. Maybe he can't brush off every newspaperman who approaches him, or just clam up on him. Maybe he must make a real effort to be a little cooperative. . . . You've got to come out of that shell."

It was no secret that Mantle had contentious relationships with many of the writers who covered the Yankees, and word had gotten around the league. Mickey was also shy and didn't like talking about himself. DeWitt explained that he was no longer a rookie but a team leader who needed to make the extra effort to cooperate with the press. He could no longer be rude and unfriendly or cut off reporters with curt, one-word answers. In spring training, it quickly became obvious that Mantle had turned a page in his dealings with the press. He was also trying to be more patient and selective at the plate, which even opposing players noticed.

"I saw Mantle looked different down in St. Petersburg," said the Cardinals' Stan Musial. "It was the first time [since 1951] that he'd ever looked real sharp in the spring. He'd always struck out a lot before, but this year he was letting the bad pitches go by. And he hit a lot of real long homers even down there, where the background isn't good for hitting. If he hits .400 or 60 home runs this season, I can't say I'll be surprised. He has all the qualifications."

Mantle especially had the qualifications to take on Babe Ruth's legendary home run record.

In the twenty-nine years since Ruth's record-setting season with the 1927 Yankees, several players had challenged the home run mark, but all had faded during the second half of the season. In 1932, Jimmy Foxx had forty-one home runs by the end of the July but had finished with fifty-eight. Ruth himself had thirty home runs by the end of June in two other seasons but had been unable to surpass his own record. By midsummer of 1956, Mantle's pace in the challenge to Ruth's record began to slacken, in part because of increasing pain in his chronically ailing right knee. In July, he hit only a handful of home runs but bounced back in August by hitting twelve. In August, even President Dwight Eisenhower joined the Mantle frenzy. He attended a Yankees game against the Senators at Griffith Stadium, where he asked Mantle to hit a home run for him. In the seventh inning, Mantle obliged. Mickey went into September with forty-seven home runs, needing fourteen to break Ruth's record.

Had he been healthy, Mickey might have made a stronger assault against The Babe. Mantle, though, pulled a groin muscle while he was running the bases during the first week of September and didn't homer in the first ten games of the month. He had been leading in all three categories of the Triple Crown—batting average, runs batted in, and home runs—but soon was passed by Ted Williams in the batting average race. At the age of thirty-eight, the Splendid Splinter was on the verge of ruining Mantle's chances at winning the Triple Crown. Mickey was now also pressing, swinging at bad pitches outside the strike zone. Each time he struck out or popped up weakly, he exploded with profanity-laced temper tantrums and wild attacks on the dugout water cooler. The ghost of Babe Ruth was getting to him. Mantle spiraled into an awful five-for-thirty-four slump, his worst of the season. Mickey Mantle added his name to those who had pursued Ruth into September and failed. He did not hit his fiftieth home run until September 17 in an extra inning game off of White Sox left-hander Billy Pierce in Comiskey Park. It was just his third homer of the month, though it clinched the pennant for the Yankees. But with the pressure of Ruth's record off his shoulders, Mickey could focus on his head-to-head batting average race with Williams. Though nursing the muscle pull, Mantle was leading Williams by four points going into the final series of the season, in which the Yankees hosted the Red Sox. It was one of the few times that Stengel wanted to keep him out of the lineup to rest him for the World Series, but Mickey insisted on playing.

"I didn't want to be sitting on the bench with the batting title at stake," Mantle said afterward.

Mickey connected for his fifty-second home run in the first game and only pinch-hit in the second game where he added an RBI when he walked with the bases loaded. Meanwhile, Williams got only one hit in the first two games and then conceded the batting title to Mantle by sitting out the season finale. Mickey drove in a run on a pinch-hit ground ball. He finished the season batting .353, beating Williams by eight points. Mantle's pinch-hit run batted in was his 130th of the season, allowing him to nudge out the Tigers' Al Kaline by two RBI.

Mickey Mantle had won the Triple Crown. He was the first Triple Crown winner since Ted Williams in 1947.

The Yankees capped it off by beating the Dodgers in the World Series that was made especially memorable by Don Larsen's perfect game in game 5, a feat saved by Mantle's full-speed running catch of a four-hundred-foot blow to deep left center field in the fifth inning. Mickey would call it "the best catch I ever made."

"There would have been no perfect game for Larsen without what Mantle did to catch Hodges' line drive," the *Washington Post*'s Shirley Povich would later write. "That ball was certain to fall in until a flying Mantle reached the scene from nowhere and speared it backhanded. Larsen should have blown him a kiss."

Larsen might have blown him a double kiss. Not only did Mickey save the perfect game, but also he won the game. Through three innings, Larsen had been matched in perfection by the Dodgers' Sal Maglie, who earlier had pitched a no-hitter for Brooklyn in the home stretch of their pennant race. Then in the fourth inning, Mickey shattered Maglie's own perfect game by pulling a curveball down the right field line where it barely cleared the foul pole at Yankee Stadium's 296-foot mark. It was all the scoring that Larsen and the Yankees would need.

Two days later, when the Yankees won the World Series for their seventeenth championship, Mickey Mantle's greatest season was in the history books. The only thing that could have topped it would have been breaking Babe Ruth's record, which he had threatened all season. Mickey, though, was looking forward to doing that. In his mind, it was inevitable, and he was putting Babe Ruth on notice.

"I'd rather have won the Triple Crown than to have broken Babe Ruth's record," Mickey told broadcaster Len Morton at season's end, "because I doubt that I'll ever have another chance to win the Triple Crown, but I think that if I get to play another twelve to fourteen years, that I'll break Babe Ruth's record."

Epilogue

The Greatest

Greatness is a property for which no man can receive credit too soon; it must be possessed long before it is acknowledged.
　　　　　　　　　　　　　　　　　—RALPH WALDO EMERSON

IN THE DAYS BEFORE THANKSGIVING, MICKEY TOOK MERLYN TO A MOVIE theater in downtown Dallas to see *Around the World in 80 Days*, an adventure-comedy and their first night on the town since the World Series. The theater had just darkened as they settled into their seats when they heard the familiar da-da-da-ruhn da-da-da-ruhn-da-ruhn pomp of a Movietone News reel. Up on the screen was Casey Stengel holding a king's crown over Mickey's head. Mantle is smiling from ear to ear and holds three bats over his shoulder. Each bat has a different number in black—.353, 52, and 130—representing his league-leading figures in batting average, home runs, and RBIs. Mickey and Casey clown around and then we hear the announcer's voice:

"Baseball has crowned a new king—Mickey Mantle of the New York Yankees—who last week received his Triple Crown for leading the American League in batting average, home runs, and runs batted in. It's a rare feat—something that neither the great Babe Ruth nor Mickey's predecessor, Joe DiMaggio, ever did—and manager Casey Stengel said, quote, you ain't seen nothing yet, end quote. Indeed King Mickey Mantle is fulfilling predictions that he'll break all of Ruth's records before he's done."

In 1956, with the Triple Crown season teasing of what could lie ahead, Mickey Mantle stood at what he now believed to be his destiny's footstep—the greatness predicted and expected of him—and so close to that goal that he felt fully confident of reaching it. He had no idea that his dream, the goal he was chasing, is an illusion that drives men and women to a breaking point from which there is no return. That was good. It is not true that people stop pursuing dreams because they grow old, Gabriel García Márquez, the Mantle of his trade, later wrote—they grow old because they stop pursuing dreams.

Mickey would never break Babe Ruth's single season home run record, though he would challenge it again in 1961 and come up short again. That didn't matter. It is meaningless. Roger Maris, Mark McGwire, Sammy Sosa, and Barry Bonds would all hit more than sixty home runs in a season. They all broke Ruth's record, and they all pale in comparison to his greatness, like scoops of mellorine compared to real ice cream. For greatness and being the greatest lies beyond numbers, which themselves are nothing more than that equally illusory green light that teased Gatsby at the end of Daisy's dock.

When Mantle died in 1995, I sensed a sadness among his friends and fans—visibly so among those who overflowed Lovers Lane United Methodist Church in Dallas, where his memorial service was held— that perhaps had as much to do with his failure to accomplish his quest of being the greatest ever as with his actual tragic passing. Maybe with Mickey Mantle one is indistinguishable from the other.

━◦━

For Merlyn Mantle, Mickey's death equated to the collapse of her world that at the time seemed total, overwhelming, and relentless. Devastated, she was lost for a while in a sea of grief until her sons and friends urged her to take comfort at the outpouring of love for Mickey from teammates, fans, and much of America, which had been moved in his final days as he carried his afflictions with grace and humor. The thousands of letters of support that Mantle received after his transplant operation had surprised both Mickey and Merlyn as they discovered that the public could forgive and forget. America chose instead to remember his baseball greatness and the national heroic role into which he was cast. It was an experience that inspired Merlyn to dedicate the last decade and a half of her life to protecting and enhancing Mickey's legacy—his place in the history of the game. Ultimately, she went to her grave convinced that the love of her life had firmly established himself as the greatest baseball player of all time. Since then she has been joined by experts in the game who have come to share her belief, spurred largely by the statistical analysis craze that has taken over baseball as well as the reassessment of Mickey and his career now as baseball prepares in 2020 to commemorate the twenty-fifth anniversary of his passing.

How good could have Mickey Mantle been if he had taken care of himself? That has been the common refrain that always seems to emerge from a popular national pastime among fans, former teammates, baseball people, and sportswriters. How good was Mantle, and could he have been the greatest ballplayer if he had played on two healthy legs? The mythology of Mickey Mantle makes him untouchable by any player in the modern era and is surpassed perhaps only by that of Babe Ruth. And perhaps what made Mantle more endearing than the Bambino was the evident flaw of a blown-out leg from his rookie season, a hero playing his entire career with his humanity on his sleeves. What's that quote attributed to Achilles? "The gods envy us. They envy us because we're mortal, because any moment may be our last. Everything is more beautiful because we're doomed." Or as the young Jane Leavy put it in recalling her childhood love for Mantle, "I felt that he carried a sense that he was damaged and so did I." Jane, author of *The Last Boy: Mickey Mantle and the End of America's Childhood*, had been born premature "with a damaged right leg as precarious as The Mick's." So why so many of us loved Mantle and prayed for his health and his heroics is understandable. The high priest keeping watch over the speculation of how good Mantle was has been John Thorn, a lifelong baseball fan who typifies the baby boomers who grew up basking in the golden era of the game in which Mickey Mantle blossomed with his baseball exploits. As the official historian of major league baseball, Thorn today is also among its leading scholars with intimate knowledge of sabermetrics, the science of learning about baseball through objective evidence being used to measure the game and its players in new ways. Through sabermetrics, Thorn maintains, Mickey Mantle "looks great" and possibly closer to Babe Ruth and Lou Gehrig in a different era. This is not an endorsement of Mantle as the greatest but just an acknowledgment of him having moved comfortably into the conversation of who is the greatest.

Who is the greatest of all time, of course, is argumentative. Those kinds of debates are the essence of what makes baseball, and other sports, so beloved by fans: Bragging rights abound over who was the best center fielder in New York in the midfifties—Mickey, Willie, or The Duke. Was DiMaggio's fifty-six-game hitting streak or Ted Williams's .406 batting average the crowning achievement of the 1941 season? How would the Mantle-Maris 1961 Yankees have fared against the 1927 Murderers Row team of Ruth and Gehrig? Should Joe DiMaggio have been introduced as "baseball's greatest living ballplayer," as he demanded for his appearances, while Willie Mays and Hank Aaron were still alive and equally in the conversation for that title?

Baseball is stats, the heart of sabermetrics, but John Thorn cautions that the true measure of greatness requires more. "The myth counts," he concedes. "The story counts. It's not just stats." *Not everything that can be counted counts, and not everything that counts can be counted.* Einstein. Or William Bruce Cameron. No one can be sure. We know it wasn't Mickey Mantle.

What's not debatable is that the constant over time, as *Mantle: The Best There Ever Was* details, has been Mickey's popularity. It evolved into a religion of its own, heightened as he excelled despite the injuries and as fans watched him hobble up to the plate every day with his legs heavily bandaged and in obvious pain. His believers worshipped him even more as he continued to put up big numbers throughout this time. Today, in death, Mantle's popularity is unmatched. His greatness is obscured by the legend that grew around him. As Allen Barra, author of *Mickey and Willie: The Parallel Lives of Baseball's Golden Age*, summed up in his 2002 analysis for the *New York Times*, "However underrated he was at times by the press, fans and even his own manager, Casey Stengel, who, incredibly, did not include him on his all-time all-star team, Mantle, at his peak, most likely was the greatest combination of power and speed baseball has ever seen."

Yet as the late Harvard professor and baseball fan Stephen Jay Gould wrote, in pointed response to those preoccupied with alternative histories,

"To hell with what might have been. No one can reach personal perfection in a complex world filled with distraction. Williams had his best years cut short by World War II and Korea; DiMaggio played in the wrong park; Shoeless Joe Jackson, acquitted by the courts, was executed by major league baseball. What happened is all we have. By this absolute and irrefragable standard, Mantle was the greatest ballplayer of his time."

In advancing his theory of Mantle as the greatest, Professor Gould even used a season that fans and experts often overlook when praising Mickey—1957—which he argued was "probably the greatest single season by any player in baseball's modern era."

"Mantle's achievements in 1957 have been masked by a conspiracy of circumstances, including comparison with his showier stats of the year before and the fact that his career-best batting average of .365 came in second to Ted Williams's .388," Gould wrote in "Mickey Mantle: The Man versus the Myth," from his collection of essays *Triumph and Tragedy in Mudville: A Lifelong Passion for Baseball*. "In 1957 Mantle had a career high of 146 walks, with only 75 strikeouts. (In no other year did he come even close to this nearly two-to-one ratio of walks to strikeouts; in ten of eighteen seasons with the Yanks, he struck out more often than he walked.) This cornucopia of walks limited his official at-bats to 474 and didn't provide enough opportunity for accumulating those (largely misleading) stats that count absolute numbers rather than percentages—RBIs and home runs for example. Superficial glances have led to an undervaluing of Mantle's greatest season. "Sabermetrics (or baseball number crunching) has its limits and cannot substitute for the day-to-day knowledge of professionals who shared the playing field with Mantle, yet numerical arguments command our respect when so many different methods lead to the same conclusion. As [sabermetrics founder] Bill James points out in his *Historical Baseball Abstract*, all proposed measures of offensive performance—from his own runs created for outs consumed, to Thomas Boswell's total average, Barry Codell's base-out percentage, Thomas Cover's offensive earned run average, and Pete Palmer's overall rating in *The Hidden Game [of Baseball]*—judge Mantle's 1957 season as unsurpassed during the modern era. Consider just one daunting statistic: Mantle's on-base percentage of .512. Imagine getting on base more often than making an out—especially given the old saw that, in baseball, even the greatest fail about twice as often as they succeed. No player since Mantle in 1957 has come close to an on-base percentage of .500. Willie Mays reached .425 in his best year."

Perhaps nowhere in all of American literature can one find a storied career more dramatic and touching of an archetypal innocent who becomes a national hero, flaws and all, than that portrayed in real life by Mickey Mantle. He was every bit the leading figure in baseball that Babe Ruth had been in his era, as the idol of millions of youngsters throughout the country. But they lived and played in Americas that were as different as the games of baseball in those periods. Both those times were simpler than our time in the twenty-first century, and baseball too. Therein lies the challenge of comparing eras, players, and achievements from those epochs. It is foolish to even seriously try, but then who was it that said we will nevertheless do foolish things, so why not do them with enthusiasm? And that's what has hooked us from our childhoods to adulthood—the foolishness of games like baseball and to indulge in them with no holding back.

Mickey Mantle was undoubtedly the best switch-hitter of all time. There can be no argument about that. Add the World Series championships—seven of them, the dozen American League pennants, the World Series home run record, the Triple Crown year of 1956, the momentous season of 1957 that Stephen Jay Gould argues as his greatest, and then the 1961 campaign with a team that was arguably as good as Babe Ruth's 1927 Yankees, if not better. Then there were the three Most Valuable Player awards in 1956, 1957, and 1962—and the fourth MVP of which he was so clearly robbed.

Yes, robbed. Look at Mantle's 1964 season when he led the American League in on-base average (.426) and slugging (.591) for what sabermetrics analysts would later figure to be a league-leading OPS of 1.017. This would be Mickey's last outstanding season, even as he struggled with knee, groin, and hamstring injuries. But his thirty-five home runs were third best in the league, and he drove in 111 runs and finished fourth in hitting with a .303 average. More importantly, he managed to play 143 games in leading the Yankees to the pennant. Mantle, though, lost the MVP balloting to the Baltimore Orioles' sensational third baseman Brooks Robinson who batted .317 with 118 RBIs. However, as Yankee historian Peter Golenbock so poignantly wrote, Robinson "didn't come close to Mantle's other stats and . . . didn't pick his team out of the rubble to win the pennant. [He] got the MVP award. It wasn't a bad choice. It just wasn't the correct one."

Consequently, in my mind, based on criteria that gives as much weight to winning pennants and World Series championships as to individual statistics, the competition for the title of the greatest of all time comes down to Ruth and Mantle, with DiMaggio on the outside and then that group of Willie Mays, Hank Aaron, and Ted Williams. I know this penalizes players who weren't on great teams that could win World Series titles. But in my mind, that immeasurable in the individual statistics becomes inseparable from greatness. In football, would many experts or fans be calling Tom Brady the greatest quarterback of all time if he hadn't won a record five Super Bowls for the New England Patriots? Team sports are about winning championships, and individual players who put up great statistics become multimillionaire superstars, but greatness still lies on another plane. How else can you judge if Mantle made his teammates better except through championships, and his teammates certainly admired Mickey more than any other star on the Yankees. So did his opponents. No less a baseball star than Al Kaline of the Detroit Tigers, when he was taunted by a young fan who said, "You're not half as good as Mickey Mantle," replied, "Son, nobody is half as good as Mickey Mantle."

Understandably, this is why I'm convinced there is something that sabermetrics and its analytics miss about Mickey Mantle. The thing about *not everything that counts can be counted* again. While all the experts have long discounted Mantle's numbers in his off-seasons and lamented his bum legs, there has always been one thing that was missing: Mickey Mantle's determination and his impact on his teammates. What the analytics didn't show us about Mantle was the heart and determination it took just to take the field day after day with his damaged legs. Heart and determination, much like World Series championships themselves, are unquantifiable aspects of Mantle that have never shown up in the statistics and analytics.

But don't cry for Mickey. He still comes off incredible well in the analytics known as Wins Above Replacement, known commonly by the acronym WAR, a powerful statistic created though a complex formula that takes into account everything that a player accomplishes. That statistic asks the question, "If this player were injured and his team had to replace him with a minor leaguer or someone from the bench, how much value would the team be losing?"

The formula for determining a player's WAR favors Mantle because he was a center fielder, which is more difficult to play than left field, where Ted Williams played. Center fielders also have more value than first basemen, so that helped place Mantle ahead of Lou Gehrig.

In his Triple Crown season of 1956, when he batted .353, hit 52 home runs, and batted in 130 runs, Mantle had a WAR of 12.9, the highest of the modern era beginning in 1947. Mickey's WAR in the following season was 12.5. In the history of the game, the only player who recorded higher was Babe Ruth with a WAR of 14.7 in 1923 and 14.0 in 1921. Willie Mays's best WAR was 11.0, Lou Gehrig's was 12.0, and Ted Williams's top was 11.8. Barry Bonds's best three seasons produced WAR numbers of 12.5, 12.4, and 12.2, although they were done while he was using performance-enhancing drugs.

There was also more that went into Mantle WAR in 1956 and 1957. He was an outstanding base runner, with statistics that were surprising considering he was a power hitter. Among them are his stolen bases, in which he had a higher success rate than even Willie Mays. But what made Mickey stand out in those seasons was the gap between his batting average and the batting average of other American Leaguers who would have replaced him in this WAR formula. In 1956, American Leaguers batted .260 compared to Mantle's .353. In 1957, they hit .257 compared to Mantle's .365.

In the eyes of sabermetrics experts, though, batting averages are thought to be a misleading statistic. They prefer On Base Plus Slugging Percentage, more commonly known as OPS, which adds on-base percentage and slugging percentage for a number that combines the two—and is meant to compare how often a hitter reaches base with how well he can hit for average and for power. So among sabermetrics analysts, OPS is widely considered one of the best evaluative tools for hitters. So let's go there. In 1956, the OPS among American Leaguers was .735 compared to Mantle's 1.169. In 1957, Mickey's OPS was even better at 1.177 compared to .708 among the league's average.

Add to all that the continuing evolution of analytics in baseball that will undoubtedly take reevaluations of the game's present and past players to new discoveries. And in that, Mantle like Ruth can rest comfortably. They are, as the line goes in their second great game, golf, "the leaders in the clubhouse." So, are we witnessing a historic rethinking in the way all athletes are judged and on how some players transcend their own personal statistical limitations to elevate their teams to an ultimate achievement of championships?

Finally, there is the question that every Mickey Mantle fan eventually asks: if he's not the greatest ballplayer, then why are Mickey Mantle baseball cards more valuable than others? Worth repeating: In early 2018, a mint-condition Mickey Mantle 1952 Topps card sold for a whopping $2.88 million, second only to a T206 Honus Wagner that fetched $3.12 million in 2016. In the collectable trade, the 1952 Topps Mickey Mantle card and four other Mantle cards rank higher in value than the No. 6 card, of Ted Williams. There is also what GoldenAgeBaseballCards.com calls "The Greatest Baseball Card Ever," whose symbolic value is unmatched. This is Mantle's 1956 Topps card, showing Mickey's face with the background of a 1951 action photograph: Mantle leaping over the short fence in Yankee Stadium's right field to steal a home run from a hitter. There is a ball in his glove, though the ball had actually sailed over his head in a dinger. But it is young Mickey Mantle at his athletic peak a few weeks before the tragic injury in the World Series. "This card reflects what all Mickey Mantle fans believe," notes the site. "Had he not hurt his knee, Mantle would have been the greatest player ever."

"In fact, it adds to the legend and the possibility," says cultural historian and baseball blogger William Szczepanek, "that at a specific point in time Mantle may be considered the greatest player ever."

As Merlyn Mantle kept believing to her end, that day is coming. She could see it. So have others. They call it the Mickey Mantle mystique, and it lives on, perhaps greater in death than when he was alive.

I mentioned that to Merlyn the last time I spoke to her as I was mentally scrambling to say something positive about her insistence that Mantle was the greatest. All I could think of at that moment was the mystique of the late Jim Morrison, and I asked her if she remembered that classic 1981 *Rolling Stone* magazine cover of the Doors' singer with the headline "He's hot, he's sexy, and he's dead."

"Oh, my God!" she said, as the idea slowly registered. "I never saw that. It's fabulous." Then, as it hit her as to why I had alluded to those words about Morrison, Merlyn added, "But isn't that something you could say about Mickey as well?"

"That's what I was thinking," I said.

"Oh, dear lord." She stopped and lingered on the thought for a moment. "You know, Mickey being the way he was and that crazy sense of humor of his, that's something he would have *loved* on his gravestone."

Author's Note

My late friend Carlos Fuentes, the Mexican writer and diplomat, used to say that the only way you can come to know someone is by making sure you have figuratively closed off all doors to what you have known of them in the past. This becomes almost impossible for someone like Mantle whose life transcends decades and has become a national institution, as if his image has been carved into our Olympus of pop culture.

You try, though, by talking to those who knew him best. For that I relied heavily on the more than 250 conversations with ex-teammates, friends, and family whom I interviewed while working on my original biography, *Mickey Mantle: America's Prodigal Son* (2002), and the additional 108 interviews for my dual biography *DiMag & Mick: Sibling Rivals, Yankee Blood Brothers* (2016). For *Mantle: The Best There Ever Was*, I also used interviews with dozens of additional sources, and I was most fortunate in having the treasure trove of two of the women in Mickey's life.

The title was changed from "Mantle: The Man, the Myth, the Mick" to *Mantle: The Best There Ever Was* by the publisher, Rowman & Littlefield.

When Meryln Mantle reached out to me in late 2006, she and I talked about a great number of things. We reminisced about the conversations she and I had back in the early 1970s. I reminded her that I had kept my word in not using that material, though I had tried to get her permission for its use in *Mickey Mantle: America's Prodigal Son*. She appreciated that I had honored my promise to not use that material until after she and Mickey had passed away. I assured her I would wait until the appropriate time after her death to write this book. The notes from those conversations were packed away with all my reporting and research material from the 1970s. It has been only in the past year that I was able to locate those boxes in storage for inclusion in my journalism and book archives being donated to the Texas collection at my alma mater, Baylor University. In finding that material, I also hit the mother lode. In addition to notes of my conversations with Merlyn, I found additional notes I'd forgotten about many of the conversations and interviews with Mickey during that time. These were notes that were not among the material I had used on Mantle for the two previous books of the trilogy. In early 1974, we had relocated from Dallas to Houston, packing up books and research material in shipping boxes, some of which remained sealed through that move as well as through subsequent moves over the years to Cambridge, Massachusetts, and then to storage in Southern California. Those notes provide the bulk of the previously unpublished interviews with Mickey, Merlyn, and Billy Martin, who was manager of the Detroit Tigers during that time and whom I met through Mantle when Billy visited them in Dallas.

Mickey may have been a hero of his present, but he was haunted by his past. In his later years, there were numerous incidents of nervous exhaustion. In the early 1970s, playing golf and drinking on the nineteenth hole, he often talked about dreams and reminiscences that took hold of him sometimes as daydreams. Re-creating them in a book was a nightmare of its own on exactly how to source the material and transition to and from the narrative in which they are framed. For the dreams I did not want to rely on traditional methods of attribution that too often only serve to restrict a reader's flow. Writer friends suggested changing verb tenses, re-creating Mickey's dreams in the present tense, and that's how I have worked them into the book for the most part, starting with the scene that introduces part 1.

For *Mantle: The Best There Ever Was*, I also relied on the recollections of Holly Brooke, Mickey's girlfriend during his 1951 rookie season and on-and-off-again lover over the years. She is a source many biographers, myself included, wanted to interview over the years. However, none of us could locate her, and some off us concluded that perhaps she had passed way. Then in 2006, just weeks before Merlyn Mantle called my then agent Mike Hamilburg wishing to talk to me, I received an e-mail from someone whose correspondence would prove equally fortuitous.

Mr. Castro:

I was recently "googling" for information on my Aunt Holly (Brooke) and came across the following: "Castro maintains Mutt Mantle controlled his son's personal life, disapproving of Mantle's relationship with showgirl Holly Brooke and insisting that he . . . ."

I'm looking forward to reading your book and getting a different perspective from the stories I grew up with from Aunt Holly. I cringe when I see articles portraying her as a "showgirl"; Holly was much more than showgirl . . . she was an artist (with paintings hanging in Gracie Mansion), a columnist (the one I recall is "The Babbling Brooke"), she performed on Broadway in plays such as "Portrait of a Queen," she is also the Aunt/Great Aunt of Robert Sean Leonard and Brett Harrison, close friends to stars such as Jimmy Durante and Roy Rodgers [sic], she worked as a lab technician on the Manhattan Project (where she lost her sense of smell in an accident), I could go on and on . . . she has led quite a life. The one thing she has always wanted to do but never gotten around to finishing is an autobiography.

The great news is that she is alive and well (she visited for Christmas). She just recently gave me an autographed photo Mickey gave her back in the days when they were engaged (I'm not sure if it is a copy or original. . . . Holly insists she gave me the original, but it looks like it may be a copy). I know a slightly different version of how Mickey Mantle married his hometown sweetheart, but there's no reason to go into any of that; might just cause folks pain that will do no one any good. Suffice to say, Holly and Mickey remained close friends until he passed away.

Keith Huylebroeck (pronounced holly-brooke . . . hence her stage name)

Bethlehem, PA

Keith Huylebroeck eventually put me in contact with Holly Brooke, and it began a decade-long friendship until her death in 2017. I was extremely fortunate because journalists and authors had been looking for her since the 1950s. She was an important missing link to Mantle from his rookie year. But she was more. It turned out she stayed in touch with

Mickey even after he married Merlyn in December 1951, resuming her affair with him at various times through the mid-1960s. She was blessed with an incredible memory and a seemingly encyclopedic knowledge of New York in that golden age, as well as of Mantle's life and his friendship and relationship with Joe DiMaggio.

The story in this book of Mantle and Billy Martin meeting with Cardinal Spellman in 1956 came from Holly. So did some of the details of Mickey's time in Kansas City in 1951, and the scene of Mantle and his teammates meeting Ernest Hemingway at Toots Shor's along with the material in that entire chapter, including the redhead with Mickey in the phone booth. The redhead was Holly.

Most memorable of all was her recollection of at least one telephone call of encouragement she says Mantle received from DiMaggio that summer of 1951 when the Yankees had demoted the slumping Mickey to Kansas City, then one of the team's minor league affiliates. According to Brooke, she was staying with Mantle in Kansas City while he was in the minors and witnessed Mickey receiving that call. She also strongly denied that Mantle, either as a rookie or later when they were involved in an extramarital affair, would become physically ill whenever DiMaggio visited the Yankee clubhouse as portrayed in Billy Crystal's endearing but flawed HBO film, *61*, about Mantle and Roger Maris's chase of Babe Ruth's single-season home run record.

Holly Brooke's corroboration of my earlier interviews with the other two most significant women in Mantle's life—wife Merlyn and Greer Johnson, his companion during the last decade of his life—and longtime DiMaggio pal Reno Barsocchini provided virtually unassailable confirmation that Joe and Mickey's true relationship was hardly what the world had been led to believe it had been. Their accounts revealed for the first time that much to the contrary of the long-held myth of DiMaggio and Mantle as unfriendly antagonists, the relationship between the two men was actually that of symbiotic teammates and heroes cast into the national spotlight in 1951—DiMaggio's final season and Mantle's rookie year—and lasting until Mickey's death in 1995. It debunks all those DiMaggio-can't-stand-Mantle-and-vice-versa stories as being untrue and at best as the well-intentioned made-up stories of Mickey's teammates attempting to protect him from the boogeyman they created of DiMaggio—though Mickey Mantle really needed no protection. Mickey more than held his own with the fabled Yankee Clipper on the field, and today he is perhaps remembered more fondly than DiMaggio by their fans.

I first met Mickey Mantle in 1970, the year after his retirement and shortly after he had returned to Dallas from a frustrating season as a coach of the New York Yankees. Mickey had lived in Dallas since the late 1950s, and only earlier that year I had joined the reporting staff of the *Dallas Times Herald* right out of college. One of the first things I did upon going to work at the *Times Herald* was to check the Mickey Mantle files at the newspaper's morgue. I was stunned to see the scarcity of any Mantle clips since his retirement. No lifestyle pieces, no Mick-in-retirement articles. You would have thought Mantle didn't reside in Dallas. A couple of national pieces had been written about Mickey in retirement but nothing locally. I lobbied for an assignment to interview Mantle, which came my way because no one else was interested. Heck, my editors themselves weren't interested.

When I first contacted Mantle, I started getting a sense of why no one was writing about him. Even after I explained that his home telephone number had been in our city desk files, Mickey seemed miffed. I remember his words as something that might have come from Yogi Berra. "Well," Mickey said over the phone, "I only gave out that number so that I could be reached whenever someone needed to talk to me."

Mickey was close to an hour late to our lunch interview. As I write in the book, he had wanted to meet at a trendy burger shop in the Turtle Creek section of North Dallas. When he finally arrived, Mickey apologized in a matter-of-fact manner. He said, "There was a screw-up on our tee time this morning."

I was immediately blown away, not because I was finally meeting my boyhood hero, face-to-face, but because as I saw him—slightly red-eyed, smiling crookedly, slurring some of his words—I thought to myself, my God, it's like meeting my father. They were both heroes, and they were both drinkers. And not happy drunks either. Of course, I didn't tell Mickey he reminded me of my father. Nor did I tell my father that he reminded me of Mickey. But from experience, I had an understanding of how to deal with Mantle. An interview, a formal question-and-answer interview, was out of the question. Instead, over charbroiled cheeseburgers and beers, Mickey rambled in a disjointed exercise of free association for which I wasn't prepared.

We talked for close to two hours that afternoon, and I remember being panic-stricken the longer we talked because I feared that I actually had little to use in a traditional story about Mickey in retirement. He would clam up when the conversation turned to things he was doing now. A bowling alley bearing Mickey's name in Dallas had closed down, and then reopened, and Mickey was unclear as to what the status of it was. He didn't want to talk about his investments, and he was equally evasive on questions about his life with his sons. There was one comment I wrote several times in my notebook: "We're doing a lot more things together now, that's for sure."

My time with Mickey might have ended that afternoon had we not started talking about golf, one of the few things over which he showed any passion. I happened to live in a townhouse complex that was adjacent to the Preston Trail Golf Club in far North Dallas. Mickey was a member of Preston Trail. I wasn't—this was one of the most exclusive golf courses in Dallas—but I'd sneaked onto the course a few times and attended the Byron Nelson Classic at Preston Trail earlier that year. So when Mickey told me of a particularly tricky par 5 that he said he had driven the length of with a slight breeze, I knew exactly which one he was talking about. I was a duffer, but golf is the consummate game for eternal optimists. The next thing I knew, I had a golf date with Mickey a few days later. We played with two other members from whom Mickey cajoled a stroke per hole handicap for me, even though I kept assuring him I wasn't that bad. "Believe me," he said to me, "you are." We won all eighteen holes at $10 a hole, and Mickey won a side bet with each of the two members. He insisted I keep the winnings from the main bet, and I sensed that, in a way, Mickey got as big a kick out of winning $100 bets from each of the two men as he did from a World Series share when he was playing baseball.

As for the interview itself, I think it was Gore Vidal who described interviews like these as "encounters"—and I had several of these types of encounters with Mickey in the 1970s and in the 1980s. In 1973, I was working for the PBS *Newsroom* show that Jim Lehrer had created in Dallas, and we wanted Mantle to appear on our live show to discuss the young Texas Rangers baseball team. Since I knew Mickey, I contacted him and we immediately faced two insurmountable problems. First, Mickey wanted to be paid. He had no idea what PBS was but thought if it was live he should be paid. Second, Mickey really didn't want to appear live but wanted the interview to be taped, which went against the format of the show. The whole thing was a wash. In 1985, while at *Sports Illustrated*, I proposed and had approval for a Mickey Mantle profile that resulted in several phone conversations with Mickey, and equally as many broken dates for face-to-face meetings. As we were to learn later, Mickey was drinking himself to death during these years. His family life was also not good. There were ongoing problems with his son Billy, and he and Merlyn were breaking up. They didn't divorce, but they lived apart for almost the last decade of his life. I spoke with him twice in late 1994, planning to meet with him during an upcoming card show appearance on the West Coast. But then he had to cancel the show because of stomach problems that worsened until his death.

Although I spoke to Merlyn Mantle numerous times in the 1970s, as I acknowledged in my Mantle biography, she did not cooperate with me as I was later researching that book, having learned that I was relying on interviews with Greer Johnson. Merlyn had bitterly resented Mickey's relationship with Johnson and denied access to anyone whom she knew to be working with Johnson. When Mantle was hospitalized and dying in 1995, the Mantle family went so far as not permitting her to visit Mickey on his deathbed, refusing to allow her to bid him good-bye. The Mantles also tried to keep her from attending Mickey's memorial service. And although I had notes from Mickey's conversations in the early 1970s with Greer, I honored Merlyn's request that I not write about it until after her death. She died in 2009.

Through all those years, Mickey continued his close friendship with Holly Brooke. They remained lovers even after Mantle's marriage, and her recollections reveal that Mickey regularly unloaded his heart to her about what was sometimes a turbulent married life. Holly continued working as an actress as well as a painter and writer, raising her son as a single mom and later marrying Broadway producer Henry Clay Blaney.

"Mickey Mantle was just a wonderful man," Holly said, summing him up. "He's also the most honest man I've ever met in my whole life. Mickey just would not tell a lie. He would try not to hurt anybody. I don't know how many people you can say that about. He was remarkable."

Sadly, Holly Brooke—aka Marie Huylebroeck and Lady Holly Blaney—died at her home off Central Park in Manhattan April 9, 2018. She was ninety-four.

Acknowledgments

Mantle: The Best There Ever Was would not have been possible without the assistance of many individuals.

My heartfelt appreciation and gratitude goes out to Merlyn Mantle for her gracious hospitality back in the 1970s when I met her through Mickey and then for reaching out to me in the years after publication of *Mickey Mantle: America's Prodigal Son.* Her love for Mickey and her kindness and consideration in thinking of me planted the seed for this book.

Merlyn reached out through my late agent and friend Mike Hamilburg, her acquaintance from years ago when his father Mitchell produced *Safe at Home*, the 1962 sports comedy that costarred Mantle and Roger Maris, capitalizing on their national fame from their 1961 chase of Babe Ruth's home run record.

Mike Hamilburg was always ready with Mickey Mantle stories. He had many. He represented my 2002 Mantle biography and left me a ton of memories and countless personal files about Mantle, Maris, and *Safe at Home*, which was filmed in Fort Lauderdale and Pompano Beach, Florida.

Holly Brooke has been a good friend and source whose recollections of her life with Mickey Mantle in New York in 1951 and later were critical to the development and writing of the book, as they were for *DiMag & Mick: Sibling Rivals, Yankee Blood Brothers.*

James Bacon, my former desk mate at the *Los Angeles Herald Examiner*, was an inspiring mentor with his friendship and countless stories about Hollywood stars from Sinatra to Marilyn, not to mention his whiskey and his introduction to numerous contacts, among them Reno Barsocchini, Joe DiMaggio's longtime friend.

Pete Rose was magnanimous in sharing his memories and recollections of the time he spent with Mantle and some of his Yankee teammates and in helping me understand the unique culture and dynamics of the major league clubhouse.

Andrew Vilacky and Tom Catal of the Mickey Mantle Museum in Cooperstown have always been extraordinarily gracious and generous in their hospitality and friendship with me and my family, as well as in sharing their library for use in this and other books.

Greer Johnson, Mantle's "soul mate" the last ten years of his life, was extremely kind in reminiscing about Mickey and graciously trusting me with her memories and remembering Mickey's conversations with her about his father, DiMaggio, Roger Maris, and many of the other important people in her life. This book, like *Mickey Mantle: America's Prodigal Son*, would not be as complete in its assessment of Mantle without her assistance.

The late Ray Mantle, one of Mickey's brothers, was gracious in sharing memories of growing up with Mickey, especially in clearing up discrepancies in other accounts of Mantle's early life. Ray also offered his own personal insight into Mickey's relationship with their father and Mickey's friendship with Billy Martin.

Stephen Jay Gould was a paleontologist at Harvard whom I met in 1976 when I was a Nieman fellow at the university and discovered we shared a childhood in which Mickey Mantle was all we could think about. He had all these theories even then about how Mantle had been the greatest ballplayer ever and became even more convinced with the advent of sabermetrics late in his shortened life.

A number of people were helpful in providing information or putting me in touch with prospective interviewees in researching Mantle over the years but especially helpful were DiMaggio biographer Richard Ben Cramer, who shared his thoughts on why he believed Joe and Mickey intensely disliked each other; author Phil Berger, who graciously shared his insights and contacts on Mantle, the subject of one of his numerous books; and Michael A. Stoner, attorney for Greer Johnson. Writer friends have been equally kind in reading parts of this book and offering feedback, among them Peter Golenbock, Tom Wolfe, Randy Taraborrelli, Bob Vickrey, and Teo Davis.

Special thanks to these individuals for their support or assistance in tangible and intangible ways: Hank Aaron, Marty Appel, Ed Attanasio, Jim Bacon, Penni Barnett, Jim Bellows, Keven Bellows, Yogi Berra, Hollis Biddle, Jim Bouton, Jennifer Boyd, Jimmy Breslin, Jerry Brown, Jeff Brynan, Jim Bunning, Ken Burns, George W. Bush, Claudia Caballero, Al Campanis, Elissa Walker Campbell, Dave Campbell, Ruben Castaneda, Paul Cohen, John B. Connally, Dino Costa, Bob Costas, Kevin Costner, Warren Cowan, Billy Crystal, Francis Dale, Cody Decker, Carl Dias, Joe DiMaggio, James Duarte, Mel Durslag, Tom Eggebeen, Carl Erskine, Roy Firestone, Robert Fitzgerald, Randy Flowers, Whitey Ford, Don Forst, Dudley Freeman, Arthur Fuentes, Carlos Fuentes, Randy Galloway, Peter Gammons, Paul Gelb, Cathie Flahive Gilmore, Mikal Gilmore, Carole Player Golden, Peter Golenbock, Johnny Grant, Kathy Griffin, Carlos Guerra, Chris Gwynn, David Halberstam, Denis Hamill, Mike Hamilburg, Arnold Hano, Thomas Harris, Lew Harris, Jickey Harwell, Don Henley, Mickey Herskowitz, Tom Hoffarth, Joe Holley, Ken Holley, Ed Hunter, Matty Ianniello, Alex Jacinto, Derek Jeter, Chipper Jones, David Justice, Ron Kaye, Ray Kelly, Jennifer Kemp, Liudmila Konovalova, Dennis King, Sandy Koufax, Steve Kraly, Doug Krikorian, Tony Kubek, Ring Lardner Jr., Don Larsen, Chris LaSalle, Jean LaSalle, Lisa LaSalle, Frances LaSalle Castro, Tommy Lasorda, Tim Layana, Timothy Leary, Jane Leavy, Jill Lieber, Carole Lieberman, Mike Lupica, Ralph Lynn, Michael Moldovan, Sara Moldovan, Willie Mays, Barbara McBride-Smith, Julie McCullough, Mark McGwire, David McHam, Frank Messer, Lidia Montemayor, Jim Montgomery, Louis F. Moret, Dennis Mukai, Mark Mulvoy, John Murphy, Stan Musial, Joe Namath, Jack Nelson, Don Newcombe, Peter O'Malley, Edward James Olmos, Bill Orozco, Robert Patrick, Dick Patyrak, Octavio Paz, Thomas Pettigrew, Vic Prado, Robert Redford, Jimmie Reese, Pee Wee Reese, John Reilly, Liz Reilly, Rick Reilly, Bobby Richardson, Wanda Rickerby, Phil Rizzuto, Tim Robbins, Phil Alden Robinson, Gregory Rodriguez, Jim Rome, Carol Rose, Chris Russo, Emilio Sanchez, Richard Sandomir, Susan Sarandon, Dick Schaap, Dutch Schroeder, Vin Scully, Diane K.

Shah, Gail Sheehy, Charley Sheen, Ron Shelton, Bob Sheppard, Blackie Sherrod, Ivan Shouse, Buck Showalter, T. J. Simers, Paul Simon, Marty Singer, Bill Skowron, George Solotaire, Lee Strasberg, Susan Strasberg, Ben Stein, George Steinbrenner, Sallie Taggart, Gay Talese, Don Tanner, J. Randy Taraborrelli, Joe Torre, John Tuthill, Peter Ueberroth, Keith Urban, George Vecsey, Antonio Villaraigosa, Sander Vanocur, Robert Vickrey, Don Wanlass, Tommy West, Ted Williams, Tom Wolfe, Clare Wood, Gene Woodling, Steve Wulf, and Don Zimmer.

My appreciation to the entire staff of the Baseball Hall of Fame Museum Library in Cooperstown, New York, for their cooperation on so many levels. Thanks also to the library staffs of *Time* and *Sports Illustrated*; *Sporting News*, Associated Press, *Los Angeles Times*, *New York Times*, *New York Post*, *New York Daily News*, *Newsday*, *Washington Post*, *Boston Globe*, *Dallas Morning News*, *Houston Chronicle*, *Detroit Free Press*, *Kansas City Star*, *Oklahoman*, and *Tulsa World*; ESPN Archives, MLB.com, the New York Yankees, Susan Naulty of the Richard Nixon Presidential Library in Yorba Linda, California, and the National Archives and Records Administration; the reference departments at the New York Public Library, Beverly Hills Public Library, Santa Monica Public Library, Dallas Public Library, and Library of Congress; and the administration of the Commerce (Oklahoma) Unified School District.

I want to thank, too, Christina Kahrl, my editor on my Mickey Mantle biography at Brassey's Inc., for her sensitive editing and commentary on drafts of the manuscript. Christina isn't just a great editor but also one of the most knowledgeable baseball writers in America. Although she wasn't involved in editing *Mantle: The Best There Ever Was*, her contributions on *Mickey Mantle: America's Prodigal Son* were invaluable in developing this book.

At Rowman & Littlefield, my editor Christen Karniski has been a patient, tireless advocate who has treated me and this manuscript with more tenderness than we may deserve, with the confidence that it is a special and important book. The same is true with Leticia Gomez, my agent of recent years. My gratitude goes out to her for her friendship and diligent work.

As always, I am especially indebted to my late parents: my mother, Maria Emma, for being the soul and strength of my family and always encouraging me to pursue my dreams and to listen to God's voice; my father, Antonio Sr., for his courage and support, not to mention turning me on to baseball and Mickey Mantle. By the way, Mom went to her grave believing that a steady, unsuspecting diet of the slightly sour Mexican *crema* with Kahlúa would have cured Mickey of his drinking problem back in the 1970s. She swore that's what did it in curing Dad.

Special gratitude again goes out to my muse, Jeter, the prince of all Labrador retrievers.

This book might never have been written without the inspiration and sacrifice of my wife and our sons. Both Trey and Ryan have always been supportive as their old man disappears to work on his books. My wife Renee, the fairest of them all, has known the personal importance to me in completing this third book in my Mickey Mantle trilogy—willing to sacrifice vacations, movie nights, and more for whatever research and work the project required. That work on this book included more than the usual. Many of my interviews were tape-recorded. But there were numerous instances in which Renee was put in the position of what seemed like she was deciphering the Rosetta stone. Sometimes the only person who can read my handwriting, she had to make sense of my chicken-scratching on aging notes of conversations and interviews from years ago with Holly Brooke, the Mantles, and others. Even on our second honeymoon throughout Paris and Rome last summer, Renee kept insisting that the experience was fuel for wrapping up this project. As I have long said, her love and devotion—and the love of my sons—are my proof once again that there is a God.

Bibliography

Appel, Marty. *Pinstripe Empire: The New York Yankees from Before the Babe to After the Boss.* New York: Bloomsbury USA, 2012.

Berger, Phil. *Mickey Mantle.* New York: Park Lane Press, 1998.

Canale, Larry. *Mickey Mantle: The Classic Photography of Ozzie Sweet.* Richmond, VA: Tuff Stuff Books, 1998.

Castro, Tony. *DiMag & Mick: Sibling Rivals, Yankee Blood Brothers.* Guilford, CT: Lyons Press, 2016.

———. *Mickey Mantle: America's Prodigal Son.* Dulles, VA: Brassey's Books, 2002.

Cataneo, David. *I Remember Joe DiMaggio: Personal Memories of the Yankee Clipper by the People Who Knew Him Best.* New York: Cumberland House, 2001.

Clavin, Tom. *The DiMaggios: Three Brothers, Their Passion for Baseball, Their Pursuit of the American Dream.* New York: Ecco, 2013.

Cramer, Richard Ben. *Joe DiMaggio: The Hero's Life.* New York: Simon & Schuster, 2000.

Creamer, Robert W. *Babe: The Legend Comes to Life.* Evanston, IL: Holtzman Press, 1974.

———. *Stengel: His Life and Times.* New York: Simon & Schuster, 1984.

Creamer, Robert W., and Sports Illustrated. *Mantle Remembered* (SI Presents). New York: Warner Books, 1995.

Durso, Joseph. *Casey: The Life and Legend of Charles Dillon Stengel.* New Jersey: Prentice Hall, 1967.

Engelberg, Morris, and Marv Schneider. *DiMaggio: Setting the Record Straight.* New York: Motorbooks International, 2003.

Falkner, David. *The Last Hero: The Life of Mickey Mantle.* New York: Simon & Schuster, 1995.

Flynn, George. *Lewis B. Hershey, Mr. Selective Service.* Chapel Hill: University of North Carolina Press, 1985.

Ford, Whitey, and Mickey Mantle. *Whitey and Mickey: A Joint Autobiography of the Yankee Years.* New York: TK, 1987.

Golenbock, Peter. *Dynasty: The New York Yankees, 1949–1964.* Chicago: Contemporary Books, 2000.

———. *Wild, High and Tight: The Life and Death of Billy Martin.* New York: St. Martin's Press, 1994.

Gould, Stephen Jay. *Triumph and Tragedy in Mudville: A Lifelong Passion for Baseball.* New York: Norton, 2003.

Hart, Jeffrey. *When the Going Was Good: American Life in the Fifties.* New York: Crown, 1982.

Hines, Rick, Mark Larson, and Dave Platta. *Mickey Mantle Memorabilia.* New York: Krause, 1993.

Kennedy, Kostya. *56: Joe DiMaggio and the Last Magic Number in Sports.* New York: Sports Illustrated, 2011.

Lansky, Sandra, and William Stadiem. *Daughter of the King: Growing Up in Gangland.* New York: Weinstein Books, 2014.

Leavy, Jane. *The Last Boy: Mickey Mantle and the End of America's Childhood.* New York: Harper, 2010.

Leinwand, Gerald. *Heroism in America.* New York: Franklin Watts, 1996.

Linn, Ed. *Hitter: The Life and Turmoils of Ted Williams.* New York: Harcourt Brace, 1993.

Mantle, Merlyn, with Herb Gluck. *The Mick.* New York: Doubleday, 1985.

Mantle, Merlyn, and Mickey Herskowitz. *All My Octobers.* New York: HarperCollins, 1994.

Mantle, Merlyn, Mickey E. Mantle, David Mantle, and Dan Mantle. *A Hero All His Life.* New York: HarperCollins, 1996.

Mantle, Mickey, and Phil Pepe. *My Favorite Summer, 1956.* New York: Doubleday, 1991.

Roberts, Randy, and Johnny Smith. *A Season in the Sun: The Rise of Mickey Mantle.* New York: Basic Books, 2018.

Robinson, Ray. *Iron Horse: Lou Gehrig in His Time.* New York: Norton, 1990.

Schoor, Gene. *The Illustrated History of Mickey Mantle.* New York: Carroll & Graf, 1996.

Smith, Marshall, and John Rohde. *Memories of Mickey Mantle: My Very Best Friend.* Bronxville, NY: Adventure Quest, 1996.

Index

About the Author

Tony Castro is an American historian and author of seven books, including the bestselling *Mickey Mantle: America's Prodigal Son*, which the *New York Times* has hailed as the definitive biography of the New York Yankees baseball icon. *Mantle: The Best There Ever Was* is the concluding book of his Mickey Mantle trilogy, the second of which is *DiMag & Mick: Sibling Rivals, Yankee Blood Brothers*.

A Nieman fellow at Harvard University and a graduate of Baylor, Tony is also the author of critically acclaimed biographies of Ernest Hemingway, Cesar Chavez, and baseball legends Lou Gehrig and Babe Ruth. He is currently working on a biography of Napoleon Bonaparte.

Tony lives in Los Angeles with his wife, Renee LaSalle, and Jeter, their black Labrador retriever. Their two grown sons, Ryan and Trey, also reside in Southern California.